CRΕΤΕ
TRAVEL AND ARCHAEOLOGICAL GUIDE

ANNA KOFOU

EKDOTIKE ATHENON S.A.

Contributors:

• Caves: **Anna Petrochilou**
  President of the Greek Speleological Association

  Museums and Archaeological Sites
• Siteia and Aghios Nikolaos: **Nikos Papadakis**
  Former Director of Museums
• Chania and Rethymnon: **Stavroula Markoulaki**
  Former Director of Museums
• Historical Museum of Herakleion and Byzantine Monuments: **Manolis Borboudakis**
  Director of Byzantine Antiquities

• Cretan Myths: **Evangelos N. Roussos**, Ph.D.

• Flora of Crete: **George Sfikas**
  Researcher of Greek Flora

Publisher: Christiana G. Christopoulou
Translation: Philip Ramp,
revised by Alexandra Doumas and Richard Witt
Artistic supervision: Spyros Karachristos
Photo research: Georgia Moschovakou
Editor: Maria Koursi
Photographs: Archive of Ekdotike Athenon,
Nikos Kontos, Nikos Desyllas, Michalis Kouvidis
DTP: E. Varvakis Co.
Printed and bound by Metron S.A. - Ekdotike Hellados

ISBN: 960-213-426-7
Copyright © 2006 by Ekdotike Athenon S.A.
34, Akademias St., Athens 106 72
Printed and bound in Greece

CONTENTS

GEOGRAPHICAL INFORMATION .. 5
Land, People, Mountains-Plateaux,
Ravines, Plains, Rivers and Lakes, Coast-
line, Communications, Climate, Cultiva-
tion and Production, Geological Past,
Flora, Fauna.

CRETAN MYTHS 19
Gods and Heroes, Birth of Zeus, Zeus
and Europa, Kingdom of Minos, Talos,
Art during the Minoan Period, Pasiphae
and the Minotaur, Ariadne and Theseus,
Daidalos and Ikaros.

HISTORICAL REVIEW 33

Archaeological Excavations 35

History 35
Neolithic Period (6000-2600 B.C.), Pre-
Palace Period (2600-2000 B.C.), Old
Palace Period (1900-1700 B.C.), New
Palace Period (1700-1450 B.C.), Post-
Palace Period (1450-110 B.C.), Proto-
Geometric Period (1100-900 B.C.) Geo-
metric and Orientalizing Periods (900-
650 B.C.). Archaic Period (650-500
B.C.), Classical and Hellenistic Periods
(500-67 B.C.), Roman Period (67 B.C.-
A.D. 330), First Byzantine Period (330-
824), Arab Occupation (824-961), Second
Byzantine Period (961-1204/10). Venetian
Occupation (1204-1669), Turkish Occu-
pation (1669-1898), Modern Times.

TOURING 87

Herakleion 88
History of the Town, Tour of the Town.

The museums 95
Archaeological Museum, Historical
Museum of Crete, Church of Saint
Catherine - Collection of Byzantine Icons.
Excursions 1-7. Archaeological Site of
Knossos, Archaeological Site of
Archanes, Archaeological Site of Phais-
tos, Archaeological Site of Aghia Triada,
Archaeological Site of Tylissos, Sedoni
Cave, Idaian Cave, Kastelli Pediados
(Venetian fortress), Eileithyia Cave,
Archaeological Site of Malia, Milatos
Cave, Diktaian Cave.

Aghios Nikolaos 190
History of the Town, Archaeological
Museum. Excursions 8-11. Connections
for Spinalonga, Church of Panaghia Kera
at Kritsa, Archaeological Site of Gournia, Chamezi Folk Museum.

Siteia 213
Archaeological Museum. Excursions 12-
13. Archaeological Site of Zakros, Toplou
Monastery, Kapsa Monastery, Melidoni
Cave. Excursion 14.

Rethymnon 234
History of the Town, Archaeological
Museum. Excursions 15-18. Arkadi
Monastery, Amari Valley, Preveli Mona-
stery, Kourna Lake.

Chania 255
History of the Town, Tour of the Town,
Archaeological Museum. Excursions 19-
26. Gouverneto Cave, Chrysopigi
Monastery, Askyphou Plateau, Samaria
Ravine. Graeco-Roman town of Elyros,
Kasteli (Kisamos), Chrysoskalitissa
Monastery, Kastelli Selino.

Geographical information

The land

Crete is the largest island in Greece and the fifth largest in the Mediterranean after Sicily, Sardinia, Cyprus and Corsica. It has an area of 8261 sq. km. (8303 sq. km. when the islets of Gavdos and Dia are included) and a coastline 1046 km. long. Crete is in essence a mountain range which lies athwart the Aegean Sea to the south. At the same time it is a link between Asia and Europe. Its unique geographical position between Europe, Asia and Africa determined its historical course both throughout antiquity and in more modern times. It has an elongated shape; at its longest it is 260 km. from west to east and at its widest 60 km. The island is a good deal narrower at certain points, such as in the region of Hierapetra where it is only 12 km. wide. To the south it is bordered by the Libyan Sea, to the west the Myrtoon Sea, to the east the Karpathion Sea and to the north the Cretan Sea. Its coastline, which consists of both sandy beaches and rocky shores, is framed by the small islets of Kouphonisi, Gaidouronisi, Dia, Aghioi Pantes, Spinalonga, Gavdos, etc.

The famous beach of Vaï on the NE shore of Crete.

Gavdos, which is in the Libyan Sea, is the southernmost point of Europe.

According to the latest census (1981) Crete has 502,165 inhabitants. Administratively, the island is divided into four Prefectures (Nomes) which from west to east are: the Prefecture of Chania, with Chania as the capital, the Prefecture of Rethymnon, with Rethymnon as the capital, the Prefecture of Herakleion, with Herakleion as the capital, and the Prefecture of Lasithi, with Aghios Nikolaos as the capital. Herakleion is both the capital of the island and the largest town (101,634 inhabitants).

The People

The inhabitants of Crete belong to the so-called Mediterranean type. The population is mainly concentrated in the six large towns on the island – the capitals of the four prefectures, Hierapetra and Siteia – and employed in trade, handicrafts, tourism and the like. The remainder of its inhabitants are principally engaged in farming and livestock raising.

Nearly all Cretans, but above all those who live in the market towns and the villages, maintain time-honoured customs and manners. In the countryside one encounters many elderly Cretan men dressed in the traditional outfit (baggy trousers and headscarf). Women, on the other hand, no longer wear their splendidly embroidered traditional costumes, although

they do continue to weave folk embroideries distinguished for their decorative wealth and colourful compositions. In Crete, more than any other region of Greece, familial and kinship bonds remain close, and Cretan hospitality, is renowned. Many other traditions are also preserved, such as the music, which is played on the ancient Cretan *lyra* (a three-stringed instrument), the dances (*pendozalis, chaniotikos, ortses, siteiakos, malevyzytikos* and *sousta*) and the songs called *mandinades*. The Cretans are famous for their indomitable spirit and their love of freedom and independence. That is why they played a leading role in all the struggles of the Greek nation, writing brilliant pages of heroic history. Those who travel to the towns and villages of Crete will come to know the outstanding beauty of its people.

The Mountains - The Plateaux

The high mountains are one of the characteristics of the Cretan landscape. They are composed of limestone. The geological upheavals which created basins and plateaux also formed a large number of impressive caves, many of which were used for religious purposes during antiquity. The mountains of

Cretan girls in local dress.

The traditional dances of Crete are of particular interest. Extremely lively, they are usually accompanied by traditional instruments.

Crete make up a section of the Dinaric-Taurus chain, which starts in the Dinaric Alps and comprises the mountains of Albania, Pindus, the Peloponnese, Kythera-Antikythera, Crete, Karpathos and Rhodes, and ends in Taurus in Asia Minor. These massifs form three large mountain complexes, each with its own personality. Between the ranges lie the mountainous or semi-mountainous zones which cover the greater part of the land. There is a third lower zone along the coast and in the interior. In western Crete are the White Mountains or Madares, a large mountain complex with scores of peaks, the highest of which is Pachnes (2453 m. a.s.l.). Ida or Psiloreitis, a single elongated mountain mass whose highest peak is Timios Stavros (2456 m. a.s.l.), constitutes the main mountain complex and is also the highest point in Crete. On the western side of eastern Crete is Dikte or the Lasithian Mountains, a range with many peaks, the highest being the anonymous "2148". The well-known plateau of Lasithi (402 sq. km.) spreads out between the peaks. On the south side of the island are lower mountains such as Kedros (1777 m. a.s.l.), which is separated from the Ida mountain range by the Amari valley. There is another small mountain range north of Ida, Kouloukonas, known in antiquity as the Tallaia mountains. The Mylopotamos valley lies between them. Mount Kophinas (the Asterousia Mountains, highest peak 1231 m. a.s.l.) lies to the south of the

Snow-capped peak of Psiloreitis.

plain of Mesara. Finally, there are two large mountain complexes in the province of Siteia: to the west the Siteian mountains (the highest peaks are Kliros, 1320 m. a.s.l. and Aphendis Kavousi, 1476 m. a.s.l.) and to the east lower mountains (the highest peaks are Playia, 819 m. a.s.l. and Prinias, 803 m. a.s.l.). Moreover, every peninsula has its own lower mountain range.

There are three mountaineering clubs in Crete, at Herakleion, Chania and Rethymnon. There are three shelters for climbers in the mountains of Crete:

in the White Mountains situated at Kallergis (1680 m. a.s.l.) which holds 30 people, and at Volika (1480 m. a.s.l.) which holds 40 people. Both of them belong to the Mountaineering League of Chania. On Psiloreitis, situated at Prinos (1100 m. a.s.l.), is another refuge which holds 16 people and belongs to the Mountaineering League of Herakleion.

Another characteristic of the land in Crete is the numerous plateaux which are generally located in the middle zone of the mountains and which act as rainwater collectors in the winter. Several of these plateaux are fertile and densely populated. Others are used only for grazing. Unquestionably, the most beautiful and impressive of these is the Lasithi plateau, which is surrounded by the peaks of Dikte and lies at a height of approximately 900 m. a.s.l.). It is as heavily populated today as it was in antiquity. Also of importance are the plateaux of Omalos in the White Mountains at a height of 700 m. a.s.l., Nida on Psiloreitis at a height of roughly 1400 m. a.s.l. and Askyphou near the Idaian Cave. The plateaux that are at a high altitude (such as Omalos) are only inhabited in summer and are relatively easy to reach.

The Ravines

One of the principal features of the Cretan landscape is the many ravines which cut through the island from north to south. Most of them start in the mountainous zone and end near the sea. Their role in preserving the rare flora and fauna of the island is enormous, because they are the only regions that remain far-removed from all human activity. The best known, both for its size and its beauty, is the ravine of Samaria, the famous "Pharangas" which is 18 km. long and which ranges from 3 m. wide at its narrowest point to 150 m. and requires five to seven hours to traverse.

A small mountain stream with cold water runs along its bottom. In walking the length of the ravine one has to cross this stream forty-seven times. At many points the vertical walls of the ravine reach a height of 500 m., while the mountain peaks that surround it (Gigilos, Volakias, Zaranokephala, Paches) are over 2000 m. high.

On the slopes of the ravine are cypress forests (Cypressus sempervirens) in their true, wild form with horizontal branches, and pine trees of the Pinus brutia type. There are plane trees at the bottom. The ravine is also full of rare Cretan wild flowers.

Here is also the last refuge of the Cretan wild-goat (the kri-kri) which is why the region has been declared a National Forest, meaning that hunting, lumbering, the cutting of wild flowers and staying overnight in the ravine are prohibited.

Other large ravines in Crete are the Imbriotiko, between the villages of Imbros and Chora Sphakion, the Kourtaliotiko, where the historic Preveli Monastery is located, the Topoliano, near the village of Topolia, where besides the thousands of deciduous plane trees there are some evergreen plane trees as well, and the Prasiano, in the Prefecture of Rethymnon.

The Plains

There are no large plains in Crete but between the mountain complexes are several small, fertile tracts, and there are some others at certain coastal locations on the north side of the island, mainly at the back of bays. The most important of these is the plain of Mesara (Prefecture of Herakleion) on the south side of central Crete. Mesara played an important part in the history of the island, and because of its fertility has always been the granary of Crete. During Minoan times there were important installations and palaces there (Phaistos, Aghia Triada). Also noteworthy are the plains of Kisamos, Kydonia, Apokoronas and Kantanos (Prefecture of Chania) and of Rethymnon-Mylopotamos and Aghios Vasileios (Prefecture of Rethymnon). In the Prefecture of Herakleion is the plain of Herakleion and the plain of Pediada. In the Prefecture of Lasithi is the plain of Hierapetra. Besides the plains, the cultivable land extends up the smooth slopes of the mountains, frequently to a considerable height above sea level.

The Rivers and Lakes

There are no important rivers in Crete. Most of them would be better characterized as dry stream beds because in the summer they have little or no water. Yeropotamos, Koiliaris, Anapodiaris and Megas Potamos are some of the better known rivers. There are only two lakes, that of Kournas in the province of Apokoronas and that of Aghios Nikolaos in the town of that name on the gulf of Mirabello. Because of the limestone composition of the mountains, spring water is not abundant in Crete. The largest number of existing springs is in western Crete and along the southern coast.

The Coastline

The coasts of Crete are diverse, indented and of a large variety of forms with dozens of bays, capes and peninsulas, both large and small. The northern shores are an ideal place for summer holidays, swimming and water sports. The southern coasts, which are more isolated, have a beauty all their own to offer those who are seeking a quite life close to nature.

Communications

Crete has a well-developed road network, especially on the northern side. Regular flights connect the island to

The famous ravine of Samaria.

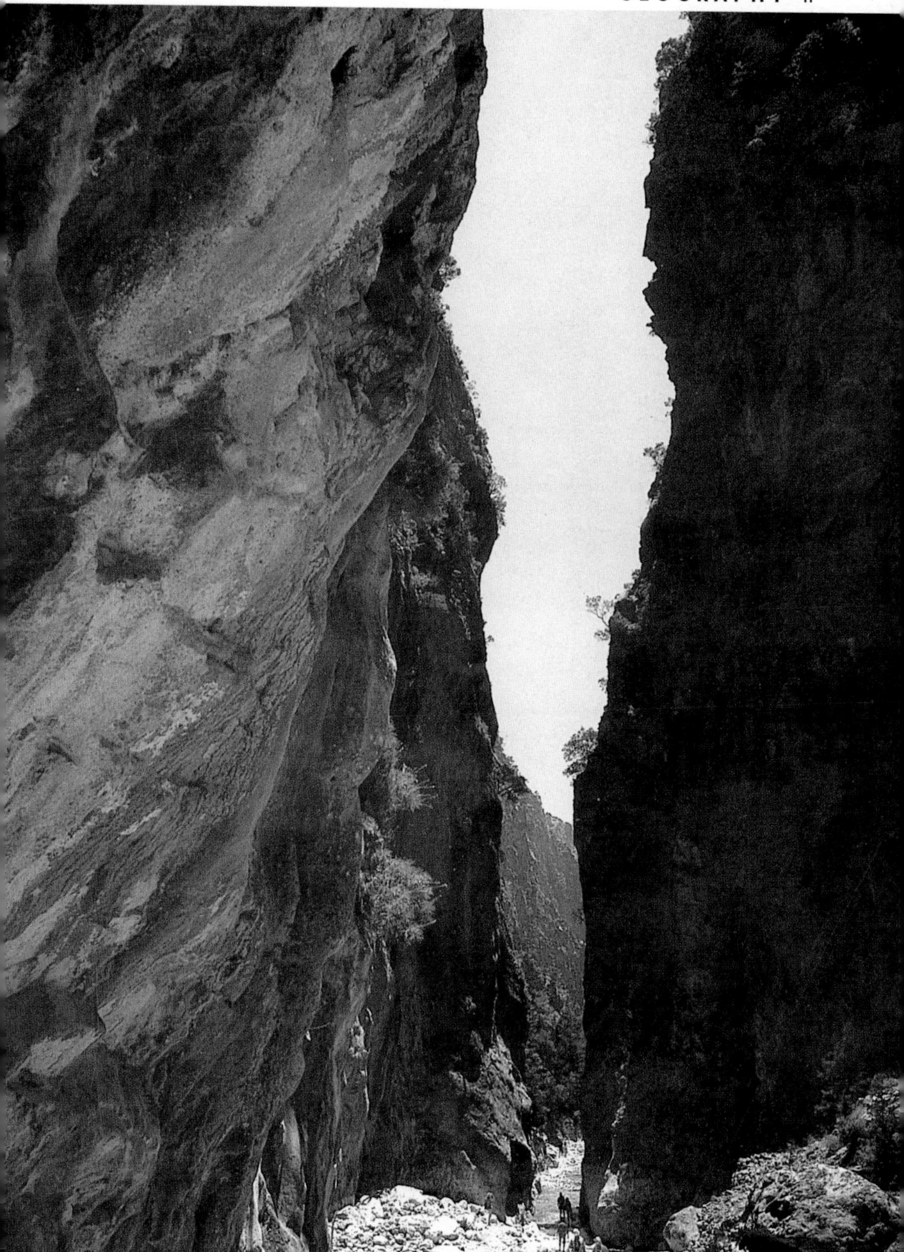

The beach of Palaiokastro.

Athens (from airports in Chania, Herakleion and Siteia) while in the summer it also has connections to Paros, Mykonos, Santorini and Rhodes.

The most important harbours on the island are also on its north side (Souda, Chania, Kisamos, Herakleion, Rethymnon, Aghios Nikolaos and Siteia). The commercial and maritime traffic on the island is principally conducted through the two harbours on its north coast (Chania and Herakleion) with daily connections to Piraeus (more than one departure) and to the rest of the islands in the Aegean and, in summer, Cyprus. Kisamos (Kasteli) is connected to the Peloponnese (Gythion, Monemvasia, Neapolis) and Kythera by regularly scheduled car ferries. The harbours on the Libyan Sea have little activity with the exception of Kaloi Limenes and Hierapetra. Small motorboats connect the south coast of Crete with Gavdos, the only inhabited islet of all those that surround Crete.

The Climate

Crete's climate is mild and healthy, without dramatic changes, and is classified as a temperate, marine climate. Winter is generally mild with snowfall only in the high mountains, rain on the plains and a great deal of sunshine. The summer is hot and dry, warmer in eastern Crete and particularly hot on the shores of the Libyan Sea. This mild, warm climate favours the cultivation of trees, vegetables and plants throughout

Matala.

the year which in other areas of Greece are cultivated only in summer.

Cultivation and Production

Despite its mountainous soil, Crete is generally fertile, with extensive cultivation and production of a large variety of agricultural products. Walnuts and the tasty Cretan chestnuts are produced in the mountains. Olive groves and vineyards predominate in the middle zone. Apart from the grapes from which the excellent Cretan wines are produced, several table varieties are grown and exported to Europe. There is also considerable production of the choice Cretan raisins (sultanas). Citrus fruits, principally the orange and the tangerine, are cultivated on the plains, as are various vegetables; the olive is found throughout the island.

Other Cretan agricultural products are carob beans, fava, mountain tea, broad beans, oregano and flax. On the plains and in the warmer parts there are also many greenhouses which produce tomatoes, cucumbers, aubergines and bananas all year round. Bananas and avocados are also grown outdoors in some places.

Beekeeping and livestock raising are particularly well-developed on the island. Crete is famous for its delicious cheeses: *graviera*, *myzithra* and *anthotyro*.

The Geological Past

The morphology of Crete is the result of various geological phenomena and tectonic movements.

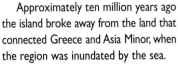

Milking sheep in Anogeia.

Shepherd in a Cretan meadow.

Approximately ten million years ago the island broke away from the land that connected Greece and Asia Minor, when the region was inundated by the sea.

During the Pleistocene, 1-3 million years ago, Crete acquired its present shape, more or less, and the high Cretan mountains were formed. The geological transformations and alterations in the climatological conditions influenced life on the island. Many large mammals such as *Elephas antiquus*, the dwarf *Elephas creticus*, hippopotamuses, rhinoceroses and wild cattle, deer and bison that originally lived on the island, disappeared. Only the wild goats, virtually identical with those of the present day, survived. The first inhabitants, organized in small groups, are thought to have arrived on the island around 6000-5000 B.C., though more recent investigation indicates that human beings have lived there since Palaeolithic times.

During this period it seems that Crete was a lush island with dense forests. These forests survived to a degree during the following centuries since, according to evidence, Crete exported cypress timber to all the surrounding lands during Minoan times. In Homeric times Psiloreitis was covered with forests to which it also owes its name in antiquity – Idi – from the Doric word *Ida*, which meant trees for lumber, forest, or wood-covered mountain. Very little is left today of these ancient forests. Their destruction and the deforestation of the mountains is due mainly to the havoc caused by the various invaders of the island, the worst offenders being the Venetians and the Turks. Moreover, stock-raising and the lack of water and rivers contributed to the devastation resulting in less than one-tenth of the surface of the land being covered by forest. Dry scrubland now prevails.

The Flora

Even though the vegetation of Crete is limited, as we have noted, the flora is nonetheless exceptionally rich in terms of variety. According to the calculations of experts there are almost 2000 species of plants on the island. Of these, some 160 are exclusive to Crete. One can observe this large variety of plants from the plains and the shores all the way to the mountain heights. In spring all these flowers in bloom offer a gorgeous sight. Dry scrub predominates in summer though oleander and osier bloom in the ravines. But the plants begin to turn green with the first rains in autumn. Anemones are abundant in winter in the leeward areas and narcissus appear in the Mirabello valley at the end of January. Slightly later, the various orchids, the Persian buttercup (*Ranunculus asiaticus*) and the asphodels begin to flower. Most of the rare Cretan plants grow in the ravines or on the steep mountain slopes. Some of these are: *Ebenus cretica, Linum arboreum, Campanula pelviformis, Staechelina arborea*, and *Petromarcula pinnata*.

On the plains and high peaks other plants flourish: *Tulipa bakeri, Tulipa saxatilis, Anchusa caespitosa, Erysinum raulinii, Dianthus juniperinus, Dianthus pulviniformis, Crocus oreocreticus, Asperula idaea, Arum idaeum, Scabiosa albocincta, Scabiosa minoana* and many others.

Rare plants are also found on the plains and along the shores. An example is the Cretan palm tree (*Phoenix Theophrastii*) which is unique in the world and which grows along the beach at Vaï and is one of the sights of the island; there are also *Pancratium maritimum, Centaurea pumilio, Anthemis tomentella, Anthemis filicaulis, Eryngium ternatum, Teucrium cuneifolium* etc.

Finally, there are some very interesting and beautiful plants which grow both near the sea and in the mountains or semi-mountainous regions such as: *Cyclamen creticum, Gladiolus italicus, Chrysanthemum coronarium, Cistus villosus-creticus* etc.

Cretan "kouloura" and fresh fruit.

Many of the plants endemic to Crete are found in relative abundance while others have become extremely rare because of the destruction of their habitat or over-collecting. In the latter must be listed the famous Diktamo (*Origanum dictamnus*) and the gorgeous *Paeonia clusii* with its pure white flowers.

An outstanding feature of the Crete flora is the evergreen variety of plane tree, unique in the world.

Crete also has the deciduous plane tree known throughout the eastern Mediterranean, *Platanus orientalis*. In certain regions, however, one finds trees of the same species which keep their leaves throughout the year and have been given the special name of *varietas cretica*.

The Fauna

Besides its rich flora Crete also has an exceptionally interesting fauna. In addition to the usual animals that one encounters in Greece such as the hare, the hedgehog, various rodents and bats, one finds the unique Cretan wild goat (*Capra aegagrus-cretica*), the *Kri-Kri* or *Agrimi*, which has a very distinctive and impressive appearance. Today it survives only in the White Mountains, in the National Forest of Samaria and on the neighbouring islets of Dia, Thodorou and Aghioi Pantes. In antiquity, and especially Minoan times, there were a large number of wild goats on the island and they had a pre-eminent place in Minoan religion as sacred animals, which can be seen from the numerous de-pictions of them in the art of the period.

Other interesting mammals on Crete are the Cretan marten (*Martes foina-bunites*), the Cretan badger or Arkalos (*Meles meles-arcalus*), the Cretan wild cat or Phourogatos (*Felis silvestris-agrius*), the Cretan weasel or *Kaloyannou* (*Mustela nivalis galinthias*) and *Acomus mimus*, the Cretan "prickly rat", unique in the world.

The Cretan golden eagle (*Aquila chrysaetus*) and the lammergeyer (*Gypaetus barbatus*) a subspecies unique in the world, stand out among the birds. Crete is famous for its many vultures (*Gyps fulvus*) which roost in the Cretan mountains and ravines; the island is also an important stop for migratory birds on their way each spring from Africa to Europe and returning each autumn.

a. Persian buttercup (Ranunculus asiaticus).
b. Cistus villosus-creticus.
c. Wild daisies (Chrysanthemum coronarium).
d. Sea Lily (Pancratium maritimum).
e. Anemone coronaria.
f. Rock tulip (Tulipa saxatilis).

Cretan myths

Gods and Heroes

The oldest Cretan myths speak of the remarkable organization of life during the Minoan period, the "god-given" laws of the Cretan state, its power and its spread over a large radius to the islands and mainland regions nearest the island. These myths also speak of its wealth and technological development and of certain individuals who, through their exceptional abilities, were the inspiration for noble institutions and incomparable achievements, protecting their people from all evil forces.

These myths, at least as they have been handed down by ancient Greek authors, constrained by the criteria of official Greek religion and political experience, mainly echo a strong tradition of worship of sidereal bodies and the floruit of Minoan civilization, with power concentrated in the figure of Minos. Thus,

on the one hand the cults of the Sun (Helios) and the Moon (Selene) have traits in common along the southeastern coast of the Mediterranean; the worship of "Asterius Zeus" and Astarte involving magical rites for rain and vegetation, mystery dances and festivals, such as the "bull-contests", together with primitive forms of worship in the large caves of Crete – the "Idaian Antron" and the "Diktaian Antron" – seem to have been the motive forces for the formation of the myths of Zeus and Europa, Minos and Pasiphae, Talos and Daidalos, the Minotaur and the Labyrinth, Ariadne, Diktynna and Britomartis.

On the other hand, the traditions concerning local headmen and eponymous heroes, and the memory of the power of Minoan Crete and its vast extent, with colonies both in and outside Crete, seem to have led to the formation of myths about Rhadamanthys, Sarpedon, Gortys, Kydon, Deukalion, Idomeneas, Katreas and Althaimenes, Miletos, Pamdareos, Kaunos and Byblis, heroes who, without exception, are presented as the ancestors or descendants of Minos.

The Birth of Zeus

According to mythological tradition, Crete took its name from a daughter of the oldest Cretan king, Asterius, who is none other than "Asterius Zeus", and its history starts at exactly the same time as that of Zeus, who himself was born and bred on Crete ("Cretan-born"

The slaying of the Minotaur by Theseus and all the adventures connected with it constitute one of the most exciting myths of Crete. Here, Theseus again rushes with his sword at the Minotaur which, seeing that its end is near, wounded and powerless, begs him for mercy, as does Minos, who has hurried to assist the monster. (Red-figure krater. Circa 470 B.C. Ferrara, Museo Archeologico di Spina).

So that Kronos would not hear the crying
of the infant Zeus, who was growing up
in secret in a cave on Mount Ida, the
well-armed Kouretes danced and beat on
their shields. Here, the Kouretes try to
drown the infant's wailing by beating on
their shields. The child is depicted in the
arms of the Nymph Amaltheia. (Roman
architectural relief from the reign of
Augustus. Paris, Louvre).

Zeus in the guise of a bull
abducts Europa. (Red-figure krater.
Early 5th century B.C.
Archaeological Museum, Tarquinia).

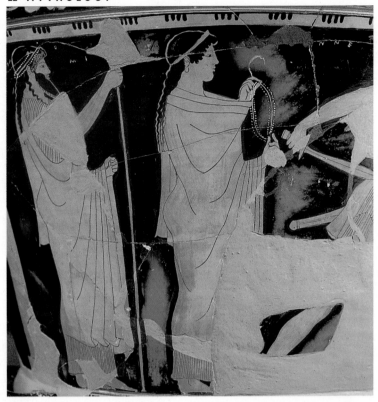

Minos proved to be a worthy king of Crete. He brought wealth and power to his country which he ruled wisely and justly. Here, dignified and holding the sceptre given to him by Zeus himself, Minos is depicted with one of his children, Ariadne, whose name is associated with a great hero, Theseus, and a much loved god, Dionysos.
(Detail from a red-figure krater. Circa 470 B.C. Athens, National Archaeological Museum).

Zeus). Concerning the birth of Zeus it is said that his father, Kronos, when he was still king of the Heavens, had heard from his parents, Uranos and Mother Earth (Gaia), that as soon as one of his children was powerful enough he would seize his throne. Thus, the moment that each child was born, Kronos immediately swallowed it and kept it inside him to be certain that it would do him no harm. Rhea, his wife, was inconsolable over this dreadful practice which left her no children to enjoy. When it was time for her to bring her last son, Zeus, into the world, she begged Uranus and Mother Earth to help her hide the child from his father. Uranos and Mother Earth listened to Rhea and were moved to pity. So when Zeus was born, Mother Earth herself took him to Crete and hid him on "Mount Aegean" or, as others said, Mother Earth led Rhea to Crete and helped her give birth to her son there. Then she gave Kronos a rock wrapped in swaddling clothes which he swallowed unsuspectingly. So Kronos would not hear the baby crying, the Kouretes, the good-natured demons of Crete, stood outside the cave where the infant was hidden, dancing and beating loudly on their bronze shields.

The divine infant was fed with the milk of a goat, Amaltheia. Later, when Zeus became the king of the gods, he honoured her in particular, setting her image among the stars in the heavens, as the constellation of Capricorn. Zeus himself wore her hide and made it his impenetrable shield, the famous "Aegis", in his war against the Titans, and the horn of Amaltheia became the symbol of abundance (the Horn of Plenty).

Others say that Amaltheia was a nymph and that she along with Idi and Adrasteia, or other nymphs, raised Zeus. Thus, the divine infant grew quickly both in body and mind; when he felt sure of his strength he went and found Kronos and fought with him. Being superior in strength and guile, he defeated him; Kronos then vomited forth all the children he had swallowed,

including, first of all, the stone that had been put in the place of Zeus. Zeus took this stone and placed it on Parnassus, at the Delphic Oracle, so that gods and humans alike would always see it and admire and venerate his power.

Zeus and Europa

Zeus, it is said, started the Cretan race, when he coupled with the beautiful princess Europa, whom he brought to Crete from the shores of Phoenicia.

According to the myth, one beautiful morning, when Europa and her girl friends were gathering flowers in a meadow near the shore, Zeus approached them. He had transformed himself into a very gentle, snow-white bull, his powerful young body the epitome of grace, lighted by two innocent eyes and crowned by two horns like gold half-moons. Peacefully chewing his cud he drew near the girls and lay down at the feet of Europa. The girls were enchanted and taking courage began to look him over in amazement. After a while, Europa leapt onto his shoulders laughing happily. Then the animal jumped up in a flash and raced into the sea. The girl, holding on to his back and trying not to fall off, cried out in despair but her friends had scattered in panic.

Thus, with Europa on his back, Zeus crossed the sea and reached the shores of Crete. In Crete the Horae had prepared the bridal bed in the Diktaian Cave. But others say that Zeus coupled with Europa in Gortyn, under a plane tree, which has never lost its leaves since that time. It is even said that during the "divine wedding" the great god offered his beloved three unique gifts: Talos, a bronze giant, who protected all of Crete, a gold dog who could catch all game, and a quiver with arrows that never missed their mark.

Europa bore three sons: Minos, Rhadamanthys and Sarpedon.

The Reign of Minos

It was believed that Minos with his gold sceptre, which had been given him by his father Zeus, managed to unify under his rule the more than one hundred cities of Crete from his centre at Knossos; to rule both on the island and abroad; to build a powerful fleet; to drive the pirates from the sea; to contain the barbarians; to build new towns on the island and in the surrounding islands and to govern his countless subjects with laws that Zeus had taught him. During his time the town grew in size and beauty, the arts were developed and people lived in peace, affluent and secure.

For thousands of years people kept alive the memory of Minos and his iron will and unrivalled justice, a reputation which even followed him to Hades where, as chief justice – higher than Rhadamanthys and Aiakos – he judged the dead, which both East and West sent to the Underworld daily. Minos used his great power to organize his state in an admirable fashion. His legislation, which his subjects believed was devised with the advice of his father, Zeus, remained in the memory of mankind for thousands of years.

In order to govern this large state more easily Minos is said to have divided it into three districts: the first faced Asia and its centre was Knossos, the largest town in Crete and the one most loved by Minos, for which reason he made it his permanent base. The second district faced Africa and had Phaistos, another large town, as its centre, while the third faced Europe and had Kydonia as its centre. Minos appointed his brother Rhadamanthys as his representative in the administration. It is said that his other brother, Sarpedon, went to Lycia and founded his own kingdom there. It is also said that Minos himself had taught Rhadamanthys to settle differences between people, to oversee the application of the law, but principally to judge the cases at the capital of the state, Knossos. Minos entrusted the dispensation of justice in the villages to Talos.

Talos

Talos was an "animated" giant made of bronze, the guard of Crete. It is said he was made by Hephaistos on behalf of Minos or Zeus, who offered him to Europa as a wedding gift. Others say that he was the last descendant of the bronze race and others that his father was Kres and that he himself became the father of Phaistos and the grandfather of Rhadamanthys. Finally, for others Talos was the brother of Rhadamanthys, the third brother of Minos, or an official in his service.

Just as Rhadamanthys was the judge in people's disputes at Knossos, it is said that Talos was the judge for all the rest of Crete. With the bronze tablets of the law on his shoulders, he made a circuit of the entire island three times a year, going from village to village and showing the subjects of Minos what was right and proper.

According to another tradition, Talos was not only the "guardian of the law" but was also the real "armed" guard of Crete and made his circuit not three times a year, but three times a day. Surveying the sea from high up on the cliffs, he hurled large rocks onto hostile ships which dared to approach Cretan shores. If a foreigner had the audacity to set foot on the land of Minos, Talos would jump into the fire and with his red-hot bronze body squeeze the enemy to his chest and burn him alive. He laughed thunderously every time he exterminated an enemy of Crete in this fashion.

But the final hour arrived even for Talos. When the Argonauts sailed past Crete, Talos hurled rocks at the *Argo* and would not let it approach. Medea, using her magical powers, either bewitched the giant from afar and paralyzed him or promised to make him immortal. In this way she managed to approach him. The bronze giant was

Talos, the bronze giant of Crete, slowly dies, wounded by the Argonauts when they reached the island with the sorceress Medea. Here, however, two of the Argonauts, the Dioskouroi, Kastor and Polydeukes (Pollux), comfort him in his final moments, perhaps because people considered the two heroes to be their protectors and saviours in the face of death. (Detail from a red-figure krater. 400-390 B.C. Ruvo, Museo Jatta).

practically invulnerable but he had only one vein which started in his neck and ended at his ankle, where it was stoppered with a pin or a fine membrane. Medea pulled out the pin or punctured the membrane and the ichor, the divine fluid the hero had in him instead of blood, flowed out like moulten lead and Talos fell to the ground dead, like a giant pine tree.

There are others who say that Medea undid Talos by driving him mad and yet others that Poias, the father of Philoktetes, struck him with a poisoned arrow.

Art in the Age of Minos

During the age of Minos, when people began to live in peace and enjoy their wealth and the fine things of life, Daidalos, the most famous craftsman in the world, arrived in Crete to adorn it with the most wonderful works. It is said that most tools were first conceived in his mind and that he had no equal in architecture and sculpture.

The statues that Daidalos made were like living people because they could see and walk and their bodies could assume any position. Until that time artists had made statues with an erect and immobile body, legs together, arms straight down the sides and the eyes with half-closed lids. Daidalos was the first to give them various postures, with their legs apart, arms outstretched or raised and the addition of realistic eyes. Thus, it was said that the statues

of Daidalos had to be tied down so they would not run away.

Daidalos, whose fame had preceded him, won the friendship of Minos in Crete. The great king open-handedly spent from the wealth of his empire so that this renowned craftsman could embellish the island with his beautiful works. Thus, Daidalos built the large Cretan palaces with their lavish halls, the statues and altars, the baths and the Labyrinth, where the Minotaur was kept locked up, and the marble dance floor where the daughter of Minos, Ariadne, danced with her girlfriends during the major festivals.

Pasiphae and the Minotaur

In order to be recognized as the king of all Crete it is said that Minos called on Poseidon to send him a sign that this was the wish of the gods. At that moment a bull of incomparable beauty leapt from the waves. Minos did not sacrifice this bull to Poseidon as he should have, but kept it for himself and sacrificed another. The god, however, became furious with Minos and, to punish him, caused his wife, Pasiphae, to fall in love with the bull, a passion as frenzied as it was unnatural.

Pasiphae, in her desire to mate with the handsome animal, found help from Daidalos; he covered the outside of a wooden cow with a real cow's hide and pulled it on wheels to a meadow where Poseidon's bull was grazing. The bull approached the fake cow and Pasiphae,

The Minotaur was the fruit of the love between
Pasiphae and the bull of Crete. With the head of a bull
and the body of a man, this monster lived in the
Labyrinth and fed on human flesh. In the illustration,
Pasiphae seems engrossed with the infant Minotaur
she nurses in her lap. (Interior of an Etruscan krater.
340-320 B.C. Paris, Bibliothèque Nationale).

who was hidden inside, managed to mate with it.

From their union was born the Minotaur, a monster with a bull's head and a human body. Minos did not kill the Minotaur but shut it up in the labyrinth, one of Daidalos' greatest works which lay beneath the palace and was very easy to enter but practically impossible to get out of, at least for someone who was unfamiliar with it. That was because this peculiar structure had many corridors full of complicated turns which more often than not led nowhere. The king put his enemies in this labyrinth to get rid of them, for the Minotaur lived and fed on human blood.

Ariadne and Theseus

Ariadne was the daughter of Minos and Pasiphae. She saw Theseus but once and immediately fell in love with him. Theseus was among the youths that Athens, which was considered responsible for the murder of one of the sons of Minos, Androgeas, was forced to pay as a blood tribute to Crete. These young people were destined to be fed to the Minotaur in the labyrinth.

Theseus was the most handsome of all those the Athenian boat brought to Knossos that year. He was the son of the King of Athens, Aegeus, or of the god Poseidon himself, and had voluntarily decided to accompany his unfortunate companions, hoping to find a way to save his homeland from this degradation once and for all.

When Ariadne learned of his intent, she offered her assistance after she had made him swear that if he succeeded he would take her with him and make her his wife. According to the terms of vassalage, Athens was obliged to send its children as food for the Minotaur as long as it lived. Consequently, in order to rescue his homeland, Theseus had to kill the monster. And in order to save himself after this deed, he had to find a way out of the labyrinth.

Ariadne found out from Daidalos, the architect of the labyrinth, that if one took a ball of thread and tied one end to the entrance, one would be able, by holding on to the thread, to go as far as one wished into the labyrinth and to return to the light of day without difficulty by reeling in the thread.

Thus, Ariadne gave Theseus the thread and the necessary directions. Theseus reached the centre of the labyrinth, found the Minotaur, struggled with it, defeated it and then grabbed it by the mane and ran his sword through it, letting the blood pour out as an offering to Poseidon. Ariadne joined Theseus in his escape, after he had killed the Minotaur.

Returning from Crete, Theseus's boat first landed on the island of Dia, which was later called Naxos, or on an island that lies off the shore of Knossos. There Ariadne made love with Theseus – it is said that Stamphylos and Oinopion or Demophon and Akamas, the children of Theseus, were born from this union –

and on the same night Theseus left and she never saw him again.

Some versions of the tale claim that Theseus yearned for Aegle, the daughter of Panopeas, in Athens. Others say that Athena appeared to him in a dream and ordered him to leave Ariadne and return to his homeland immediately or that Dionysos appeared and threatened him with disaster if he did not leave Ariadne, or even that Dionysos appeared in person and took the princess for himself. According to this account the god presented himself as loving and kind and made love to her, after he had offered her a pure gold crown, made by Hephaistos, which was so bright that later the gods put it in the heavens to shine among the other stars.

Daidalos and Ikaros

After he had made the wooden cow for Pasiphae to mate with Poseidon's bull, Daidalos was afraid of the punishment that awaited him if his part in the queen's adultery ever became known. Thus he decided to leave while he still had the chance. Pasiphae helped him and secretly gave him a boat to take him wherever he wanted to go. Daidalos took Ikaros, the son he had had by Naukrate, one of the king's slaves, with him and left Crete for good. As they sailed east from the Cyclades Ikaros slipped and fell into the sea and drowned. Daidalos buried his child on a nearby island which since then has been called Ikaria and the surrounding water, the Ikarian Sea.

Ariadne sleeps at the side of Theseus, as shown by the winged form of Sleep hovering over her head.
The hero suddenly rises, startled by the unexpected presence of Athena who commands him to abandon the princess. (Detail from a red-figure Attic lekythos. Circa 460 B.C. Tarantas, Museo Archeologico Nazionale).

Daidalos continued on his way alone till he reached Sicily which was then called Sikania. He went to Kamikos or Amikos where Acrigentum was later built. There he was received hospitably and offered the patronage of King Kokalos.

According to one variation of this myth, Minos learned what Daidalos had done before he left Crete and went looking for him to punish him. But Pasiphae had hidden him in a safe place. Then Minos, unable to find him, issued an order to his men to search all the ships that were about to leave Cretan harbours, promising a large reward to anyone who managed to ferret out Daidalos and bring him in.

When Daidalos saw there was no way to escape from Crete, he racked his brain to think of some way to save himself. In the end, observing the birds who flew unmolested from place to place, he decided to get out of his difficult position by following their example. So, he collected the feathers of all kinds of flying things, wove them together, sealed them with wax and made wings for himself and his son. One day father and son flew off like birds, leaving Crete and the authority of the king behind. During their journey the young Ikaros, rejoicing in his flight over the dazzling Aegean, went up even higher, for he was lighter than his father, and got too close to the sun. The wax melted, the wings disintegrated and Ikaros plunged into the sea and drowned. Daidalos continued flying on alone and reached Sicily.

Others say that Daidalos and Ikaros left Crete in a normal way by boat and that Daidalos invented sails. Thus, with a strong wind on the stern and the dexterous manoeuvres of Daidalos, the boat sped across the water and pulled away from Minos' galleys. Those who saw the sails of the ship disappearing over the horizon thought that Daidalos and Ikaros had made wings and were flying.

Daidalos remained in Sicily, which he reached after his escape from Crete, for a long time, under the patronage of King Kokalos and made things that were admired not only by the people of that period but much later as well.

Meanwhile, Minos, who had lost track of Daidalos, took his fleet and went from place to place, looking for him. Wherever he went Minos brought out a triton shell and a thread and promised a large reward to anyone who could pass the thread through the shell. Minos knew that only one person could do this, namely Daidalos, who had built the labyrinth.

After going from country to country Minos finally reached Sicily, went to Kamikos and found the King. He showed him the shell and to his surprise saw that Kokalos found nothing difficult about it. Minos eagerly awaited the outcome while Kokalos left and went in secret to Daidalos and showed him what Minos wanted. Without hesitation, Daidalos bored a hole at the point of the shell, took the end of the thread, tied it to an ant and had it enter the front of the shell where it made its way to the back. Kokalos proudly went to Minos and showed him his accomplishment. Minos was now certain that Daidalos was hidden there and immediately demanded his surrender. Kokalos promised he would do what he asked and then invited him to stay in his palace. Minos accepted and shortly after he was found dead in his bath.

Concerning his inglorious end, it is said that Daidalos instructed the daughters of Kokalos on how to hold Minos in the hot bath water till he succumbed or that the girls poured scalding water or boiling pitch over him.

The sad story of Ikaros is illustrated here in four scenes. Left, Daidalos, his father, finishes one of the wings he and Ikaros will fit to their backs so as to escape from Crete by flying. Behind him, a female form, perhaps the personification of Craftsmanship, helps him in his task. In the second scene, Ikaros tries on the wings. A Fate raises a closed eiliton containing his destiny. Right, holding a laurel branch, Apollo turns to look at them. Further on, the hero boldly flies in the sky. In the final scene, and while the Fate to the left has now opened the eiliton, Ikaros lies lifeless on a lush hill, undoubtedly in Ikaria.

The local god(?) watches from above. (Roman sarcophagus. Shortly after the middle of the 2nd century B.C. Messina, Museo Nazionale).

Historical review

The geographical position of Crete was definitive for its historical course down through the ages. Situated between three continents – Europe, Asia and Africa – it was at the junction of the major cultural currents and at the cross-roads of conflicting geopolitical interests and bloody clashes. On Cretan soil were hatched and developed features of civilization which marked the history of mankind. At the same time the island paid a heavy price because of its strategic position and was repeatedly invaded and periodically conquered, which contributed to the destruction of the existing civilization, the lowering of living standards and the subsequent misery of the inhabitants. However, through successive restructurings new forms of social coexistence were forged, new intellectual values arose and new material and cultural creations appeared which left their indelible mark on Crete and the historical role of the Cretans.

Colour relief of the "Prince of the Lilies" or the "Priest-King". The figure is wearing a Minoan loincloth and a crown of lilies and peacock feathers. Palace of Knossos (circa 1500 B.C.). Herakleion Museum.

Certainly the memory of the remote and glorious past, the Minoan period, survived in the ancient world by means of Greek mythology. Mythology, however, cannot be considered an adequate substitute for historical reality. Due to the successful efforts of Greek and foreign archaeologists, historians and linguists who have brought and are bringing to light the material artefacts of Minoan civilization, the Cretan past has been significantly illuminated.

Moreover, during recent times archaeological excavations and historical research have been extended into more modern periods, revealing the physiognomy of Crete in its entirety.

Nevertheless, the distant past of mankind on the island during those periods from which there is no written information (Neolithic) or those periods from which written testimony (hieroglyphics, Linear A) has been found but not yet deciphered, continues to keep its secrets and continually challenges the experts.

Endeavouring to systematize our knowledge of these periods, two of the most important specialists on Minoan civilization, the Englishman Sir Arthur Evans, the excavator of Knossos at the beginning of the century, and, more recently, the Greek Nikolaos Platon, have formulated two different systems of dating.

Evans gave the name of the mythical king Minos of Knossos to the time between the end of the Neolithic period (2600 B.C.) and the end of the second millennium (1100 B.C.). Based on archaeological finds, pottery in particular, and their comparison with similar finds in Egypt, Evans divided this period of 1500 years into three phases: Early Minoan (EM), 2600-2000 B.C., Middle Minoan (MM), 2000-1600 B.C. and Late Minoan (LM), 1600-1100 B.C. Each stage was divided into three sub-periods with Latin numerals, such as Early Minoan, I, II, III and the abbreviations, EMI, EMII, EMIII.

Professor N. Platon based his system primarily on important events that took place on the island, revealed by the development, the erection and the destruction of the palaces of Minoan Crete. Thus, he divided this same period into four rather than three stages: Pre-Palace (2600-1900 B.C.), Old Palace (1900-1700 B.C.), New Palace (1700-1450 B.C.) and Post-Palace (1450-1100 B.C.). To assist experts each period is divided into phases, i.e., Old Palace I, II, III, etc

To help the reader of this Guide and the visitor to the antiquities and museums of Crete, the chronology of Professor Platon has been adopted.

During the presentation of each specific period, however, the subdivisions of Evans have been added to the titles of the chapters, in parenthesis and abbreviated.

CHRONOLOGICAL CHART OF THE HISTORY OF CRETE

Neolithic period	6000-2600 B.C.	Hellenistic period	330-67 B.C.
Pre-Palace period (EMI, II, III and MMIa)	2600-1900 B.C.	Graeco-Roman period	67 B.C.-330 A.C.
Old Palace period (MMIb, II)	1900-1700 B.C.	First Byzantine period	330-824
New Palace period (MM III and LM I)	1700-1450 B.C.	Arab occupation	824-961
Post-Palace period (LM II, III)	1450-1100 B.C.	Second Byzantine period	961-1204/10
Proto-Geometric period	1100-900 B.C.	Venetian occupation	1204/10-1669
Geometric and Orientalizing period	900-650 B.C.	Turkish occupation	1669-1898
Archaic period	650-500 B.C.	Cretan Republic	1898-1913
Classical period	500-330 B.C.	Province of Greece	1913 to the present

ARCHAEOLOGICAL EXCAVATIONS

Archaeological excavations in Crete began after the middle of the 19th century. In 1878 the Herakleiote antiquarian, Minos Kalokairinos, discovered the palace of Knossos and carried out preliminary excavations. The Society for the Promotion of Education, the President of which was Joseph Chatzidakis, in cooperation with the Italian archaeologist, Frederico Halbherr, excavated the cave known as the "Idaian Antron" in 1884. Joseph Chatzidakis also discovered the Eileithyia cave at Amnisos. In the same year (1884) the Gortyn inscription, a famous and important text of ancient Greece, was brought to light.

The granting of autonomy to Crete gave Greek and foreign archaeologists the opportunity to conduct brilliant excavations. Evans and his staff uncovered the Minoan palace of Knossos, the "royal villa", houses around the palace, the "Royal Tomb" at Isopatos, while S. Xanthoudidis excavated the tombs of Mesara and other areas of Crete. In the following years artefacts from cemeteries, settlements and caves were discovered over the entire island.

The archaeological activity of Greek and foreign archaeologists (from the British, Italian, French and American Schools of Archaeology) reached their peak after World War II, bringing to light valuable data and examples of all forms of art which are of assistance in examining and reconstructing, in part, all aspects of life in Minoan Crete.

The amount of objects still hidden beneath the Cretan soil is indicated by the unique discoveries of N. Platon at the Palace of Zakros and of Yannis and Efi Sakellarakis at the unplundered cemetery and palace complex of Archanes, where excavations are continuing.

HISTORY

Neolithic Period (6000-2600 B.C.)

Archaeological and historical testimony confirms a human presence on Crete for at least 8000 years. With the end of the Ice Age the preconditions were created, throughout the eastern Mediterranean, for the organization of life based upon farming, livestock raising and permanent dwellings.

The people built houses which, as is demonstrated by the ruins at Knossos, Phaistos and Magasa in Siteia, had ground floors of stone and upper storeys of mud brick and branches. The people continued to use caves, which are numerous on the island, though only on a seasonal basis. Well-known caves are Platyvola, Yeranio and Ellinospilio at Afrata in western Crete, the Eileithyia and Stravomyti caves in central Crete, and Trapeza of Lasithi in eastern Crete. They buried their dead in the depths of these and other caves or in pits close to the settlements.

The hammers and axes they used were made of stone. Other utensils were made of bone, while tools were made of obsidian from Melos, which proves that they were in contact with neighbouring islands. Their vessels, however, judging by the fragments found in caves and settlements, had a primitive shape with only rudimentary decoration and are inferior to those found from the same period in the rest of Greece.

During this period religion was practised primarily in caves dedicated to the goddess of fertility represented by the squat (steatopygic) figurines of her, found not only in Crete but throughout the eastern Mediterranean.

Pre-Palace Period (EM, MMIa) 2600-1900 B.C.

During the first centuries of the third millennium there was an increase in the population. The use of bronze for making tools had already begun in the neighbouring regions (the Cyclades, Asia Minor, Egypt) thereby improving the conditions of life. Although the rate of development quickened in the middle of the millennium there are no indications of migrations of people to Crete. Nevertheless, closer contact with neighbouring islands contributed to this development.

The following period, seven centuries long (2600-1900 B.C.) was called Pre-Palace and is divided into four phases.

Agriculture made advances during the early phases. Later, bronze objects existed alongside the stone and clay ones but were considerably improved in quality and craftsmanship. This may have been due to the fact that contacts with the neighbouring islands became more frequent.

Special importance was placed on the interment of the dead. In addition to the burials in caves and the crevices of rocks, tholos tombs also began to make their appearance in Central Crete.

Neolithic clay figure from Hierapetra (height 14.5 cm.).
Herakleion Museum.

These are monumental structures with thick walls and an unsupported domed roof. The most important tholos tombs discovered so far are at Mesara and Archanes.

Significant cultural activity and a change in the way of life characterizes the second phase of the Pre-Palace period. Besides fishing, farming and live-stock raising the inhabitants now began to expand their activities in seafaring and trade. They travelled further and further afield. In order to make copper into bronze, a stronger material, they needed tin, which they brought from foreign countries in exchange for their own, mainly agricultural, products. One of the results of the development of trade was the emergence of economic forces which, in their turn, brought about social distinctions, leading to rad-ical structural changes in the way socie-ty was governed.

The discovery of settlements out-side Hierapetra, at Vasiliki and Myrtos, with large houses which are surround-ed by smaller and more makeshift dwellings, leads to the conclusion that during this period, in the fertile and strategic positions, powerful local lords arose, who concentrated economic power in their hands. This is confirmed by the architecture of the dwellings with their sturdy walls covered in dark red plaster, numerous rooms, work-shops and store-rooms.

Religion was another definite fea-ture of life then. The goddess of fertility continued to be worshipped in caves, as well as in small sanctuaries at the high-est point of the settlements. The fig-urines of her were made of steatite, ivory and marble, and some imitate the Cycladic ones from the same period.

As wealth was accumulated and pot-tery, stone-work and metalwork devel-oped, the various tools and utensils were made in a way which served not only practical needs but satisfied the increasingly refined artistic sense of the inhabitants.

In many parts of Crete, the archaeo-logical pick has brought to light settle-ments and cemeteries of the period which have enriched our knowledge of the rapid cultural development taking place. The most important finds came from the necropolis on the islet of Mochlos, between Siteia and Aghios Nikolaos, which was at that time a peninsula with a double harbour, and from the burial caves at Maronia, Zakros and Trapeza and the settle-ments of Vasiliki and Myrtos, the tho-los tombs at Mesara and the ceme-tery at Phourni of Archanes as well as elsewhere.

For the first time, some kind of pot-ter's wheel was used for the making of clay pots.

Although metal utensils have been found, it is the weapons, tools and in particular the jewellery which reveal the metalwork of the period to us. Of true distinction are the gold diadems, metal pins and necklaces from the necropolis of Mochlos and the tholos tombs of Mesara and Archanes.

The use of semi-precious stones, such as amethyst, sard, agate, rock crystal etc., combined with gold, was widespread. During the final phase of the Pre-Palace period the jewellery worn by both men and women was of the highest quality, including necklaces of sard, rock crystal and amethyst. Gold-working was highly developed and the combination of gold with rock crystal is impressive, as is fili- gree and granulation. A characteristic example is the tiny effigy of a frog from Koumasa with exquisitely delicate gran- ulation and the minute cylinder from Kalathiana with filigree decoration.

The carving of soft materials such as bone and ivory from Egypt and Syria is often sublime: used for figurines and seals with a variety of figures, both ani- mal and human.

At the end of this phase the large set- tlements were destroyed or deserted. These included Vasiliki (which, however, was rebuilt) and Myrtos, while new set- tlements were created in other areas.

Nevertheless, daily life and cultural activity continued unabated. There was some craft specialization and the vari- ous occupational groups became estab- lished. The artisans made up the middle class, while commerce was in the hands of a special class which developed in those communities at opportune loca- tions. Agricultural products, livestock and handicrafts were the major exports.

The sealstones were among the most

important works of art during this peri- od. They were used not only as orna- ments and charms, but also in a practi- cal way, for the sealing of doors, chests and the like.

The seals which carried hieroglyphic representations (i.e., a fourteen-sided seal from Archanes) were of special signifi- cance and are considered the first exam- ples of writing from those early years.

All the cultural indicators were on the rise, preparing the ground for the dawning of the Old Palace period (Mid- dle Minoan Ib, II). It was around then that burial customs acquired more importance. There continued to be tho- los tombs at Mesara, Krasi, Myrini of Siteia and Archanes. To some of these small rooms were added, which served as ossuaries or as places for the cult of the dead.

Old Palace period (MMIb, II) 1900-1700 B.C.

The transformation observed in Crete around 1900 B.C. was a sudden one because the first palaces appeared then, which meant that power was concen- trated in a few centres on the island. It is known from other sources that dur- ing those years in Greece, the Aegean and Asia Minor there were upheavals and movements of population groups. The Cretans reacted to these upheavals by uniting under two or three kings.

It is certain that no new populations came to Crete even at that time. This concentration of power and wealth, which had existed to some degree previously, led to an unprecedented cultural development in the Aegean area.

For the next five centuries the palaces became the main centres of brilliance. The largest palace was built at Knossos, on the north central plain of the island where there had been a large settlement for centuries. Another palace, Phaistos, was erected to the south, on the plain of Mesara. Its position, on top of a hill, where there had been previous settlements, was chosen so that it could control the sea. During the same period, palaces were built at Malia (east of Knossos) and at Zakros (on the southeastern side of the island). A palatial complex was erected at Archanes, another possibly at Chania (so-called Kydonia) and one at Monastiraki, Rethymnon.

Around the palaces were unfortified towns, a feature which proves that the various local archons lived in harmony with each other under the central authority of the king, whose seat was at Knossos. The dwellings of the nobility, the officials and the priests were usually next to the palaces. These were also multi-storeyed, built of stone, clay and wooden beams (obviously to make them resistant to earthquakes) with double-leaved doors and windows.

A noteworthy private residence with decorated walls and floors, stairways and corridors, which was found at Malia, belongs to this category.

Despite the fact that the remains from the palaces of the Old Palace period are not numerous, the reconstruction of their architecture is not impossible. They were multi-storeyed with square rooms and many corridors around a central court and with a host of storerooms and sanctuaries. The interior spaces were splendidly decorated with frescoes and gypsum plaques.

The technical works, especially the drainage systems, are particularly impressive. An entire network with a suitable slope led to a central sewer deep enough for a person to walk through upright. The plumbing was equally well developed. The water came through clay pipes to the palace of Knossos from a spring on the slopes of Mount Juktas, a distance of ten kilometers. At Phaistos, however, and Malia the water supply came from cisterns, while at Zakros it came from wells/springs.

The multitude of workshops and storage areas leads one to the conclusion that the palaces covered needs a great deal broader than simply those of their residents. In the storerooms were amassed products not only from the royal fields but also from the contributions or taxes of the king's subjects, while the products of the workshops were sufficient to cover the needs of both the local market and export. This shows that trade, at least export trade, was controlled by the palaces.

Objects from Crete have been found in Egypt and areas of the Middle East. The treasure of Minoan silver objects in

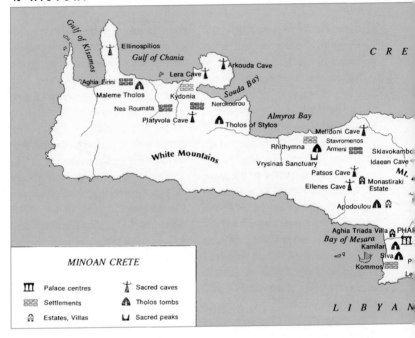

MINOAN CRETE

♨	Palace centres	🏕	Sacred caves
⊞⊞⊞	Settlements	♤	Tholos tombs
⌂	Estates, Villas	⊔	Sacred peaks

the temple of Byblos in Phoenicia and a similar treasure at Tod in Egypt are mentioned.

In the tombs of Abydos, from the 12th Egyptian dynasty, marvellous Cretan Kamares ware vases decorated with rosettes and garlands were found together with Egyptian ones. Similar finds have been uncovered in Cyprus, with which the Cretans maintained close commercial ties mainly in order to avail themselves of its abundant copper. The two-way nature of commercial relations is confirmed by the discovery in the Minoan centres of Crete of Egyptian stone vessels and figurines, sarcophagi and Oriental cylinder seals.

The development of external trade along the coasts of the Mediterranean took on such enormous dimensions that historians speak of the Minoan thalassocracy. On certain islands, such as Melos and Kythera, the existence of Minoan installations has been confirmed; they were obviously Cretan commercial stations.

Our knowledge concerning Minoan ships of this period is limited, and is derived from a handful of sealstones depicting sailing ships with 1-3 masts, which often have oars as well, and from small, terracotta models.

During the same period the roads to the interior of the island were paved with flagstones; they connected its northern with its southern side. At the

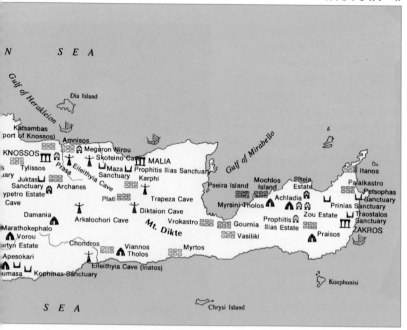

N   S E A

Gulf of Heraklion

Dia Island

Katsambas
port of Knossos)
Amnisos
KNOSSOS
Megaron Nirou
Skoteino Cave   MALIA
Tylissos   Prasa   Eileithyia   Maza   Prophitis Ilias Sanctuary
uary   Sanctuary   Cave   Karphi
Juktas   Archanes
ypetro Estate   Plati   Trapeza Cave
Cave   Diktaion Cave
Damania   Arkalochori Cave   Vrokastro   Gournia
Marathokephalo   Mt. Dikte   Vasiliki
Vorou
rtyn Estate   Chondros
Apesokari   Viannos   Myrtos
umasa   Kophinas Sanctuary   Tholos
Eileithyia Cave (Inatos)

Gulf of Mirabello

Itanos
Mochlos   Siteia
Pseira Island   Island   Estate   Palaikastro
Achladia   Petsophas
Myrsini Tholos   Sanctuary
Zou Estate   Prinias Sanctuary
Prophitis   Traostalos
Ilias Estate   Sanctuary
Praisos   ZAKROS

Kouphonisi

S E A   Chrysi Island

same time agriculture also expanded through the construction of the first large irrigation projects.

All these projects, together with the marvellous palace structures verify the existence of an advanced class of engineers, architects and artisans.

There was also a burgeoning in pottery. The vases display a variety of shapes and great decorative wealth. Kamares ware was the dominant style. The surfaces of the vases were black-coated with elegant decorative motifs painted on them, in a variety of combinations, in white and red. The style was called Kamares ware because the first vessels of this type were found in the Kamares cave on Psiloreitis in 1884. Furthermore,

Map of Minoan Crete showing the main sites where excavations have brought to light remains of the Minoan civilization.

the perfecting of the potter's wheel permitted vases to be made with very thin walls (eggshell ware).

The large storage jars are also charming in their own way, decorated as they are with numerous bands, handles and applied plastic ornamentation. There was a significant upsurge in clay miniatures, particularly figurines. Some of these depict human figures in an attitude of prayer. The men are presented naked, wearing only the Cretan girdle, and some have a knife at the waist. The women wore luxurious garments and artistic diadems. A large number of religious vessels and implements were made during the same period.

The role of religion was strengthened from one end of the island to the other. The priests occupied a high position in the Minoan social hierarchy. Religious qualities and perhaps even divine powers appear to have been attributed to the king himself. Large sections of the palaces were dedicated to the goddess. Divine worship also took place in the outdoor or covered sanctuaries on the tops of hills and mountains, such as the Peak Sanctuary on Juktas (Archanes), Profitis Ilias (Malia), Vrysina (Rethymnon), Kophinas, Petsophas (Palaikastro), Pisokephalo (Siteia) and Kalo Chorio (Pediada). At these sanctuaries the divinity was worshipped using fire and figurines, both animal and human. The triple nature of the female deity can be discerned: the heavenly (with doves), the chthonic (with snakes) and the earthly (*Potnia Theron* - Mistress of Animals).

There are changes in burial customs, since tholos tombs are no longer built and there is an increase in the number of individual inhumations in clay jars (*pithoi*). Small clay sarcophagi appear for the first time.

Writing now changed from ideograms to hieroglyphics with stylized pictures and incisions.

Hieroglyphic depictions and texts have been found on seals, tablets, staffs and discs of clay, as well as on various

Clay figurine of an armed man in an attitude of worship, from the peak sanctuary of Petsophas. (Old Palace period). Herakleion Museum.

Clay sealing with impression of a male figure and ideograms. Herakleion Museum.

objects such as the stone altar of the palace of Malia and the double axe from the Arkalochori cave. But the greatest mass of hieroglyphic archives were found gathered in special rooms at the palaces of Knossos and Malia.

The use of hieroglyphic script continued up to the beginning of the New Palace period, when Linear A writing began to appear, with which it co-existed for a period of time.

The most important hieroglyphic text is the famous clay disc from Phaistos which is dated to 1700-1600 B.C. and is definitely of a sacred, ceremonial nature. It was stamped on both sides of the disc, spiralling in from the edge to

the centre, where impressions made by movable seals depict human forms, parts of the body, tools, implements, weapons, animals, plants, a boxing glove and even ships. This was in effect the first form of printing. A total of 241 marks can be seen, of 45 different types, which are divided into groups separated by vertical lines. Despite the endeavours of experts the text has not been deciphered. Originally it was considered to be of Hittite or Asian origin because it was different from the other Minoan texts. In any case, investigators have confirmed that the hieroglyphics of Minoan Crete, despite their apparent relationship to those of Egypt, are a local invention. Various local systems evolved throughout the island. In the specific case of the Phaistos Disc certain of its Minoan symbols and their arrangement are reminiscent of the gold ring found at Mavrospilaio from Arkalochori; this reinforces the hypothesis concerning the indigenous character of the hieroglyphics.

Seal-making, however, is what truly reveals the artistic skill of the Minoans.

Many seals have survived *in toto*, while of others only their impression on clay remains. Seal-making used mainly semi-precious stones (amethyst, sard, rock crystal, agate, meteorite). The shapes are prismatic and three- or four-sided, and the designs depict various forms and objects from daily life.

Around 1700 B.C. a powerful earthquake shook a large area of western

Asia and the eastern Mediterranean from Troy to Palestine and the islands of the Aegean. In Crete it caused the destruction of the old palaces. Nevertheless, life did not come to a halt and soon a new, even more brilliant period began, the New Palace period.

New Palace Period (MMIII, LMI) 1700-1450 B.C.

The approximately two and a half centuries following the destructive earthquakes of 1700 B.C. could be called the "golden age" of Minoan Crete. Historians have dubbed it New Palace because of the breathtaking new palaces that were erected on the sites of the old.

From a comparison of the features before and after the destruction of the old palaces, it becomes obvious that there was no foreign invasion because if there had been it would have brought about a fundamental transformation in the character of the civilization and the composition of the population. The indigenous powers found the strength, the means and the proper organizational coherence to mount a tremendous effort, not only toward reconstruction but toward the renewal of their civilization on a higher level.

The unique Phaistos disc with hieroglyphics (both sides). (Circa 1600 B.C.). Herakleion Museum.

Because of the numerous excavations which were begun by the British archaeologist Arthur Evans at the beginning of the present century and which have been continued up to the present by noteworthy Greek and foreign archaeologists, we have a nearly complete picture of the life and civilization of Minoan Crete during the period of its greatest glory.

The priority that was given to the rebuilding of the palaces is explained by the fact that they were the foci of the economic, social, religious and political life of the country, which is why they are enormous in area and grand beyond measure. The palace of Knossos covers an area of 22,000 sq. m., Phaistos and Malia nearly 9000 sq. m. and Zakros 7-8000 sq. m. To these four large palaces must be added the villa at Aghia Triada, with an area of 6000 sq. m., and the palace building of Archanes. It is estimated that the roofed areas (apartments, storerooms, workshops etc.) of Knossos covered 1500 sq. m.

It is worth mentioning that the architects who designed them followed the same basic principles in arrangement of spaces in all the complexes, with a central and western court, stairways, propylaia, light wells, and so forth. The courts were the lungs of the buildings, supplying ventilation and lighting to the rooms and allowing people to move in all directions. Both of them were filled with people during religious festivals. This explains the altars, braziers, gran-

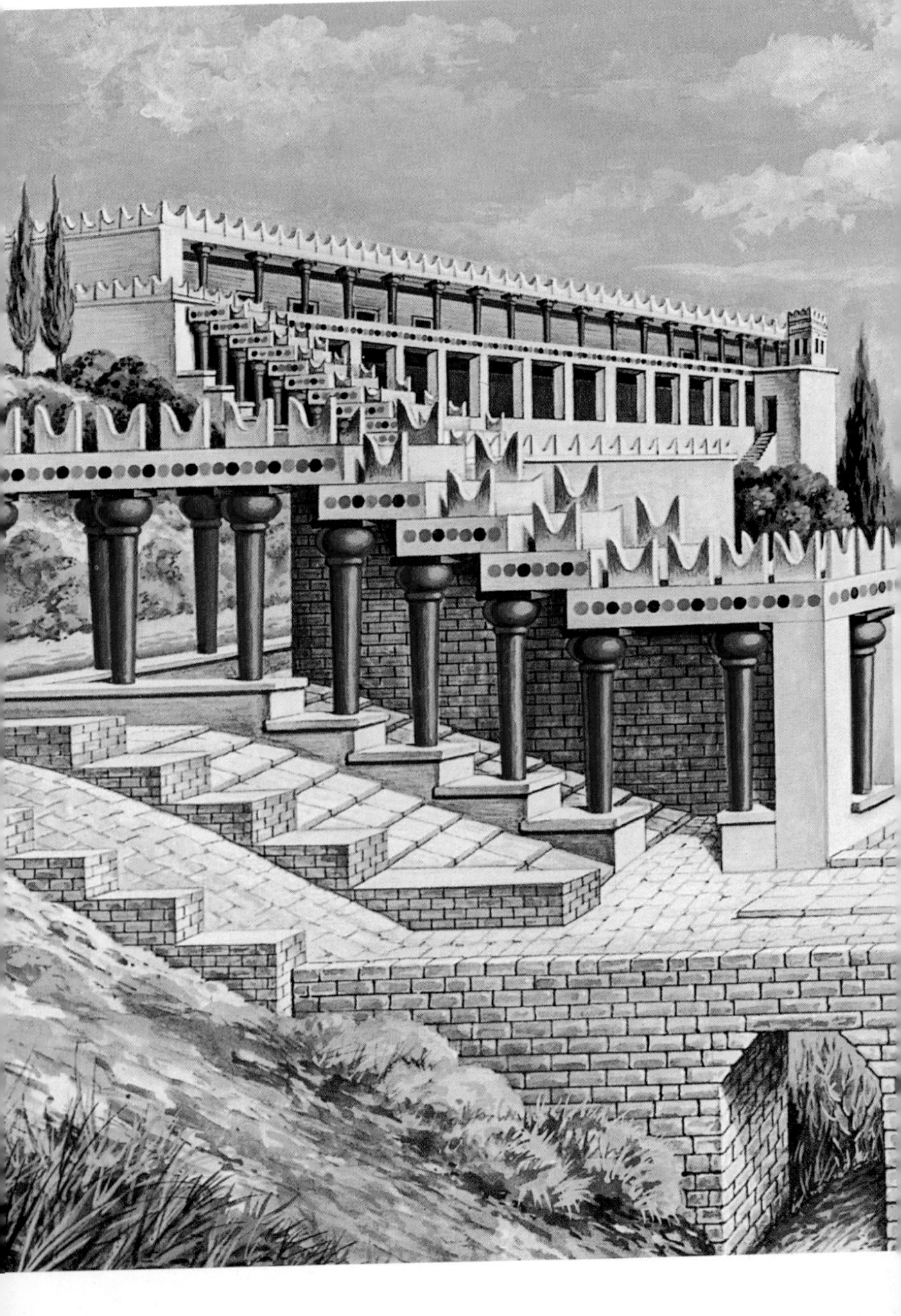

aries and sacred symbols found there.

The various kinds of apartments are not in the same place in all the palaces. Nevertheless, the cult rooms are always in the west wing. Naturally, the royal apartments were in the best spot in terms of lighting, ventilation, view, ease of communication, etc.

The storage systems were organized according to their purpose; the sacred ones next to the sacred areas, the royal ones next to the royal workshops, those for common implements next to the servants' quarters, etc. The building materials used came from neighbouring quarries or forests. With the experiences of the earthquakes fresh in their memory, the engineers combined stones with wooden beams when building the walls, to give elasticity to the structure. The columns were made of tree trunks which were placed upside down, with the widest part at the top, while the floors were of green slate with interstices of red plaster. The water and drainage systems, already well-developed during the Old Palace period, appear to have been improved.

Other large and luxurious structures, either around the palaces or at a considerable distance from them were also built at this time.

There are several theories concerning their use. Most probably they were residences of the local archons or landholders or even of a class of nobles who obviously operated under the control of the royal authority.

Reconstruction of the stairway entrance to the Palace of Knossos.

Reconstruction of the façade of the west wing of the Palace of Knossos.

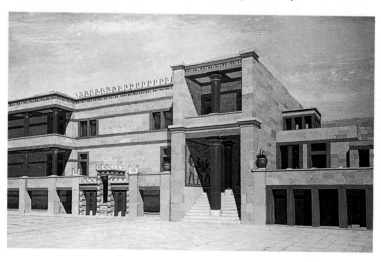

Scattered throughout the country-side of west and central but primarily eastern Crete are building complexes which from their location and the arrangement of their internal spaces could be considered country houses or farms. The most important are at Skla-vokambos, Nirou Chani, Vathypetro and Vitsila in the region of Lykastros, Metropolis Gortyn in central Crete, Plati in Lasithi, Pyrgos in Myrtos, the farms at Siteia, Zou, Achladia, Profitis Ilias, Makryyalos and Epano Zakros in eastern Crete, and Nerokouros in western Crete (Chania).

The various dwellings, wich had thir-ty to fifty rooms, also housed installa-tions that were indispensable to an agricultural economy and handicrafts: a wine press for the grapes, an olive oil press, built-in tubs for the kneading of the clay, spaces for the firing of the small vases and for spreading out the unfired vessels, places for dyeing, etc. Looms were also set up, which shows that weaving was advanced and quite widespread.

All these finds confirm the complete autonomy of the inhabitants of these rural dwellings. At Vathypetro and Epano Zakros in particular, the installa-tions for wine-making have been quite well-preserved, while at Zou in Siteia the pottery workshops are impressive.

Still, a large number of the inhabi-tants of the island lived in the towns, which in certain areas had developed into substantial cities. Large architectur-al units have been excavated at Malia, Zakros, Gournia, Palaikastro, Mochlos and Pseira, from which the town-plan of that period becomes comprehensible, with large blocks of adjoining houses.

The circumferential roads and the ones at right angles to them were usu-ally stone-paved (such as at Gournia and Zakros) while the uphill ones were stepped.

Each town appears to have had its own special character, which is demon-strated to a degree by the economic and social conditions which prevailed there. In wealthy Zakros, which was the eastern gateway for Cretan commerce, large well-built houses with many rooms were found, which were used for a variety of occupations. North of Za-kros, in the settlement of Palaikastro, courts and narrow winding streets di-vided extensive clocks. In Gournia, small two-storey houses were found, clearly the dwellings of farmers, artisans and sailors. The settlement uncovered on the island of Pseira in the gulf of Mirabello was a maritime commercial centre. It was built amphitheatrically on the leeward side, overlooking the har-bour. The wealthy houses of the mer-chants were decorated with relief fres-coes, in no way inferior to those at Knossos.

Special mention must be made of the well-equipped harbours which have been located at many points on the island. Amnisos – the harbour of Knos-sos – appears to have lived on in mem-

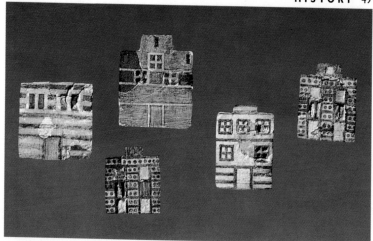

Facades of multi-storey houses in faience (height 3-5 cm.). (1700-1600 B.C.). Herakleion Museum.

ory for many centuries because Homer makes mention of it, at least five centuries later. Other harbours have been found near Aghioi Theodoroi, Nirou Chani and at Malia. The harbour of Phaistos was at Kommos, to the west of Mesara.

The development of large urban centres throughout the island increased the needs for communication links. The already extensive road network of the Middle Minoan period became even denser and was augmented by many bridges, guard houses and inns which showed the prosperity and commercial activity of the Cretans.

Worthy of note is the viaduct which connected the palace of Knossos with an arcade supported on columns. In front of the viaduct was a guest-house with dining rooms, dormitories, hot baths and water troughs for animals.

All these technical projects, and in particular the development of the harbours, demonstrate the intense commercial activity of the Cretans during the New Palace period. Crete now constituted the commercial centre of the entire central and eastern Mediterranean.

Maritime depots, which were called "Minoes", were also established outside Crete on many islands, such as Kythera, Kea, Rhodes, Thera, Melos, Skopelos and in areas of continental Greece, Aghios Stephanos, Lakonia and Asia Minor (Miletus). Minoan commercial activity is also confirmed on the shores of Asia and Africa, in Cyprus and Sicily. Written Egyptian sources mention that sea trade was carried out by the "Keftiu". Egyptian wall-paintings show the Keftiu bringing gifts to the Egyptian kings. Their appearance leaves no doubt that they are Cretans. The headdress, the characteristic attire, and the marvellously wrought gifts they are holding are the same as those which are depicted on the frescoes in Crete.

Just as in the earlier periods, handicrafts as well as agricultural products from the island were in demand on the international markets, particularly the choice wine and the aromatic olive oil. It also seems that Cretans successfully applied themselves to transit trade and dealt in Lebanese cedar from one end of the Mediterranean to the other.

During this period the Minoan ships were significantly improved. Depictions on seals and pottery show them with oars and masts, rams and gunwales, even rudders, bridges and deck cabins.

The peaceful life on the island does not mean that the Minoans of that period had nothing to do with military matters. Excavations have revealed a large number of defensive and offensive weapons, such as spears and javelins with reinforced points, long swords, a variety of daggers and cheek guards.

The social organization must not have undergone any essential changes. Certainly the abundance and the wealth would strengthen the class of nobles. The beautiful spacious houses in the large urban centres show what a comfortable life the merchants and sailors led. On the other hand the development of farming, the perfecting of agricultural equipment and the construction of large irrigation projects (such as the Linies irrigation system on the Lasithi plateau) also raised the standard of living of the tillers of the soil. Moreover, the artisans were now in a more advantageous position in relation to the preceding periods.

The wealth and variety of finds testify to the flourishing of handicrafts, which appear to also have developed inside the dwellings where the women played their part, especially in the case of weaving. It is worth noting how the aromatic and therapeutic herbs of Crete – some of which are still called by their Minoan names – were exploited, creating a class of artisans who specialized in perfume-making and pharmaceuticals. Similar improvement can be seen in the production of pigments, principally from minerals but also from seashells, such as porphyry from the murex shell which was widely applied to wall-painting.

The Minoans were also characterized by their deep religiosity. As we have already mentioned, areas were set

The famous faience figurine of the "Snake Goddess" found at Knossos (1600-1580 B.C.). Herakleion Museum.

Multicoloured stone sarcophagus of Aghia Triada with religious scenes (circa 1400 B.C.). Herakleion Museum.

aside in the palaces for religious purposes. They contained the lustral basins, as well as fountains, stepped altars, offering tables, marble altars and a host of sacred objects decorated with horns.

At certain times religious festivals were held in the sacred precincts. People came to these gatherings not only to worship, but also to be entertained. Along with their lavish offerings to the divinity, the faithful augmented the resources of the public treasury.

Society continued to have a theocratic character. The kings were at the same time the great high priests. These features are confirmed by various depictions from the period in which the king wears a crown and a necklace of lilies and holds peacock feathers, symbols of his religious authority.

Some experts believe that the name "Minos" is the title for the king, just as "Pharaoh" was the title of the supreme ruler in Egypt. There must have been some hierarchy among the members of the royal family. The queen undoubtedly occupied a high position.

The fact that the divinity who continued to be worshipped was the fertility goddess emphasizes the woman's role in Minoan Crete. The religious figurines of the goddess which are found both in the religious precincts of the palaces and on the sacred mountain peaks and hills, are truly impressive. Some show her holding snakes in her hands and wearing a heavy garment which leaves her breasts bare.

An important religious symbol of this period was the double axe, the so-called *labrys*, which is carved on the pillars of the sacred rooms of the palace of Knossos and is a symbol of supernatural power.

The care of the dead played an important part in Minoan society. All kinds of grave goods were placed in the tombs, not just plain offerings but also beauty aids and anything else the dead person might need. The entrance passage to the graves was filled in, ostensibly so the dead person would not be disturbed but, in actuality, so he would be protected from violators.

In the carved chamber tombs the dead were placed on wooden biers or in wooden sarcophagi which were later replaced by clay or even stone ones. One stone sarcophagus, obviously royal – which was found reused in a later tomb at Aghia Triada – is decorated in the manner of the wall-paintings with very interesting representations relating to the worship of the dead.

Just as in the preceding periods, a variety of burial customs were observed. The dead were interred in small caves in the hollows of hills, the sandy beaches of seaside settlements, in jars that were turned upside down and small clay sarcophagi or on wooden biers.

Tomb architecture became even more imposing. Characteristic are the tholos tombs at Kamilaris in the region of Phaistos which were built at the beginning of the 16th century, the tombs at Tekes and Kefala, between Knossos and Herakleion, and the enormous royal tomb at Isopata. The chambers were originally circular and later square with a domed or saddle roof.

The tholos tomb which was found intact in the region of Archanes is dated to the end of this period. Besides the tholos tombs, there are also a host of carved chamber tombs, most of which were found in the areas of Knossos and Phaistos.

The Temple Tomb, as Evans called it, which was excavated near the palace of Knossos, is unique in form. The burial chamber is cut into soft stone and internally faced with gypsum slabs with a blue painted roof. An antechamber led to the upper floor where the shrine was. Its form is reminiscent of the description of the tomb of Minos in Sicily where, according to tradition, he was murdered by the daughter of the local king, Kokalos.

If one carefully examines the Minoan wall-paintings, vases, sculptures, etc., one will be impressed by the position women occupied in society. They were free to participate fully in social functions. They took part in hunting expeditions and in various athletic contests, even in the most dangerous ones such as Minoan bull-leaping. Women in Minoan Crete also used a variety of cosmetics, red colour for the lips, white for the face and black for the eyes, while they plucked their eyebrows with tweezers.

One is startled by women's apparel in that period with the open bodice which left the breasts uncovered, or covered with transparent tulle. Beautiful belts were used to cinch slim waists and the skirts had repeated designs. Women's heads were usually covered by a cap or beret but when they were uncovered the hair was adorned with clasps and diadems. The coiffure ended in long curls which reached down to the shoulders while other, shorter curls highlighted the forehead.

In contrast with the women, men dressed plainly. They wore a simple, short girdle which emphasized their muscular, athletic bodies and very thin waist usually adorned with metal belts. Sport – wrestling, boxing, jumping, running etc. – was the favourite pastime of the young men. The most dangerous sport was the peculiar bull-leaping, which is depicted in a number of frescoes and other works of art.

Apart from the more energetic sports there were also board games. Checkers, dice and gaming pieces of bone were widely used. One of the most important finds is the so-called "Draughtboard", a superb work of art made from crystal, azurite, faience and ivory gilded with gold leaf and silver.

There is no doubt that the art of that period was at its zenith. The wall-paintings are its most important expres-

sion. The technical methods employed by the Minoans to fashion and preserve their artistic creations, using the fresco and secco techniques in tandem, are truly impressive.

First the surfaces of the wall were spread with thick plaster. On this was laid down a thinner layer of plaster on which was sketched the outline of the work – frequently with a string or a blunt point – and then painted on while the plaster was fresh (hence "fresco"). The colours were introduced in this way, they dried along with the plaster and became indelible. Then the secco technique was employed for the completion of the painting.

When the surface was dry, the colours were fixed with sticky substances.

Many of the frescoes are in relief, such as the bull at the entrance to Knossos, the women from Pseira, etc. The earlier paintings usually depicted the natural environment, with flowers (irises, crocuses, lilies) birds, monkeys, dolphins, as well as various special themes such as bull-leaping, the "Captain of the Blacks", the "Girl Dancer", "La Parisienne", the "Blue Bird", etc., employing astounding chromatic splendour in unique combinations.

Plaster painted with frescoes covers the sarcophagus of Aghia Triada with its unique representations.

The important art of wall-painting also had a positive effect on vase-painting. New techniques prevailed in ceram-

Fresco of women from the East Wing of the Palace of Knossos. Herakleion Museum.

ics and the vases had more elegant shapes. The motifs were chosen from the world of nature and placed on the light background of the vases with dark colours. Two styles prevailed: the floral and the marine.

Stonework also showed striking development. The stone carvers worked in basalt, porphyrite, rhyolite, obsidian, rock crystal and a variety of veined marbles, as well as chlorite and steatite. One of the most magnificent stone works is the rhyton in the shape of a lioness' head (Treasury of the Sanctuary of Knossos). The rhytons from the sanctuary of Zakros are equally well crafted while the stone vessels with relief representations from Aghia Triada and the palace of Zakros are superb.

Miniature sculpture continued to flourish. Miniature statues of faience,

gold, ivory, bronze and, more rarely, stone are truly masterpieces of inspiration, ability and artistic freedom. Well-known examples are the two famous figurines, "The Snake Goddess" made of faience and the "Bull-Leaper" of Knossos, made of ivory.

The examples of miniature art from the period are also of importance. The technique of using glass paste and faience was perfected, while ivory was also used for the *pyxides* (like the one from Katsambas), for combs, pins and mirror handles.

Gold-working also reached a high level of craftsmanship as did seal-making. A large number of pieces of jewellery made of semi-precious stones, amethyst, sard, steatite and glass paste, sometimes coated with gold, have come from the excavated tombs of the period. These were necklaces of pebbles arranged as plants, flowers and fruit as well as marine animals, insects and four-legged animals. Two of the best known pieces are the bee pendant from Malia and the accessory in the form of a divinity with birds and snakes.

The hard precious and semi-precious stones prevailed in seal-making, in lenticular and amygdaloid shapes with depictions exquisitely executed and of inexhaustible thematic wealth.

Linear A was the form of writing that held sway during the New Palace period. Specialists theorize that it constituted a development of Cretan hieroglyphics and that it expressed the same linguistic unity but its decipherment still remains an unsolved problem.

Outside Crete texts have been found in Linear A on the Aegean islands (Melos, Kea and Thera) and at sites in Mainland Greece where Minoan merchants or settlers had been a strong presence. In Cyprus this writing is considered as the starting point of the later Cypriot-Minoan period which followed its own course.

Isolated texts have been found scattered over many archaeological sites (Knossos, Malia, Archanes, Platanos, etc.) and on a variety of objects and surfaces.

Entire archives of tablets were found in the palace of Aghia Triada, in the palace of Zakros, and at Chania. Jars inscribed with Linear A were found at the palace of Zakros.

Many of the tablets must have dealt with religious matters, while the accounting nature of the writing is obvious. Indeed, experts can make out the numbers, which follow the decimal system, and the texts are written from left to right and from the top part of the list to the bottom, that is, the way we write today.

Closing this important period of the zenith of Minoan civilization it is imperative that one should note the repercussions that this development had on the broader area of Greece, islands and mainland, as well as along certain coastal areas of Asia Minor.

The enormous development of Minoan export trade during this period of approximately three centuries was accompanied by extensive cultivation of coastal and inland areas through which the cultural influence of Minoan Crete was peacefully transmitted to the surrounding peoples. This is shown most explicitly in the incredible flowering of Aegean civilization which had a great deal in common with the Minoan during this period (Thera, for example).

A more important long-term feature was the penetration of Minoan culture into the more general Greek population, around 1600 B.C.

Already by 2000 B.C. the Greeks had begun to descend from the north and settle in southern Greece. These populations – the Achaeans – would create the Mycenaean civilization in the following centuries, which was influ-

Neopalatial bronze figure of
youth in attitude of worship,
from Tylissos (1500 B.C.).
Herakleion Museum.

Steatite vessel with scenes
in relief, known as the "Cup of
the Report", from Aghia Triada
(1550-1500 B.C.). Herakleion
Museum.

enced by Minoan civilization from early on as the many finds from tombs and elsewhere demonstrate.

The Achaeans, a robust and warlike people, began to spread toward the neighbouring islands and Asia Minor in the succeeding centuries (16th and 15th) slowly creating the so-called Cretan-Mycenaean civilization.

Around 1450 B.C. all the large centres of Crete were destroyed. According to one theory this destruction was due to an invasion of foreign tribes. Another theory attributes it to the catastrophic eruption of the volcano on Thera (120 km. north of Crete), which occurred around 1500 B.C., as well as the subsequent earthquakes in 1450 B.C. Several scholars have correlated this theory with the myth of the sinking of Atlantis or the mythological Flood. Based on comparative observations of a similar eruption of the Krakatoa volcano in Indonesia (1883) the possible extent of the destruction of Crete can be reconstructed. The tidal waves carried away everything along the coast. The volcanic ash and the sulphur gas poisoned all living creatures. Successive earthquakes and fires turned the palaces and inland settlements into smouldering ruins. The brilliant New Palace civilization had reached its end.

Post-Palace Period (LMII, III) 1450-1100 B.C.

After the destruction, a new population group is observed on the island, the Greek-speaking Achaeans, who came to prevail. The installation of an Achaean dynasty based in the partially reconstructed palace of Knossos constituted the starting point for a new period in the history of Crete, which until 1380 B.C. lived under a fourth phase of the New Palace period.

The new population group also extended its presence into the interior of the island if one can judge by the discovery of a host of texts and inscriptions in Linear B script.

This script, which was deciphered in 1952 by Michael Ventris and is the third Minoan system of writing, is in a Greek Mycenaean dialect similar to the one used in the Mycenaean centres of continental and island Greece. Nearly 3000 tablets written in this script were found at the palace of Knossos. they bear many similarities to the writing on the tablets at Pylos (western Peloponnese) which are dated 150 years later.

Naturally, the presence of this new element had an affect on the entire spectrum of the political, social, cultural and economic life of the island. Despite the fact that excavations and the study of the finds are continuing it can be ascertained that for one century – until 1380 B.C. when there was a new destructive earthquake – the two races co-existed.

The trade with Africa and Egypt was undertaken in common by the Minoans and the Mycenaeans. Pottery, usually the most reliable "decipherer" of the

Sarcophagus from Hierapetra depicting men,
goats, bulls and dogs in chariot race scenes (IIth
c. B.C.). Hierapetra Archaeological Collection.

secrets of antiquity, changed style. The
so-called "Palace style" now held sway.
The designs on the vases remained con-
ventional and became stylized.

The same technique is also used in
the new frescoes at the palace, in the
"throne room", in the processional corridor and elsewhere.

The tombs also show the change.
Along with the re-usage, obviously by
the same Minoan race, of old tombs
such as the one at Isopata, there were
now tombs for the new inhabitants, the
offerings in which indicate the warlike
char-acter of the dead.

The fire of 1380 B.C., which completely destroyed Knossos, signalled the
end of the brilliant Minoan period of

the palaces. The Achaean (Mycenaean)
dynasty controlled the island and built
megara in new areas, as is clear from
various scattered ruins.

The so-called Post-Palace period
which followed on the island, though
less brilliant than the period of the peak
of Minoan civilization, cannot be considered as a period of decline. The lavish
royal tombs at Phourni of Archanes,
confirm the wealth of the new archons
and their cultural level. The Mycenaean
palace existed beside the complicated
and labyrinthine Minoan architectural
complexes but it did not prevail every-
where, while wall-painting lost its flexi-
bility and liveliness. In Aghia Triada, for
example, a large building of the period

was found, a type of Mycenaean megaron, with a complex of store-rooms, galleries and a sanctuary. Remains of a Mycenaean palace were also found at Tyiissos, while at Archanes and elsewhere many other structures were discovered.

There was a variety of burial customs with the presence of both old and new ones which confirm the co-existence of the two populations. Both in eastern and western Crete impressive unplundered graves have been excavated, such as the square tholos tombs at Maleme, near Chania, the tomb at Mouliana, where a gold mask was found, the tholos tombs at Achladia and Sphakia. Siteia, Apodoulos, Amari and Stylos of Apokoronos.

The peak years of Knossos are attested by its cemeteries as well as those of its harbour, Katsambas.

Compared with previous periods, art was in relative decline. Bronzesmithing, however, reached its peak, as it shown by the bronze vessels from Knossos and Archanes. There are also fine examples of gold rings from Mavrospilia of Knossos. Marvellous examples of the pottery of the period were found at Archanes. Sculpture supplies us with religious figurines, mainly of the goddess with raised arms, which were found in sanctuaries at Gazi, Herakleion, Gournia, Karphi, Lasithi, etc. Egyptian sources mention attacks on Egypt around 1200 B.C. by the Sea Peoples, and the inhabitants of Kaftor are

mentioned. a name which is attributed to Crete.

If the interpretation is correct, that means that towards the end of the Mycenaean period, Crete maintained a powerful fleet which was occupied with military and piratical adventures. This is confirmed by the tradition concerning its participation in the Trojan War around 1200 B.C.

Large clay figurine of the "Goddess with the doves", from Gazi, Herakleion (13th century B.C.). Herakleion Museum.

But as the 11th century approached, pockets of general decline appeared throughout Greece. The kingdoms disintegrated and trade encountered problems. The new Dorian race, also Greek-speaking, which descended from northern to southern Greece, would benefit from this, later advancing onward to the islands of the Aegean and Crete.

Proto-Geometric Period (1100-900 B.C.)

New waves of emigrants reached Crete between 1100 and 900 B.C.; they consisted of Achaeans and Dorians who knew the use of iron. Originally they settled in central Crete, but later spread over the whole island. The older inhabitants took refuge in the mountains of central and eastern Crete. Remains of settlements from this period have been found at Karphi, Lasithi, Vrokastro and Mirabello but mainly in the region of Praisos.

These inhabitants, who are referred to in source material as Eteocretans, were the descendants of the old Minoans. They preserved their customs and their linguistic idiom, as is shown by the much later Eteocretan inscriptions which were found at Praisos, written in Greek letters but in an incomprehensible language.

During this period the use of iron became general. Not only weapons, but also tools and decorative objects, such as fibulae which held the simple Dorian garment, were made of iron.

But in terms of art this period is one of co-existence and a confusion of old and new styles.

The new colonists brought with them the custom of cremating the dead which became general with the passage of time. Nevertheless, the burying of the dead continued sporadically in small tholos tombs with, or without, a small dromos.

At this time there were also certain changes in Cretan religion with a gradual transition to the Greek pantheon. The attributes of the goddess of vegetation were accorded to such deities as Diktynna, Britomartis and Ariadne, while Welchanos or Hyakinthos became identified with Zeus. The old worship of the bull was transformed into the myth of Europa.

Geometric and Orientalizing Periods (900-650 B.C.)

During this period a new political organization of the island began to appear, following the pattern of the Greek world of mainland Greece. Thus, autonomous city-states were created which, according to the testimony of ancient writers, came to total around

100. Of these, archaeological research has located at least half.

The most important were in central Crete: Knossos, Gortyn, Phaistos, Tylissos, Lyttos, Chersonnisos, Vianna, Priasos, Arkades, Rizenia and Pytion; in western Crete: Axos, Eleutherna, Lappa, Syvritos, Aptera, Kydonia, Elyros, Kisamos, Lissos, Polyrrenia, Tarra, Irtakina and in the east: Milatos, Driros, Lato, Olous, Hierapytna, Praisos, Itanos, Iteia and Ambelos.

It appears that in the main the Dorians kept the old Minoan names of towns. But they did not show a similar tolerance toward the old inhabitants who they divided into three classes, according to the resistance they had offered: the *Perioikoi* (the subjects), the *Mnoites* and the *Aphamiotes* or *Klarotes*.

The *Perioikoi* were those old inhabitants who submitted to the Dorians with little or no resistance. They were settled on the outskirts of the towns where they maintained private fields, paying the government a single tax in kind from their produce. They could also take part in the arts and commerce. They were obliged to take up arms in war but had no political rights. Nonetheless, they were governed according to their own laws, as long as these were not in conflict with the Dorian ones.

The *Mnoites* were the class which arose from those inhabitants who had offered some resistance, which is why their fields were confiscated by the State. They themselves became slaves, cultivating what had formerly been their own land on behalf of the State. The government set them to constructing public works, roads, bridges and civic structures.

The *Aphamiotes* were those who had resisted the Dorians to the bitter end. That is why they were shared out among the Dorians by lot, along with their property, as personal slaves for farming but not household occupations. It appears that the position of the *Aphamiotes* was better than that of the helots in Sparta. The model of the Dorian society of Sparta had been transferred to a large degree to Crete and the strict Dorian customs did not change much till the Classical-Hellenistic period.

The various finds from the excavations show that besides its pervasive remains of an old cultural tradition, Crete became a recipient of a variety of elements from outside. The vases that were found, mainly in the cemeteries of Fortetsa near Knossos, and at Arkades (Aphrati, Pediada) bear strong Oriental influences with some survivals of Minoan representations. Motifs such as the "tree of life", garlands and chains of poppies and lilies have their origin in the Orient. But the polychrome vases must be attributed to a Minoan legacy.

Similar Oriental influences can be seen in the metal-work, gold-work and miniature sculpture. Examples of this. are the bronze shields from the "Idaian

Antron" on Mount Ida (where the Cretan-born Zeus had already been worshipped during the Minoan period), wonderfully decorated with eagles holding sphinxes, snakes, lions, etc., in their talons. From the tombs of Fortetsa come the impressive bronze belt and quiver which depicts the abduction of a woman, the struggle of a hero with a lion.

Figurines and scarabs which were found in tombs from this period show the continuing contacts with Egypt and the influence of Egyptian art on the development of Cretan miniature sculpture. According to tradition, the sculpture of this school, with the wide spread of the legs, the projection of the arms and the open eyes is attributed to Dedalos (not the Daidalos of the Minoan myth) and his pupils.

Archaic Period
(650-550 B.C.)

The Dedalic style encountered at the end of the Geometric period reached its acme between 650 and 630 B.C. An outstanding example is the sandstone body of a statue from Eleutherna, with a beautiful knitted robe and hair reminiscent of the Egyptian wig. Of the two Archaic temples found at Prinias, the architecture of the older one, which is dated to the mid-7th century B.C., is like the small Minoan sanctuary of the post-Palace period.

The hammered bronze figurines of a young man and two women (Apollo, Leto and Artemis) from the temple of Driros belongs to the first Archaic period. From the temple of Diktaian Zeus at Palaikastro comes a beautiful clay water pipe with lions' heads for spouts, while at the temple on the acropolis of Gortyna many Dedalic clay figurines were found with the typical thick hair. Also found in the same temple was a series of votive plaques with mythological representations in relief and Oriental-style sphinxes, lions, gorgons and nude deities.

In the 7th century B.C. Crete was the most vibrant spot in all of Greece. Noteworthy artists such as the sculptors Dipoinos and Skyllis emigrated to the Peloponnese and the architects of Knossos, Chersiphron and Metagenis, settled in Ionia. They transferred their workshops there and became teachers of the great art.

In the 6th century B.C. a general decline took place in Crete. The main causes for this were, on the one hand, the withering of commercial activity and the absolute imposition of the frugal, militaristic Dorian spirit and on the other the rapid development of the Ionian commercial cities. The city-states of Crete, as on mainland Greece, were contending and warring with each other. At the same time various foreign invaders arrived on the island from Greek regions, as well as from the Asiatic coasts, and caused great material destruction while subjugating the inha-bitants.

Social life, however, remained rationally ordered with a system of laws which,

Bronze drum from the Idaian Cave (8th c. B.C.). Herakleion Museum.

Bronze helmet with winged horses in relief, from Axos (8th-7th c. B.C.). Herakleion Museum.

Three bronze statuettes from the Temple of Apollo at Driros (7th c. B.C.). Herakleion Museum.

from many points of view, were considered progressive for their time. Important information concerning this is offered by the famous twelve-column inscription of Gortyn, which is the longest inscription that has been preserved from antiquity and is considered one of the most important heirlooms of ancient civilization. Written in the 5th century B.C. in the archaic Doric dialect of Crete, it is a legal text which sets forth in detail civil law with special emphasis on inheritance and familial law. The safeguarding of the economic and inheritance rights of women is particularly striking.

Classical and Hellenistic Periods (500-67 B.C.)

While in the rest of the Greek lands a new period began to dawn that would lead to the miracle of Classical Greece,

Grave stele from Aghia Pelagia (5th c. B.C.). Herakleion Museum.

Crete withdrew to the margins of the activity going on in the Greek world.

Crete did not participate in the large military conflicts involving Hellenism – the Persian and Peloponnesian Wars. Only in the campaign of Alexander the Great is the participation of Crete mentioned in the person of their famous admiral Nearchos.

During the period of the Diadochi (*Successors*) of Alexander the Great, known as the Hellenistic period, the towns of Crete tried to secure, sometimes on their own and other times acting in concert, the protection of the powerful heads of the large Hellenistic states. Such an occasion is noted in 217/6 B.C., when all the towns of Crete decided to choose the King of Macedonia, Philip V, as the protector of the island.

This arrangement did not last for long as new civil wars broke out on the island. The anarchy that prevailed allowed the pirates, who were plundering the coasts of the eastern Mediterranean, to use those of Crete for their sorties.

The relations, however, with these terrible pirates led to Crete becoming dangerously entangled with powerful Rome. Thus, at the beginning of the 2nd century B.C., when pirates from Crete reached the Roman port of Ostia by means of the Tiber and aducted the women and children of the Roman nobles, Rome began to directly intervene in Cretan affairs.

In 71 B.C. Mark Antony tried to seize Crete, but in a naval battle near the islet of Dia he suffered total annihilation. This defeat, coupled with the mass hanging of the prisoners, led the Roman Senate to the decision to occupy Crete.

In 69 B.C. a large expeditionary force under the Consul Quintus Caecilius Metellus landed in Crete. During the next three years the towns fell one after the other into the hands of the Romans but not without heavy fighting.

In 67 B.C. Crete was subjugated by the Romans and Metellus was dubbed "Creticus" for his services and received triumphally in Rome.

Roman Period
(67 B.C.-A.D. 330)

After its subjugation by the Romans, Crete was transformed into a joint praetorian province along with Cyrene. The Roman governor settled at Gortyn, which became the capital of the island.

The population of Crete, which had shrunk a good deal during the period of the war, began to rapidly increase under conditions of peace, till at its peak it is calculated to have reached 300,000 inhabitants. The Roman installations, at Knossos in the beginning and later at Gortyn and other towns, were small in number and did not essentially alter the composition of the population.

Bronze statue of the Roman period, from Hierapetra. Herakleion Museum.

From the inscriptions that have been found it is concluded that the Greek language and by extension the Greek cultural presence was strongly preserved throughout the period. Latin was primarily the language of the government and the Roman settlers who, with the passage of time, began to come under the sway of a slow Hellenizing process.

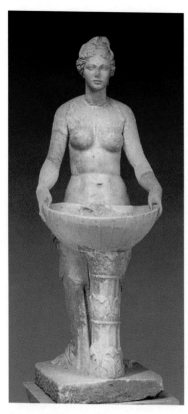

Statue of Aphrodite, Roman period. Herakleion Museum.

deities who came to the island during the years of the Roman occupation. Specifically, Isis and Sarapis were worshipped at Gortyn.

Crete was one of the first places to receive Christianity. The Apostle Paul installed his disciple and close colleague Titus, a Greek by birth, in Gortyn in the year A.D. 58; he founded the first church of which he was the bishop till his death in A.D. 105. Persecution of the Christians began early during the period of the Emperor Decius (A.D. 248-251) when ten Christians were martyred at Gortyn, the Aghioi Deka (Ten Saints) who gave their name to the present-day village.

The Roman influence on Crete can be seen in the construction of very large amphitheatres, built for the new spectacles, such as fights with wild animals and gladiators. Such amphitheatres existed in the large towns of Gortyn and Hierapytna as well as in the smaller ones. During the same period the old Greek theatres continued to operate, even though they had lost their former brilliance.

Just as in all the occupied territories, the Romans beautified the towns through the erection of large temples, prytanea, odea, agoras etc. Particularly impressive are the ruins preserved in the region of Gortyn, such as the Odeum, two theatres, two Nymphaea, the baths, the temples of Isis and Pythian Apollo, etc. At Lebena and Lissos beside the Libyan Sea, grand Asklepia were built, with extensive facilities for

Many of the old cultural institutions and old social customs (such as the public feeding) appear to have survived during this period. The same thing happened with religion. Ancient Cretan deities (Diktynna, Britomartis) were worshipped in tandem with those of the Greek pantheon (Zeus, Hermes, Demeter, etc.) and with Egyptian and oriental

the sick and visitors. The art of mosaic floors flourished during the 2nd and 3rd centuries A.D. and a special local "school" seems to have developed in western Crete (Kisamos). But in general, architecture did not cease following the traditional Greek forms, while sculpture was carried on by artists who came from Athens, Miletus, Paros and elsewhere.

First Byzantine Period
(A.D. 330-824)

The transfer of the capital of the Roman state to ancient Byzantium and the founding of Constantinople (A.D. 330) had a direct effect on the fortunes of Crete. After a brief period during which it was a section of the province of Illyrium, which belonged to Rome, Crete came under the eastern Roman Empire, headed by the Emperor Theodosius the Great (A.D. 395), and was made a separate province with a Byzantine general as its governor. These developments ended its dependence on Rome and allowed it during the following five centuries to take part in the process of transforming the old Roman state into the Greek Byzantine Empire of the East.

During that period the Christian religion spread over the island and was consolidated. Throughout the early centuries the bishopric of Crete was subject to the spiritual jurisdiction of the Pope. In the 8th century it came under the Patriarch of Constantinople.

In Early Christian and Byzantine times the spread of the Christian religion resulted in the erection of many large churches all over the island. Archaeological research has uncovered at least forty basilicas, the most important of which are at Knossos, Gortyn, Chersonnisos, Itanos, Syia and Lissos. The Panormou basilica at Rethymnon is of particular importance for its dimensions, the basilica of Almyra, Apokoronas – excavated by the archaeologist M. Borboudakis – for its mosaics, while the triple apse in the Metropolis of Kainourios, excavated by the same, is unique of its kind.

During the 8th century there were various Arab attacks on the island but these did not change the situation in any fundamental way.

Arab Occupation
(824-961)

In 824 Arab Saracens, who a few years earlier had been driven out of Spain and had settled in North Africa and Egypt, attacked Crete. Their leader Abu Hafs landed on the south coast of Crete and subjugated it in a few years. The conquest by the Arabs succeeded because of an internal crisis the Byzantine state was experiencing. It appears, however, that not the entire island was conquered (it is certain that Sphakia knew no conqueror). The old towns – and among them the "all-beautiful" capital of Gortyn – were reduced to a heap of rubble. The population sank into a long

St. Constantine (1316) by Ioannis Pagomenos, from the Church of the Assumption at Alikambos.

night of horrible slavery. Many took refuge in the mountains. But there was no ethnological change in the Cretan population, at least in the countryside. The converts to Islam, contrary to what was formerly believed, were limited.

The Arab element in the Cretan language is minor and only a few Arab place names have survived (Katsambas, Souda, Chandras, Choumeri, Atzipas). A significant event was the building of the castle of Chandax on the site of the ancient and present-day Herakleion; around this was dug a deep moat ("khandak") from which the town and the entire island took its medieval name (Candia).

During the 130 years of the Arab occupation, Crete became a centre for extensive pirate raids which spread over the entire eastern Mediterranean. Chandax acquired the notoriety of being the largest slave market in the East, where rich buyers came from the countries of Asia Minor, Arabia and North Africa. The income from the slave trade and the booty from the pirate raids allowed the Arab rulers of the island to amass incredible wealth.

For Byzantium the loss of this great island was a serious blow. That is why it repeatedly tried to restore its dominance over Crete, but without success. Finally, the Byzantine general and later Emperor of the Byzantine Empire, Nikephoros Phokas, leading a mighty fleet of war-ships equipped with Greek fire, and transport ships reached the island in 960 and began extensive operations. After months of battles and sieges the sources of resistance were eliminated and in 961 he occupied Chandax, which was ut-terly destroyed. A similar fate awaited the rest of the towns inhabited by the Arabs. Some accounts state that many thousands of Arabs were exterminated while others became prisoners of the victor. The Arab treasure on Crete was unbelievable and was transferred to the capital of Byzantium, Constantinople.

Second Byzantine Period (961-1204/10)

The Byzantines regained the island but they also inherited the vast problems of its restoration. The population had shrunk. Byzantium, with the assistance of the Church, applied itself to a systematic endeavour to secure the political domination of the island, to restore and stabilize religious conviction. Missionaries, such as Nikon the Repenter and Saint John the Hermit, the "Stranger", preached from one end of the island to the other, founding monasteries and building churches. At the same time Nikephoros Phokas settled many of his soldiers on Crete. Greek colonists also came from Asia Minor, the islands and mainland Greece.

A long and peaceful period of roughly 250 years followed, which allowed Crete not only to heal its wounds, but to achieve rapid economic progress. In 1082 the Emperor Alexis Comnenus II sent new colonists with his son Isaac led by twelve scions of the large aristocratic families of Byzantium – who became known as the *archontopouli*. Large pieces of land were parcelled out to them and they were granted important privileges, especially in western Crete. Thus the basis was established for a new Byzantine Cretan aristocracy

Fresco from Aghia Photini near Preveli. 14th century.

which would play the leading role in social and political life even during the long period of the Venetian occupation.

On the eve of the Venetian occupation the society of Crete had all the hallmarks of the contemporary Byzantine world, that is, there was a development of large land holdings and an equal growth of the power and influence of local lords. Despite the fact that the population of Crete did not reach its former high level, quite a number of towns were rebuilt and reinforced with strong walls. Moreover, many new churches were built.

Venetian Occupation
(1204-1669)

Two and a half centuries of Byzantine rule came to an end in 1204 when the leaders of the Fourth Crusade conquered Constantinople and dissolved the Empire. In the division of the property Crete went to Boniface of Montferrat, who sold it to the Venetians. In a few years the Genoese – Venice's rivals in trade in the Mediterranean – tried to bring the island under their control but finally, in 1212, the Venetians managed to impose their authority. This new period, known as the Venetian occupation, turned out to be one of the longest, lasting four and a half centuries.

The Venetian occupation is divided into two sub-periods. The first lasted till the Fall of Constantinople to the Turks (1453). It was a period of continual confrontation between the Cretans and their Venetian overlords which, however, diminished as the Byzantine Empire neared its end. The second sub-period, from the middle of the 15th till the middle of the 17th century, ended with the seizure of Chandax and the whole island by the Turks in 1669. During these two centuries, a marvellous combination of the two elements, Greek and Venetian, took place which led to an impressive cultural and social renaissance in Crete.

From the start of its rule, the Serene Republic took care to secure its control of the island, settling many Venetian families of nobles and soldiers. In one century the Venetian settlers numbered as many as 10,000, an amazing number in a period when the population of Venice itself did not exceed 60,000.

The government adopted Venetian models. The entire island, which was called the "Kingdom of Crete", was originally divided into six sextaria (like Venice itself); later it was divided into four districts; Chandax, Rethymnon, Chania and Siteia. Only in the mountainous district of Sphakia were the Venetians unable to exercise total authority, ceding to the Sphakiots a kind of local autonomy.

As in Venice, where the Doge and his councillors exercised the highest authority, so in Crete authority was exercised from Chandax by the Duca and his two councillors (the three of them constituted the Authority). The Duca governed with the assistance of various advisory councils of Venetian settlers. In the districts the administration was handled by rectors. The locals had no right to exercise public office expect for the profession of notaries (notary public) or lawyer. Only in 1500 did the locals also acquire administrative positions.

The introduction of the feudal system brought about radical changes in Cretan society and its economy. The society was divided into four classes: a) Venetian nobles, b) Cretan nobles, c) the bourgeoisie and d) the inhabitants of the countryside (villagers and townspeople, the *villiani*). The feudal fiefs which were granted to the Venetian nobility contained one or more villages and estates with a number of *villiani* or colonists. Nevertheless, three different systems of justice coexisted: the Byzantine, which governed the life of the Greek population, the feudal, which determined the relations between feudal lord and serfs, and the Venetian, which was applied mainly to the commercial and judicial sector.

From the very first moment, the new authority tried to eliminate the influence of the Orthodox Church, which kept its ties with the Ecumenical Partiarchate and by extension the revitalized Byzantine State. That is why the highest Orthodox hierarchy was replaced by the Roman Catholic, the Orthodox bishoprics were abolished and a Roman Catholic archbishop was installed at Chandax. Finally, Church property was confiscated, as were the landholdings of the ordinary people to a large degree. The locals were only allowed to keep a Protopappas ("Head Priest").

Thus, a short time after the establishment of Venetian authority uprisings are noted, in which some of the old archons played a leading role. These uprisings, which are mentioned throughout the first century of the Venetian occupation, surpassed ten in number. Several of them lasted for a few years. Indeed, when the Byzantine Empire was re-established with the recapture of Constantinople (1261) the Byzantine emperors offered their assistance to the local archons of Crete but without any real result. The most important uprisings were those of Skordilis, and Melissinos (1217-1219, 1222-1223 and 1228-1236), the Chortatzis brothers (1262-1278) and others, but the main one was started by Alexis Kallergis in 1282 and ended with a treaty in 1299 which became known as the *Pax Alexii Callergi*. This treaty granted a general amnesty to the Kallergis family and economic and social privileges while at the same time recognizing the right to choose an Orthodox bishop; it allowed for intermarriage and freedom of settlement throughout the island and permitted the emancipation of serfs.

With these privileges, as well as all the others that had already been granted by the Venetian administration to quell previous uprisings, the social and, especially, the economic conditions of the various strata of Cretan society improved significantly. Thus the two population groups, the small minority of the Roman Catholic Venetians and the majority of the Greek, Orthodox population, began to draw nearer.

Typical of this process was the revolt of 1363-1366 by the Venetian feudal lords Gradenigo and Venieri who, irate at the heavy tax burden of Venice, united with the Kallergis brothers and aided by ordinary people attempted to found an autonomous Republic of Saint Titus, after the patron saint of the island. With promises of equality between the Orthodox and the Catholic Church,

Domenicus Theotokopoulos (El Greco) was born in Herakleion in 1541, as notary documents confirm. He died at Toledo in Spain, where he lived for many years and painted his greatest works, in 1614. Self-portrait of 1563. (Paris, private collection).

they succeeded in uniting the locals and foreigners. In the end the revolt failed, but it created closer bonds between the Venetian settlers and their new homeland as well as the local population.

During the second stage of the Venetian occupation there were noteworthy social changes on the island. The feudal system began to decline because of the splitting up of the land and the debts of the feudal lords to their Jewish lenders. Venetian officials filed reports confirming the Hellenization of the Venetians, both in language and religion. But the system of serfdom continued till the end of the Venetian occupation, contributing to the wretchedness of the villagers. Various proposals for the restitution of land to the villagers came to nought. Particularly oppressive was the system of statutory labour, that is, compulsory labour on public works such as the erection of the mighty fortresses on which the villagers worked hard and outside of which they lived.

In the towns, however, the retreat of feudal society created a new distinction of classes and the bourgeoisie flourished in particular, applying itself to export trade as well.

During this period the Orthodox Church regained some of its former influence. Despite the endeavours of the Roman Catholic hierarchy, the Orthodox faith gained strength on the island. Hundreds of churches, both large and small, were built, as well as sizeable monastery complexes where many took refuge, especially villagers, for religious reasons of course, but also to avoid the oppression and the compulsory labour.

What was particularly impressive during the long period of the Venetian occupation was the development and unique evolution of intellectual life in

The fortress of Rethymnon, where the inhabitants sought refuge for 23 days on the fortified acropolis (Fortetsa) in order to avoid the repeated attacks of the Turks (From the private collection of the publisher G. Christopoulos).

Crete. The equality that characterized relations with Italy fertilized the intellectual forces of Crete with elements of the Italian Renaissance.

Already during the 14th and 15th centuries advanced forms of painting appeared which were used in the mural decoration of important monasteries (Vrondisi, Valsomonero, Gouverniotissa), and communal churches (Sklavero-chori, Episkopi, Pediada). From the 14th century painting in Crete was quite advanced and utilized contemporary Italian influences. These influences were due to the dominant presence of the Venetian element on the island, but tended to be confined to secondary traits, in no way altering the Byzantine character of the composition. On the other hand admirable painters also came from Constantinople (after its capture by the Turks), from Mystras and other regions. The painters of Constantinople brought their artistic tradition to the island. The evolution of this art, with the schematization of technique and the dominance of the principles of Classical aesthetics in the formation of the compositions, gradually led to the formation of a new school of painting, the "Cretan School",

CITTA DI CANDIA

perhaps the most important period of Greek painting after the Fall of Constantinople. The Cretan School originally retained the old Byzantine forms, created new ones and borrowed elements from Italian art, especially from the copper-plate engravings of the great Italian painters. Today very few examples of this art have been preserved in Crete itself. The best ones are in the monasteries of Mount Athos, Meteora and the museums of Greece (Byzantine Museum of Athens) and abroad. The most important representatives of the Cretan School were Theophanis, Klotzas and Damaskinosl, to name only a few. Venetian sources mention that for the period 1527-1630 alone, there were 125 painters registered in Chandax. The youthful work of Domenicus Theotoko-

Chandax during the final days of the siege. The town's fortress was built in the 16th century to confront the Turkish threat. It was besieged for 21 years, up to 1669, when its defender, Francesco Morosini, surrendered the town to the Grand Vizier Ahmed Kiupruli by treaty (Venice, Biblioteca Marciana).

poulos (El Greco), who was born in Fodele in 1541, belonged to the Cretan School, though with strong Italian influences. After studying painting in his native Crete he went to Venice at the age of twenty-five and later to Spain where he developed into one of the greatest painters of all time.

There was also a great deal of progress in education which was due on one hand to the arrival of enlightened people from Byzantium and on the other to the studies pursued by a large number of Cretans in Venice and Padua. Sources from the 17th century note the existence in Chandax of a substantial number of doctors, lawyers and notaries with degrees from Italian universities. Following an example set by Venice, lower and middle schools were founded in Crete while from the 16th century on Academies began to appear. These were intellectual societies within the framework of which discussions and lectures were organized on literary and scientific subjects. Learning was also being cultivated in the monasteries, several of which had valuable libraries which contributed to the appearance of the scholar-monk. Later a number of these men. such as Meletios Pigas, Maximos Margounios, Gerasimos Vlachos and others attained the highest offices in the hierarchy of the Orthodox Church.

Greek medieval poetic and theatrical creation flourished more in Crete than anywhere else. After the Hellenistic and Roman periods the Greek theatre revived on a new basis, particularly during the fruitful final two centuries of the Venetian occupation. The oldest examples of modern Greek poetry in Crete are the demotic songs, some of them from the Second Byzantine period, but most from the Venetian occupation. With the Byzantine tradition as their basis, Western influences created the preconditions for the birth of Cre-

tan literature. The numerous early works (13th-16th century) use both dramatic and satirical poetic dialogue. The language, with strong local peculiarities and Italian influences, was fashioned into a new written dialect which was far removed from ancient prototypes. The main literary figures during the peak period were Yorgos Chortatzis with his dramatic masterpiece *Erophile* and his comedy *Panoria*, which combined elements of the Renaissance and mythology, Vincenzos Kornaros with his drama *The Sacrifice of Abraham* and above all that masterpiece of Cretan literature *Erotokritos*, Markos Antonios Phoskolos with his comedy *Fortounatos* and others. The output of Cretan poets continued at a high level till the final years of the Venetian occupation.

Starting in the very first years of the Venetian occupation Italian architecture spread rapidly from one end of the island to the other. Italian architects designed marvellous buildings, fortresses, harbours and august churches. In a short period of time the Cretan towns took on the form of Venetian Mediterranean towns. The civic buildings – some of which still exist – were striking because of their monumental facades (loggia) while beautiful fountains decorated the spacious squares, such as the Morosini fountain with its lions, at Herakleion. Orthodox monasteries – such as Arkadi – and hundreds of churches bore the stamp of the late Gothic and Renaissance style. Most of the churches

The Venetian commander Francesco Morosini, the heroic defender of Chandax, aboard his flagship during a naval operation against the Turkish fleet shortly before the fall of the city (Venice, Biblioteca Marciana).

were single-spaced and vaulted with plain façades. In the environs of Chania the monasteries of Aghia Triada Tsangarolon, Kera Gonias, Chrysopigi and Gouvernetto faithfully followed the Venetian prototype in their facades, but the triple-conched plan of these churches was obviously due to influences from Mount Athos. These exceptionally large monasteries, such as the Arkadi Monastery, are without doubt some of the finest examples of Renaissance architecture in Greece.

The large fortresses were quite awe-inspiring; in the 16th century as the threat of a Turkish invasion became clearer, they were rebuilt to contain the suburbs of the towns and to be adapted to the needs of modern warfare. Such fortresses were built in all the towns and harbours, as well as on the islets of Gramvousa, Souda and Spinalonga. The fortress of Chandax – which was called the "Megalo Kastro" (Great Fortress) – was built over an entire century with the compulsory labour of the inhabitants of the countryside. Despite the earthquakes and the many troubles, this fortress is still considered one of the best preserved Venetian fortresses in the Mediterranean.

The great earthquakes of 1303, 1353, 1508 and 1650 as well as other smaller ones caused extensive damage to various structures. Even greater was the damage caused during the Turkish siege. Despite all that, the Venetian architectural presence remains firmly imprinted in many places on the island, on churches, fortresses and certain civic buildings.

Turkish Occupation
(1669-1898)

Throughout the last two centuries of the Venetian occupation Crete was under the continual threat of Turkish invasion. A number of times Turkish forces did manage to land at various points on the island and temporarily occupied forti-

fied towns. This happened on a large scale in 1538 when the famous admiral Hareddin Barbarrosa placed western and central Crete under his control, but was stopped outside the powerful fortress of Chandax and in the end was forced to withdraw from the island. In 1645 however, Yussuf Pasha, commander of 60,000 soldiers and 400 ships landed west of Chania. In a short space of time he captured the town, and in 1646 Rethymnon and most of the fortresses of the island. By the end of 1648 Crete had been conquered; only Chandax continued to resist.

The siege of the "Great Fortress" was one of the longest on record, lasting twenty-one years. The most modern

Cretan noblemen of the countryside (Archondoromaioi) in the 16th century (Chapel of Saint George., Voila, Siteia).

According to the description of the traveller Belon the Sphakiots wore white shirts with belts around the waist and boots. Fresco depicting the founders of the Chapel of Saint Michael (Mesa Lakkonia, Mirabello).

means and methods of siege were employed throughout its duration. Venetians and Cretans resisted stubbornly until every hope of external assistance proved to be fruitless On the 27th of September 1669, the defender of Chandax, Francesco Morosini, surrendered the town to the Grand Vizier Ahmed Kiupruli by treaty. With the exception of the small fortresses of Gramvousa, Souda and Spinalonga, which remained under Venetian rule for a few more decades, Crete came under the authority of the Sublime Porte. The new peri-

od turned out to be one of the worst in the centuries-long history of the island. The conquest was accompanied by unbelievable material destruction. During the siege many of the fortresses sustained heavy damage and had to be repaired during the following years. A large number of the churches were levelled and others converted into mosques, while the bells were removed from the rest with the exception of Arkadi Monastery. The marvellous Cathedral of Saint Titus in Chandax was converted into a magnificent mosque which took the name Vizier Cami in honour of Kiupruli, the captor of the "Great Fortress".

The vengeful wrath of the victors was turned upon the population who had put up such a stalwart defence. Large-scale slaughter took place from one end of the island to the other while thousands of inhabitants became prisoners. The oppression of the Christians by the Ottoman government and the large number of Turkish colonists who came and settled in the towns and the fertile regions, continued during the following decades. Unable to stand the unremittant misery, thousands of Cretans left the island, many of them settling in the British-ruled Ionian islands. A substantial number of the inhabitants preferred to convert to Islam to escape their tribulations, though secretly they continued to observe the rites of the Orthodox religion and were subsequently called "crypto-Christians".

Following the tactics they employed in all the areas they conquered, the Turks undertook a general reforestation of the land. The old public lands went to the Sultan while large private properties were given to Turkish officials as timars or to Islamic religious foundations as vakoufia. The Christian farmers became serfs. The tax system, which provided for only two kinds of tax, the head tax and the property tax, was very harsh in Crete, worse than in the other regions of the Turkish Empire.

Sphakia was originally the fief of Deli Hussein who later donated it as a vakuf to the holy cities' of Islam, Mecca and Medina. Thus the Sphakiots, in contrast to what older historians believed, were also obliged to pay taxes. However, because of the geographical formation of the region it was difficult for the Turkish army to set up camp there.

On the administrative side, Crete constituted a separate vilayet with Chandax as the seat of the head Pasha. There were also pashas in the three (later four) pashaliks or districts.

With the subjugation of the island by the Turks the authority of the Pope came to an end and the island returned to the embrace of the Ecumenical Partiarchate in Constantinople. The seat of the Orthodox Metropolitan was established in Chandax while as the same time the old bishoprics were re-instituted under their old names. The privileges which had been ceded to the Ecumenical Partiarchate by Sultan Mohammed II, were also extended to Crete. Despite this, the persecution of the Christians and their religious representatives continued. The misery of the clergy and the decline of its level of education contributed even more to the intellectual deadening of the general population.

But these conditions of slavery led to the outbreak of successive uprisings. In 1692 Venetian forces landed on the island and the Cretans sped to join up with them in an endeavour to drive the Turks off the island. But the failure of the enterprise turned the fury of the Ottomans against the Christian population.

A new opportunity for revolt appeared in 1770 when the Russians, during their war against the Turks, tried to rouse the enslaved Christians. The Cretans were quick to reply and led by the Sphakiot Daskaloyannis they had considerable success in the beginning. But the conclusion of peace between Russia and Turkey again left the Cretans exposed. The brunt of the Turkish rage was turned against the Sphakiots this time and their leader Daskaloyannis, who was forced to surrender and was skinned alive.

Despite all this, the revolutionary spirit ran high. On the eve of the Greek War of Independence of 1821, distinguished Cretans were initiated into the Philiki Hetaireia. The participation of Crete in the War of Independence was all inclusive. During the first three years (1821-1824) Cretan fighters were able to bring the most important part of the island under their control. Then the Sultan asked the assistance of his vassal Mehmet Ali, the Khedive of Egypt. He sent over a large number of Egyptian troops who subdued the greatest part of the island in revolt. But the following year the revolt took on new life despite the endeavours of the Turks, and the end of the War of Independence in 1828 found a large part of Crete in the hands of the rebels.

When the borders of the independent Greek state were set, the European Powers refused to include Crete within them. The Sultan ceded the island to the Khedive of Egypt as a reward for his services. But the Egyptian occupation lasted barely a decade, as an unsuccessful uprising of the Egyptians (1840) against the Sultan deprived them of Crete.

The period of 1841-1898 was the last stage of the Turkish occupation on the island. The existence of an independent Greek state, with Athens as capital, acted like a catalyst on Crete leading to new revolutionary movements aimed at union with Greece. These movements were instigated by the high-handedness of the Ottoman administration, primarily the oppression of the Christians by the Turks. In the middle of the century it appeared that the situation would improve and the European Powers forced the Ottoman Empire to adopt broad reforms. A law passed in 1856 ensured the freedom of religious worship and under certain conditions Christians could participate in the apparatus of administration. This opportunity was exploited by the "crypto-Christians" who renounced Islam. But the reaction of the Turks was violent as they saw their numbers dwindling and their former subjects, the rayahs, rising socially, economically and intellectually. Under these conditions it is not surprising that the second half of the 19th century was marked by nearly continual bloody uprisings of the Cretan people.

The most important of these – which became known as the "Great Cretan Revolution" – began in 1866 and lasted till 1868. Using reinforcements and volunteers from free Greece, the rebels scored a series of victories. The struggle experienced a number of ups and downs as powerful Turkish forces reached the island. The time-honoured method of mass resprisals, principally against non-combatants, finally brought the struggle to an end and most of the leaders fled the island. The high point of the Revolution was the holocaust at Arkadi Monastery where its defenders, together with hundreds of woman and children who had taken refuge there, preferred to blow up the powder magazine of the monastery and be buried under the rubble with nearly 1500 armed Turks, than to surrender.

Ten years later, during a new Russo-Turkish war, another revolt broke out. Under conditions similar to those of 1866-1868, the rebels succeeded in overrunning the island, except for six fortresses which remained in the hands of the Turks. The European Conference at Berlin, however, again left Crete under the domination of the Sultan who was forced, by the treaty of Halepa, to grant the Christians broad jurisdiction in the administration of the island. Of particular importance was the recognition that Greek would be the official language of the Parliament and the courts.

These reforms were soon debased by the Turkish Cretans leading to new movements and the revolution of 1895-1896. The following year (1987), using the slaughter of Christians as a pretext, a segment of the Greek army and volunteers together with the local rebels began to liberate one province after the other, the rallying cry being the union of Crete with Greece. The European Powers had been finally convinced that Turkey could not maintain control of the island. Therefore, they intervened in 1898 and set up the autonomous "Cretan Republic" under the formal suzerainty of the Sultan but with Prince George, the second son of the King of Greece, as the High Commissioner. Thus the two centuries of Turkish occupation came to a close. The new regime's security was assumed by the European Powers, which landed their forces on the island. This security was aimed at both warding off a Turkish return to the island and a unilateral declaration of union with Greece.

Under the previous conditions of slavery the Christian population on the island had been degraded and was not able to initiate any kind of cultural activity. The main pursuit of this wretched people was simple survival. Therefore, works of high art are missing from that period. The Cretans only made objects for daily use, while religious places were "decorated", for the most part, with the icons of ordinary local painters. Nevertheless, artistic feeling did not forsake the Cretans. This was mainly expressed through handicrafts and weaving, particularly in the 19th century when they are characterized by dexterity and a remarkable variety of colours and designs. The same could be said for woodcarving. Typical examples have been preserved in several monastery collections, but principally at the Herakleion Historical and Ethnographical Museum.

The long poetry tradition of the Venetian occupation was carried on, to a degree, by the folk muse, through the *rizitika* and demotic songs which were usually accompanied by stalwart dancers to the sound of the Cretan lyra. These songs set down, in lyric form, the life of subjugated Crete, with its sorrows, its joys and its unsubdued conviction.

In contrast to other historical periods, the Turkish occupation did not leave any clear stamp of its passage in the architecture of the monuments and civic structures. Most of the mosques were nothing more than converted Orthodox and Roman Catholic churches. The principal and most apparent influence was in the morphology of the towns, which slowly took on the well-known look of Turkish settlements with narrow alley-ways, usually flagstoned (*kalderimia*), enclosed porches (*hayiatia*), minarets and several distinctive fountains.

After the founding of the Greek state (1830) and the formation of the University of Athens, there was a steady rise in the level of Greek education in Crete, especially after the reforms of Hatti Humayun.

Modern Times

The settlement of 1898, which formed an autonomous Cretan Republic, only partially satisfied the longing of the Cretan people who wanted to become part of the Greek state. This longing, as well as the liberal, revolutionary spirit, remained at a fever pitch. Therefore, certain actions of the High Commissioner, which tended to impose restrictions on the people's freedoms or to introduce foreign models of administration, began to cause reactions which, finally, in 1905, led to an uprising known as the "Revolution of Therissos". The leader of the revolution was Eleftherios Venizelos, who had also led the way in the negotiations which had brought the Ottoman regime to an end. The rebels held their positions for eight months till Prince George resigned. A new Commissioner was sworn in, the former Prime Minister of Greece, Alexandros Zaimis, who called for elections. After Venizelos won the elections in Crete, an uprising of the Military League in Athens triumphed (1909); they called on him to become Prime Minister. Thereafter he took the leading role in the political life of Greece as well as in the fortunes of Hellenism till his death in 1936. Earlier (1908) the forces of the European Powers withdrew from the island and the post of High Commissioner was abolished.

The Cretans continued their endeavours to unite with Greece, issuing decrees and conducting plebiscites. Finally, union was realized through the victorious Balkan Wars of 1912-1913. Under the Treaty of London, 17-30 May, 1913, the Sultan relinquished his formal rights.

On 1/14 December, 1913, with King Constantine and Eleftherios Venizelos present, the Greek flag was raised at the Firkas fortress in Chania and the annexation of the island by Greece was completed.

As part of the Greek state, Crete shared in the fortunes of Greece in the 20th century. After the end of the Greek-Turkish war in 1922 and the agreement for the exchange of populations, all the Moslems in Crete – about 30,000 were left – were forced to leave, their place being taken by Greek refugees from Asia Minor.

The long fighting tradition of the Cretans came to the fore again during the Greek-Italian war of 1940-1941 when the Cretan Division was especially distinguished on the Albanian front. But the absence of men of fighting age on the island proved disastrous when Nazi Germany launched its attack against Greece on April 6, 1941 and, after conquering mainland Greece, began a combined air and sea invasion of Crete at the end of May. 1941.

The defense of the island was undertaken by approximately 30,000 men of the British Commonwealth (Australians, New Zealanders and British) as well as about 12,000 Greeks, mainly new recruits, cadets and state policemen, poorly armed. At their side stood the unarmed civilian population who at the time of the landing fought with whatever was at hand to repel the invaders.

The Battle of Crete, despite the fact that it only lasted for ten days (20-30

Eleftherios Venizelos (Chania 1864 - Paris 1936) who played a leading role in the political life of Greece (Athens, National Historical Museum).

May) constituted one of the most important battles of World War II and certainly the most important German airborne operation. The enormous losses suffered by their elite paratroopers created grave problems for the war plans of the German High Command which did not venture on a similar operation for the duration of the war.

The German occupation of Crete lasted for four years. During this period the indomitable spirit of the Cretans was expressed through the organization of a powerful armed resistance movement, which on the one hand pinned down large numbers of German forces on the island and on the other increased the number of victims and the amount of material destruction.

At the end of the war a long and undisturbed period of peace began, unusual in length for the stormy history of Crete. This state of affairs created the necessary preconditions for significant progress in the economy, principally in agriculture. On account of the favourable climatological conditions there was an impressive development in the cultivation of early garden vegetables in greenhouses which changed the appearance of the plains, especially in southern Crete.

There was also enormous archaeological activity by Greeks and foreigners which bore rich fruit now strikingly displayed in the wealth of exhibits at the Archaeological Museums of Herakleion, Rethymnon and Chania. The founding, a few years ago, of the University and the Polytechnic School of Crete, with branches at Rethymnon, Herakleion and Chania, and the Technical Educational School at Herakleion and Chania, outlined new horizons for broader cultural and scientific development. Despite the fact that the mention of individual personalities falls outside the scope of this guide, the legacy of the giant of Greek literature, Nikos Kazantzakis known, throughout the world, is indeed impressive.

Finally, particular mention must be made of the rapid increase in tourism. In a period of less than two decades a tourist infrastructure has been developed for the entire island.

The excellent hotels and other tourist units, in combination with the superb climate, have made Crete into one of the most important summer resorts in the Mediterranean.

Touring

The two main points of entry to Crete are the airports and harbours at Herakleion and Chania. A small number of visitors also use the harbour at Kisamos (W. Crete) and the harbour and airport at Siteia (E. Crete).

This guide contains 26 excursions which cover the entire island, practically all the summer tourist resorts and sites of archaeological interest, both along the coast and in the interior. Most of these excursions use one of the capitals of the four prefectures of Crete (Herakleion, Aghios Nikolaos, Rethymnon and Chania) as their starting point, though Siteia is used for Excursions 12 and 13, and Kisamos for Excursion 25. This method was employed because these towns have adequate tourist facilities, contain the principal museums and are the termini for connections to all parts of the island. There is a special section for each of these towns which treats its history, sites and cultural events as well as giving useful information and telephone numbers.

This guide contains the most detailed and up-to-date information on the

The beach at Vaï attracts large numbers of tourists during the summer months due to the unique scenery it offers its visitors.

archaeological sites and museums. The excursions are drawn up in a way which allows them to be completed in one day. The visitor then must make his choice depending on the time at his disposal.

The ideal way to tour is with a private or a rented car. Taxis can also be used for certain excursions. Of course, it is much less expensive to tour by bus. But this also requires more time and a careful study of the timetables. For certain highly frequented excursions (e.g. Herakleion-Knossos) one can book a place on the tours organized by the tourist agencies.

It is prudent to check the operating hours of the museums and archaeological sites by telephoning either the local offices of the National Tourist Organization (EOT) or the museums themsleves.

One is expected to dress presentably (no slacks or shorts for women) when visiting the monasteries. The monasteries are open during the day with a break of 2-2 1/2 hours at midday.

Because of the peculiarities of the road network, the calculation of the time needed for a given tour does not always correspond to the distance in kilometres. In the interior, principally the mountain road network, the average speed does not usually exceed 25-35 km. an hour. On the plains and particularly the national roads of N. and S. Crete it is possible to travel at 100 km. an hour. The roads are paved for the most part but some of these excursions use roads which are either under construction or being repaired or are simply dirt roads.

Despite the fact that Crete has a well-developed hotel system it is advisable, during the tourist season, which runs from March to November to book your rooms in advance.

HERAKLEION

Herakleion is the largest town in Crete and is the main point of entry, either by sea or by air, for visitors to the island. It is but a short distance from the most important archaeological sites (Knossos, Phaistos, Gortyn, Archanes, Malia) while its archaeological museum is considered the second most important – after Athens – in the country. Moreover, along the entire north coast of Crete, easily accessible from Herakleion, are hotel complexes, both small and large, which are especially popular with foreign visitors.

The town was quickly but haphazardly rebuilt after the destruction it sustained during World War II. Nevertheless, there are still noteworthy examples of its medieval glory, such as the Venetian harbour, the wonderfully preserved town walls with their wide moat, as well as several renovated buildings from the Venetian period.

Arrival

Eight flights a day connect Herakleion to Athens. During the summer months there are also connections to Thessaloniki, Rhodes, Mykonos and Santorini (information at the local offices of Olympic Airways in Greece and abroad).

Herakleion airport, 4 km. west of the town, has all the facilities of an international airport and during the summer months charter flights arrive directly from abroad. Buses of Olympic Airways go from the airport to the town (Eleftheria Square) as well as buses for Aghios Nikolaos. There are also car rental agencies, of all the familiar companies, located there, as well as taxis (there is a list of taxi fares to the towns in Crete in the main waiting room at the airport). You can also purchase duty-free items there.

There are two ferry boats daily from Piraeus to Herakleion. Departures from Piraeus (Karaïskakis Square) are at 6 p.m. and 7 p.m. and the journey lasts 12 hours. During the summer there is a local connection to Santorini. Also every ten days during the summer there are connections from Herakleion to Italy, Cyprus and Israel by ferry boat.

History of the Town

During antiquity there was a small harbour, the port of Knossos, called Herakleion, on the site of the present town;

Partial view of the town of Herakleion.

The Venetian fort guarding the entrance to the harbour of Herakleion.

this name was kept throughout the Roman and First Byzantine periods. When the Saracen Arabs occupied Crete (A.D. 824) they built an important town which they enclosed with strong walls. They built a large moat around it (khandak) from which the town took the Arab name Khandak or Chandax as it was called by the Byzantines or Candia as the Latins referred to it. During the years of the Venetian occupation and even later, this name – Candia – was known throughout Crete.

During the years of the Arab occupation, Chandax was a centre of international piracy and slave trading until the Byzantines recaptured it (961); one and a half centuries later it became a Venetian possession. During the Venetian occupation (1204-1669) the town was the centre of the political, social, military and commercial life of the whole island and see of the Roman Catholic Archbishop. Beautiful civic buildings were erected as well as lovely fountains. Several of these buildings as well as the impressive Morosini fountain still survive. The Venetians, to protect themselves from the uprisings of the Cretans and, in particular, the Turkish threat, built new walls which enclosed not only the old town but the suburbs as well. Their construction started in 1462 and lasted over 100 years. The material was brought from the quarries of Katsambas and Xeropotamos, but stones from the ruins of Knossos were also used. The walls were

The picturesque and colourful street of the Market, where the products of the rich Cretan soil are displayed in the open air or on covered stalls.

three kilometres long, in a triangular shape. Because of these walls, which are among the best preserved fortification works in Europe, Candia could withstand the brutal Turkish siege for twenty-one years, after the rest of Crete had already been overcome.

During the Turkish occupation the town was renamed Megalo Kastro (Great Fortress). The walls were repaired and remained strong, thereby creating an impregnable fortress and refuge for the Moslem population during the successive revolts of the Christians during the 19th century. The interior of the fortress was laid out according to the well-known system in oriental towns, with small houses and narrow streets.

With the end of the Turkish occupation, the form of the town began to change. The largest part of the old town was destroyed by earthquakes, the bombing in World War II, but principally the building of the past thirty years. The old churches, which had been converted into mosques, once more became Christian churches. The town extended outside the walls in a haphazard way and today is nearing the airport.

Tour of the town

The place to begin a visit to the sights of the old town is Eleftheria Square, where there are statues to two great Cretans, Eleftherios Venizelos and Nikos Kazantzakis.

At the beginning of Xanthoudidou St. (north side) is the Archaeological Museum, on the site of an old monastery to Saint Francis, and exactly opposite are the offices of EOT. On the west side of the square is a narrow, paved street, Daidalou, one of the most popular tourist streets with restaurants, cafeterias, boutiques, bookstalls and small hotels, which leads to the much frequented Eleftheriou Venizelou Square, known in popular parlance as the Square of the Lions, derived from the lions on the Morosini fountain located there.

A central thoroughfare, Dikaiosynis St., begins left of Daidalou, behind Eleftheria Square. On its left side are the old barracks which were built by the Venetians in the 16th century and rebuilt by the Turks. In the central block is a well-preserved Venetian portal which was brought here from the old monastery of Saint Francis. Today these buildings house the Prefecture Offices, the Courts, the Police and a section of the Tourist Police. In a small opening between the Prefecture Office and the Courts is the bust of the leader of the Revolution of 1770, Daskaloyannis and behind that the Post Office and Daskaloyannis Square.

A little further down Dikaiosynis St. meets "1866" St. on the left and El. Venizelou Square on the right. 1866 is a picturesque, bustling and colourful street on the Market where the produce of the rich Cretan soil are displayed either in the open air or covered stalls: fruits, vegetables and mountain herbs as well as meat, cheese products and the decorative wedding rolls made of dry bread. This street ends to the south at Kornarou Square (see below).

Turning right off Dikaiosynis St., 50 metres along you reach El. Venizelou Square which has many coffee houses, restaurants, bookstalls and second-hand shops as well as the well-known Fountain with the Lions, which was built in 1628 at the order of the Venetian governor Morosini. The eight bases of the fountain are decorated with Nymphs and Tritons in relief who are riding dolphins, bulls and sea monsters. The highest basin is supported on four lions but this section must belong to an earlier fountain dated to the 14th century. There was a statue of Poseidon in the basin which was demolished during the Turkish occupation. The area around this square was the centre of Venetian Candia with civic buildings and the Ducal palace which have not been preserved.

To the east, opposite the Morosini fountain, is the Venetian basilica of Saint Mark. Built in 1239, it was destroyed by an earthquake in 1303 and repaired in 1508. The Turks converted it into a mosque but today it has been renovated and is used for concerts, lectures and exhibitions.

Continuing north from El. Venizelou Square you reach the small Kallergon Square. On the left is El Greco Park (and behind that to the west the telegraph and telephone company – OTE). At the beginning of 25th Avgoustou St. (which sets off from Kallergon Square), to the right, is the Venetian Loggia, carefully rebuilt, which was the central meeting place for the nobility. Today City Hall is housed there.

Just beyond the Loggia, is the church of the patron saint of the island, Apostle Titus, with a spacious paved courtyard in front. It is not known precisely when this church was built but it is certain that during the second Byzantine period it was the Cathedral of the town. During the Venetian occupation it

became the seat of the Roman Catholic Archbishop and was renovated in 1446. However, it was destroyed by a great fire, in 1544 and rebuilt again 13 years later. The Turks converted it into a mosque and gave it the name Vizier Camr. After the earthquake of 1856 it was rebuilt once more in 1872. Inside the church is one of the most sacred relics of the Cretan Church, the skull of Saint Titus.

25th Avgoustou St. is a commercial street where the main banks, travel and shipping agencies are located; it ends at the old Venetian harbour where mainly private yachts and caiques dock now. Its entrance is guarded by the fort Rocco al Mare – or Koules – which was built for the first time at the beginning of the

14th century and again in 1523. The fort is open to the public till sunset. A ramp leads to the upper level where a small outdoor theatre has been created. Performances are given there in the summer and the view of the harbour and the fortification works is a commanding one.

West of the small harbour are the old, restored ship-yards (the Arsenals) from the 16th century, while further west is the Historical Museum and next to it the ruins of the Venetian church of Saint Peter.

The main harbour, where the cruise ships and ferry boats from Piraeus drop anchor begins on the east side of the old harbour.

The uphill Bofor avenue follows the east wall and leads back to Eleftheria Square.

The Venetian Loggia, central meeting place for the nobility. Today it houses City Hall.

The "Idomeneas Fountain" from the Turkish occupation.

The "Koubes", a fountain built by the Turks when they converted the nearby church of the Saviour into the Valide mosque. At present the building is used as a coffee house.

Besides this basic tour a second side tour is suggested. At the end of the Public Market (1866 St.) is Kornarou Square where the Valide mosque, the Church of the Saviour, was. Next to it are a kiosk and a beautiful Venetian fountain, the Bembo fountain from 1588 with coats-of-arms in relief and a headless Roman statue which the architect Zuanne Bembo brought from Hierapetra. A modern sculptural composition, depicting Aretousa and Erotokritos, from the epic poem of the same name by Kornaros, has been erected in the square at the site of the Church of the Saviour.

West of Kornarou Square, after the small squares of Arkadiou and Riga Ferraiou, are the imposing, modern Cathedral Church of Saint Minas and the Church of Saint Catherine of Sinai with a stunning collection of icons by the Cretan School (see p. 124).

Evans St., south of Kornarou Square, leads to the New Gate. Outside the gate, right, is the entrance to an outdoor theatre where theatrical performances and concerts are held in summer.

Plastira St., at the base of the interior side of the wall, heads west to the Martinengo Bastion. An uphill sidestreet goes to the upper level where the simple tomb of Nikos Kazantzakis surveys his birthplace, Herakleion.

On an equally simple plaque are inscribed his words: "I hope for nothing, I fear nothing, I am free".

The Bembo fountain with a coat-of-arms in relief and a headless Roman statue.

THE MUSEUMS

THE ARCHAEOLOGICAL MUSEUM OF HERAKLEION

The Archaeological Museum of Herakleion has the richest collection of objects from the Minoan Civilization in the world and is certainly one of the most important museums in Greece. Finds from all the periods of Crete, from Neolithic to Roman times – covering a period of six millennia – are displayed in the wonderfully arranged galleries. In the museum one finds both huge Minoan pitharia (clay jars) and tiny masterpieces of miniature sculpture and metalwork, household utensils and weapons, as well as elegant gold jewellery, while the collections of vases of all periods and styles is outstanding. The magnificent frescoes from the palace of Knossos and other archaeological sites are on the top floor of the museum, while Greek art is represented by a host a finds from the Geometric, Archaic and Classical periods.

The visitor to the Museum follows the numbered galleries which keep to chronological and thematic unities as much as possible. The cases are numbered in succession. The description which follows is intended to assist the visitor in locating the most noteworthy objects. For fuller information there is a detailed guide written by the former Director of the Museum, Dr. Yannis Sakellarakis, which is sold in the Museum bookstore.

Gallery I. Pottery from the Neolithic and Pre-Palace Periods. Neolithic finds (6500-2600 B.C.) are displayed in cases 1-2 and Pre-Palace (2600-1900 B.C.) in cases 3-18A. Of special interest are *Case 1*: the steatopygous figurine of a female divinity. *Case 2*: a marble male figurine from Knossos (No 2623). *Case 6*: clay Vasiliki mottled ware. *Case 7*: stone vases from the tombs of Mochlos. *Case 16*: a collection of seal-stones, notably a sealstone in the shape of a fly, a fourteen-sided sealstone from Archanes, a dove with its new born from Koumasa, etc. (Nos. 2251, 2260 and 516). Sealstone No. 1098 is also imported (originally from Babylon); it is dated to the 18th century B.C. *Case 17*: gold objects principally from the tombs of Mochlos and Mesara (small frog). *Case 18A*: figurines, jewellery and daggers from the Phourni cemetery.

Gallery II. Finds from the first palaces at Knossos and Malia and the peak sanctuaries of central and eastern Crete (1900-1700 B.C.). Of note are the famous Kamares ware and egg-shell vases, Also of interest are *Case 25*: faience plaques which depict fagades of two- and three-storey structures. *Case 26*: three tripod fruit bowls with decoration that resembles lace-work. *Case 21*: clay models of ships and fish, bull-shaped libation vessel, figurines of men with loin cloths and knife as well as women with elaborate head-dress and wide skirts. *Case 23*: eggshell vases, cups with extremely delicate walls, a minute gold vase. Small clay sarcophagi are also displayed in this room.

Gallery III. Pottery finds (2000-1700 B.C.), stone-work, sealstones and inscribed objects, mainly from the old palace of Phaistos. *Cases 31-39*: Kamares and barbotine vessels from Phaistos. *Case 41*: the unique clay Phaistos Disc, one of the most precious exhibits in the museum.

Gallery IV. Collection of exhibits from the New Palace period of Knossos, Malia and Phaistos (1700-1450 B.C.). *Case 57*: the Gaming Board. perhaps a kind of chess which was played with gaming pieces. *Case 50*: the two famous figurines of the chthonic "Snake Goddess" and her daughter, made of faience, examples of high art which show how women dressed in the Minoan period. *Case 51*: vase (*rhyton*) from the 16th century B.C. in the shape of a bull's head, used for libations, made of black steatite, the eyes of rock crystal and jasper and the nostrils done in white tridacna shell (the horns must have been made of gilded wood). *Case 56*: ivory figure of a "bull-leaper" in the "death-leap" over the bull. *Case 55*: wild goat and cow suckling their young, in relief. Pan from scales and stone weights. *Case 52*: royal sword with the figure of an acrobat on the hilt, from Malia. *Case 59*: alabaster libation vessel in the shape of a lioness' head, from Knossos.

Gallery V. Vases, silver utensils, sealstones, figurines, lamps from Knossos (1450-1400 B.C.). The pottery belongs to the palace style. *Case 69*: samples of Linear A and Linear B script: most of the inscriptions are from Aghia Triada, while the Linear B is from Knossos. *Case 70A*: important samples of miniature sculpture, clay model of a house found at Archanes.

Gallery VI. Exhibits from the tombs of Mesara, Knossos, Archanes, Katsambas etc. (1400-1350 B.C.). *Case 87*: gold jewellery from Knossos and Phaistos as well as the so-called "Isopata ring" from the Isopata tomb of Knossos which depicts women dancing. *Case 88*: jewellery, rings from the Archanes cemetery depict figures mourning the dead Vegetation God. Also gold boxes, necklaces, bronze mirror-discs, etc. *Case 78*: helmet made of wild boar's tusks (necropolis Knossos). Some bronze cauldrons from Tylissos.

Gallery VII. One of the most important rooms in the museum with the well-known finds from the New Palace

Superb vase (rhyton) of steatite in the form of a bull's head, the horns (now lost) were of gilded wood, the eyes of rock crystal and the outline of the nostrils in mother-of-pearl. Little Palace of Knossos, 1550-1500 B.C. (Herakleion Museum).

period (1650-1400 B.C.). Impressive double axes in wooden pillars from the Nirou megaron. *Case 94*: the "Harvesters' Vase", a libation rhyton (Aghia Triada) of black steatite depicts farmers moving two by two in procession, their tools on their shoulders, while musicians and a priest walk in front of them. *Case 96*: rhyton (Aghia Triada) with four bands of decoration which depict boxing matches, wrestling and bull sports. *Case 95*: the "Cup of the Chieftain" or "of the Report" (Aghia Triada). The relief depiction shows a young official who is offering the leader a share of the spoils from the hunt. *Case 101*: a marvellous collection of jewellery among which is the famous pendant (amulet) in the shape of two bees or hornets storing a drop of honey in a comb (Chrysolakkos cemetery at Malia). Also miniature jewellery in the shape of a duck, fish,' lion and elegant necklaces (Aghia Triada). *Case 99*: copper talents, weighing about 40 kilos each (Aghia Triada). *Case 93*: carbonized wheat, pulses, figs and fruit.

Gallery VIII. Finds from the unplundered palace of Zakros (1650-1400 B.C.). Case 109: rhyton of rock crystal. The neck is joined to the body by a gilt ring, while the handle is made of crystal beads threaded onto a bronze wire. It was restored from hundreds of pieces. *Case 111*: rhyton of green stone which was burned in the final destruction (which explains its colour variations).

The relief decoration represents a peak sanctuary with its altars, doves, sacred horns and wild goats. *Case 115*: bronze tools and a huge saw. *Case 116*: Steatite rhyton in the shape of a bull's head.

Gallery IX. Finds from the settlements of Palaikastro, Gournia, Pseira and the sanctuary at Piskokephalo. *Case 128*: amphora decorated with octopuses.

Gallery X. Artefacts from the Post-Palace period (1400-1100 B.C.). *Case 133*: large-scale figures of a goddess with her arms raised and her head decorated with symbols. *Case 140*: figures, double axes and an offering table with six vessels.

Gallery XI. Collection of vases from the Sub-Minoan and Proto-Geometric period (1100-900 B.C.). *Case 148*: pins which secured the garments of the Dorians. *Case 754*: house models.

Gallery XII. Large jars and vases in the Orientalizing style, which show foreign influences, with sphinxes, winged horses and lions. *Case 161A*: bronze votive plaque with depictions of animal offerings from the peak sanctuary at Symi Viannou. *Case 167*: decorated bronze cauldron depicts the abduction of a goddess in a ship, archers, sphinxes etc.

Gallery XIII. Collection of Minoan terracotta sarcophagi, shaped like chests and bathtubs, from various parts of Crete.

*The famous "Snake Goddess",
faience figurine. Circa 1600 B.C.
(Herakleion Museum).*

Gallery XIV. Principally frescoes from the palaces and the annexes of Knossos, as well as the Amnisos villa, the villa of Aghia Triada and the dwellings on Pseira. In the centre of the gallery is a stone sarcophagus from a tomb at Aghia Triada, decorated with frescoes which depict scenes from the worship of the dead. The main frescoes: a) *The Procession*: it decorated the "Corridor of the Procession" at the palace of Knossos. It is calculated that the frieze consisted of about 350 figures (1400 B.C.). b) *The Prince of the Lilies*: relief fresco depicting a man with a necklace of lilies and a crown of lilies and peacock feathers (from the south corridor of Knossos). c) *Bull relief*: relief fresco (1600 B.C.) from a portico at the north entrance to Knossos. The head is well-preserved, d) *Ladies in Blue*: fresco (1600 B.C.). Few authentic pieces have been preserved, e) *The Dolphins*: from the "Queen's Megaron" at Knossos (1600 B.C.) f) *Bull-Leapers*: depicts the double jump over the back of a bull (Knossos).

Gallery XV. "*La Parisienne*": fresco which depicts a young priestess beautifully combed and made-up. Also the fresco of the "*Tripartite Shrine*" (Knossos).

Gallery XVI. a) *The Saffron Gatherer*: shows a monkey gathering saffron flowers (Knossos). b) *Captain of the Blacks*: depicts an officer leading a company of black soldiers (from house at Knossos). c) *Girl Dancer*: from the "Queen's Megaron" at Knossos.

Galleries XVII and XVIII. Minoan and Greek antiquities from the Yamalakis collection, purchased by the museum in 1962. Miniature works from historical times.

Gallery XIX. Artefacts from the Archaic period. Reliefs from the Gortyn acropolis, the Prinias temple, bronze shields from the Idaian Cave.

Gallery XX. Sculptures from the Classical period to the end of the Graeco-Roman period. Statue of Aphrodite, copy of a work by Praxiteles. Larger than life size statues of Apollo, from Gortyn.

Rhyton of rock crystal found at the palace of Zakros. Circa 1450 B.C.

Kamares ware fruit bowl from Phaistos. Circa 1800 B.C.

Krater with floral decoration from the old palace of Phaistos. Circa 1800 B.C.

Amphora decorated with octopuses. An example of the "Marine Style". Circa 1450 B.C.

Beak-spouted jug with elaborate plant
decoration. Circa 1530-1500 B.C.

Ceremonial vessel from the "lustral
bassin" of Zakros. Circa 1450 B.C.

Female figure in attitude of worship, from the end of the Old Palace period or the beginning of the New Palace period.

The magnificent "Harvesters' Vase" from Aghia Triada, depicting farmers returning from work in the fields. Circa 1550-1500 B.C.

Gold necklace bead
in the form a duck from
the Palace of Knossos.
Old Palace period,
2000-1600 B.C.

Minoan gold objects.
The double axe comes from the
Arkalochori cave and the earrings come
from Mavro Spilio near Knossos.
New Palace period, 1600-1500 B.C.

Sealstones of the New Palace
period. 1600-1500 B.C.

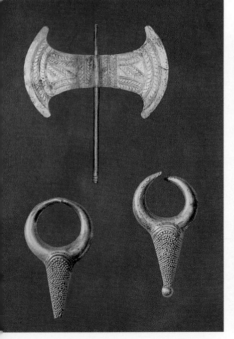

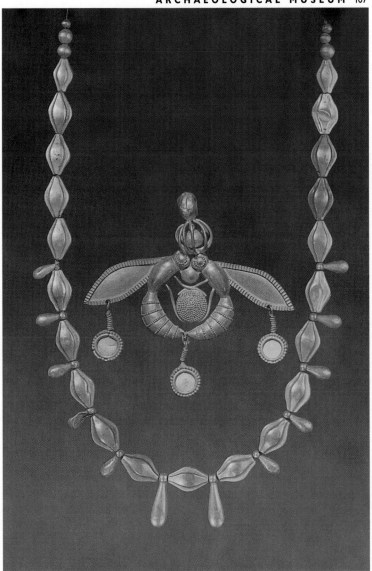

Gold necklace and gold amulet
in the form of two bees storing
a drop of honey in a comb.
Old Palace period, 2000-1600 B.C.

The famous "La Parisienne" from the palace of Knossos. Circa 1500-1450 B.C. Part of the Camp Stool Fresco.

Minoan fresco depicting the sacred sport of bull-leaping, in which both men and women took part.

Detail from the "Procession" fresco, of which only this figure, the Cup-bearer, has remained intact.

The "Blue Bird" is one of the three frescoes depicting the royal gardens of Knossos.

*Model of a small Proto-Goemetric II cir-
cular temple from Archanes, in which the
goddess can be seen with arms raised,
while on the roof there are two human
figures looking down into the temple and
an animal, possibly a dog.*

*Clay figurine of a goddess with
upraised arms and bird perched on
her head. Post-Palace period.*

*Clay model of the
Post-Palace period
from Palaikastro
representing a circle
of dancing women.
The woman in
the centre is playing
a lyre.*

*An example of the Cretan art
of clay modelling, vessel in
the form of a three-wheeled cart
drawn by three bulls.
IIth century B.C.*

THE HISTORICAL MUSEUM OF CRETE

The Historical Museum, which is housed in the Neoclassical residence of the Ka-lokairinos family, was founded in 1952, on the initiative of Andreas Kalokairi-nos, by the Society for Cretan Histori-cal Studies. It contains objects and heir-looms of early Christian, medieval and modern Cretan civilization. The collec-tions are displayed on three floors, arranged chronologically and by subject. The visit begins with the halls in the basement. The major exhibits are pre-sented according to hall.

Basement

Hall I: Sculptures from the basilica of Saint Titus at Gortyn (6th-9th century). Wellheads from Herakleion with deco-rations in relief.

Hall 2: Doorway from a Venetian build-ing in Herakleion. Architectural frag-ments from the Loggia of Herakleion (1628). Fountain from a Venetian noble's megaron, coats-of-arms of Venetian and Cretan families. Armenian inscription from the 16th century. Frieze with lions in relief.

Hall 2A: Gothic window from the church of Saint Peter. Reliefs with Christ Pantocrator and angels.

Hall 3 (corridor): Tombstones, with Venetian and Greek inscriptions. 18th-century frescoes from the residence of Fazil Bey in Herakleion.

Hall 4: Enamelled faience tiles from the Valide mosque. Inscribed Turkish tomb-stones. Inscribed founder's plaques from the churches of Saint Catherine and Saint Titus. Decorative reliefs from fountains.

Ground Floor

Left a small room fashioned into chapel with wall-paintings from the 13th to the 15th century and a wooden lectern from the 15th century.

Hall 5: Bronze light fixture from the church of Saint Titus, Gortyn, Icons, vestments and religious objects from the Byzantine period.

Hall 6: *Case 5*: Mitres, seals, clasps and lamps. *Case 10*: Byzantine coins: gold, sil-ver and copper. Copper coins from the Arab period in Crete. *Case 9*: Venetian miniature objects and silver crosses of th 15th century from the Monastery of Theologos, Mirabello. *Case 11*: Hoard of Byzantine and Venetian coins of Crete. *Case 8*: Venetian and Byzantine jewellery and Byzantine lead-bulls (*molyvdovoulla*). Collection of coins from the 16th and 17th centuries.

Hall 7: Historical heirlooms, important documents and seals of the Cretan revolutionaries the sultans' firmans. Personal effects and the desk of the first High Commissioner of Crete, Prince George.

First Floor

Corridor: Medieval maps. Photographic archives of Mourellos from the period 1867 to 1912. Photographic archives of the Battle of Crete.

Hall: (Emmanuel Tsouderos). His desk, library and personal effects. Collection of Venetian and Dutch manuscripts and maps. Complete collection of stamps from the "Cretan Republic".

Hall: (Nikos Kazantzakis). His desk and library. All the manuscripts of his work and a large part of his personal correspondence.

Second Floor

Hall 8: Woven embroideries. Cretan folk art. Carved wooden chests, various objects for daily use and musical instruments.

Hall 9: (Chrysoula Xanthoudidou). Embroideries, weaving, lace and crochet.

Hall 10: Reproduction of a typical room in a rural Cretan house.

Hall 11: Samples of Cretan household weaving, embroidery and knitting, costumes (male and female) as well as Cretan jewellery, necklaces, rings, bracelets, earrings etc. (17th-19th century).

The museum also contains collections of manuscripts, books and maps which are available to scholars with a permit from the museum.

Relief metope from the frieze of the Venetian Loggia in Herakleion with crossed high-boots and weapons.

Relief plaque bearing a double-headed eagle, the coat-of-arms of the Kallergis family and the date 1635, from the Church of the Mother of God (Theotokos), Kato Astraka, Pediados.

Relief metope from the frieze of the Venetian Loggia in Herakleion depicting an oval shield with man's face and crossed weapons.

Relief metope from the frieze of the Venetian Loggia in Herakleion depicting a round shield and torches.

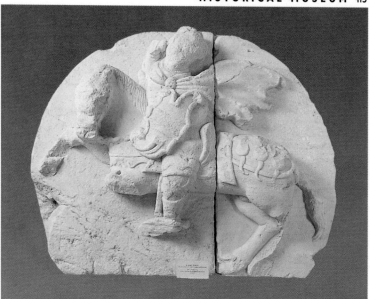

Circular marble medallion with a relief of Saint George on horseback and the coat-of-arms of the Zorzis family on the saint's shield. From the Saint George Gate of the Venetian walls of Chandax, 16th century.

Venetian tombstone with a woman in relief. Chandax, 15th century.

Round well-head depicting in relief a warrior and decorative motifs. Chandax, 13th century.

Square well-head depicting in relief hunters, heraldic lions, a griffin and a cross. Chandax, 12th century.

Gold Byzantine coin from the reign of the Emperor Nikephoros Phokas II (963-969). On the obverse the Emperor Nikephoros Phokas and the Holy Virgin (head and torso) holding a partiarchal cross and on the reverse Christ Pantocrator. From Aghies Paraskies, Herakleion.

Pair of gold filigree
earrings in the from of
a radiating rosette with
pierced beads. Unknown
provenance.
14th-15th century.

Pear-shaped gold
earrings with pearls
around the edge. On the
perforated background
a palmetto framing
a geometric motif.
Unknown provenance.
6th-7th century.

Belt embroidered with
silver and silver buckle
with embossed rosettes
and floral motifs.
From the Asomatos
Monastery, Amari.
18th century.

Portaits of the men from Anogeia, Mylopotamos, who fought the Turks. Work of the folk artist Stavrakakis at the end of the 19th century.

K. Stavrakakis

S. Niotis

K. Sbokos

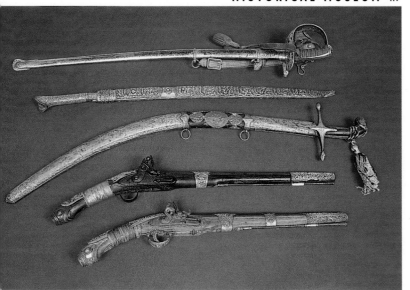

Weapons used by chieftains of the Cretan revolutions against the Turks. 18th-19th century.

Medieval Venetian breastplates, swords and stirrups from western Crete. 15th-16th century.

Wall-painting from the house of the Turk Fazil Bey in Herakieion depicting the Great

Fortress (Herakieion). 18th century.

*Interior of a traditional Cretan house
with the objects used by rural Cretans.*

*Woven band depicting knights holding
flags of the Cretan Republic.
From Krousonas, Malevizios.
19th-20th century.*

*Woven woollen bedspread with female
figures, birds and stylized floral motifs.
From Leivadia, Mylopotamos.
19th-20th century.*

CHURCH OF SAINT CATHERINE - COLLECTION OF BYZANTINE ICONS

Aghia Aikaterini Square.

The metochion of the Sinai Monastery of Saint Catherine housed a school in which illustrious men of letters of the day taught and renowned hierarchs of the Orthodox faith, such as Maxi-mos Margounios, Kyrillos Loukeris, were pupils. This educational centre played its part in the general rise in the cultural level of the age.

The church of Saint Catherine was built in 1555 and renovated in the 17th century. Today wall-paintings from the 13th and 14th centuries are exhibited there, as well as an impressive collection of Byzantine icons. Six of those from the 16th century are credited to Michail Damaskinos (a Cretan painter who worked in Crete, the Ionian islands and Venice). They belonged to the Vrondisi Monastery on Mount Ida until 1800 when they were transferred to the church of Saint Minas. Today they are exhibited among the other Byzantine icons, wall-paintings and treasures. They are: *The Adoration of the Magi*, *The Last Supper*, *The Virgin with the Burning Bush*, *"Noli me tangere"*, *The Ecumenical Council at Nicaea* and the *Divine Liturgy*.

Icon of the Second Coming. Detail showing the Angels trumpeting and the scales. Late 17th century.

West facade of the cruciform church of Saint Catherine (Aghia Aikaterini) of Sinai and the domed side-chapel of the Ten Saints (Aghioi Deka). Renaissance architecture of the 16th century.

Icon of the Virgin with Burning Bush by
Michail Damaskinos. Second half of the
16th century.

Icon of the Adoration of the Magi by Michail
Damaskinos. Second half of the 16th century.

Icon with representation of the Tree of
Jesse, who is lying on his side. It depicts
the family tree of the Holy Virgin who
dominates the representation with her
ancestors on the branches. Late 17th
century. Restored in 1906.

The Last Supper by Michail Damaskinos
in imitation of Western copper-plate
engravings, particularly those of
Marcantonio Raimondi. Second half
of the 16th century.

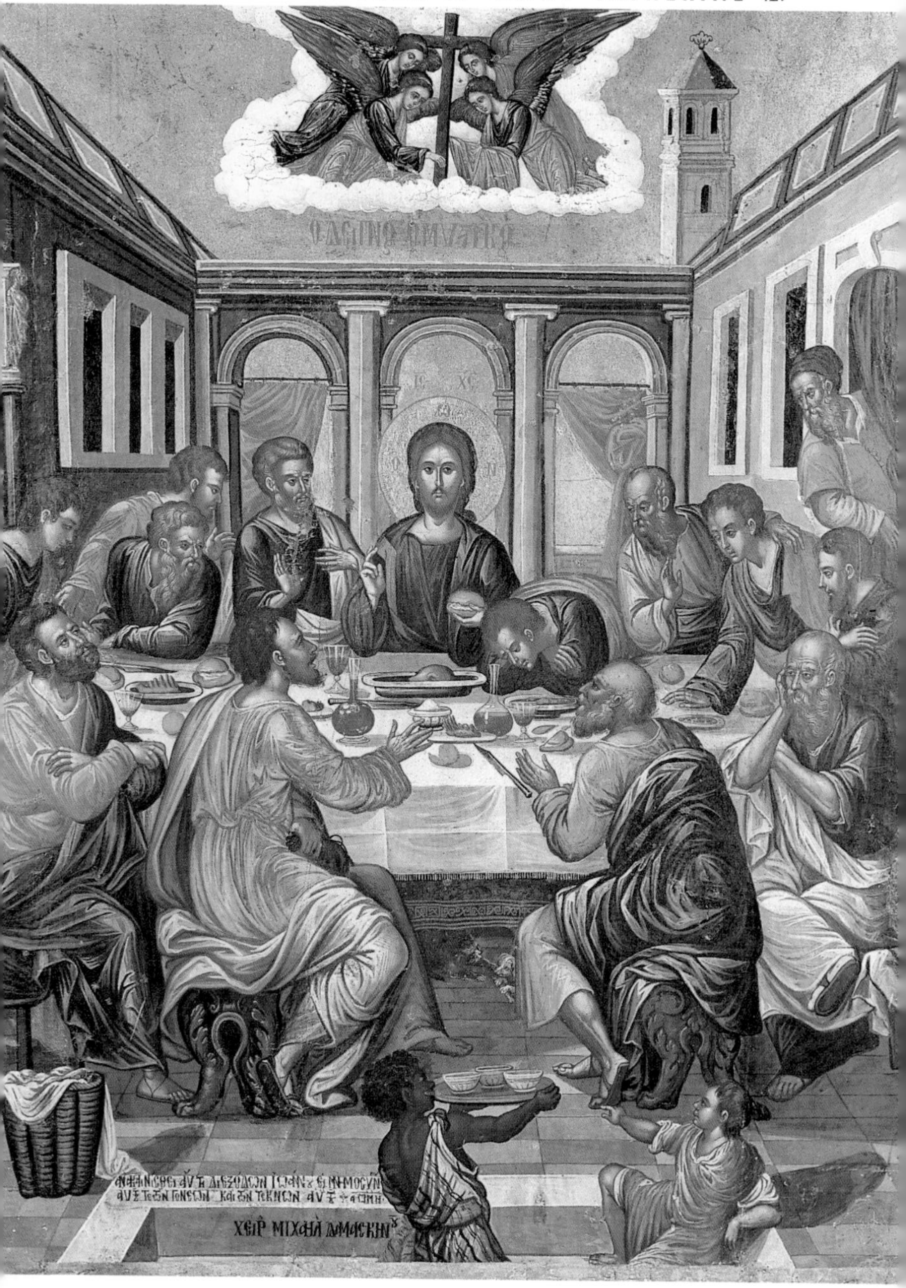

Second Coming. Detail of the Angels trumpeting. Late 17th century.

The Adoration of the Magi by Michail Damaskinos. Detail. 16th century.

TOURS

HERAKLEION: Excursion I, Knossos

The Minoan palace of Knossos lies at a distance of 5 kilometres from the centre of Herakleion. There is regular local bus service, which leaves from the central harbour.

Leaving Eleftheria Square the road continues left after the cemetery at Aghios Konstantinos. Minoan tombs have been excavated in the vicinity of Aghios Ioannis near the public road, including the famous Minoan tomb of Isopata (see Historical Review), which was destroyed by the bombing in 1942. Three and a half km. from the town is the University of Crete. This entire area was covered by the cemetery of Knossos with many hundreds of tombs from the historical period (1100-700 B.C.). Just before the archaeological site of Knossos, to the left, is the Herakleion General Hospital and right steps leading to the Roman "Villa Dionysos", which takes its name from its mosaic floor of the 2nd century A.D.

Archaeological Site of Knossos

The palace and the adjacent Minoan houses are open to visitors. Other sites in the region such as the "Little Palace", the "Royal Villa", the "Villa Dionysos", the South Royal Temple-Tomb and the

Aerial view of the archaeological site at Knossos.

Restoration drawing of the palace of Knossos.

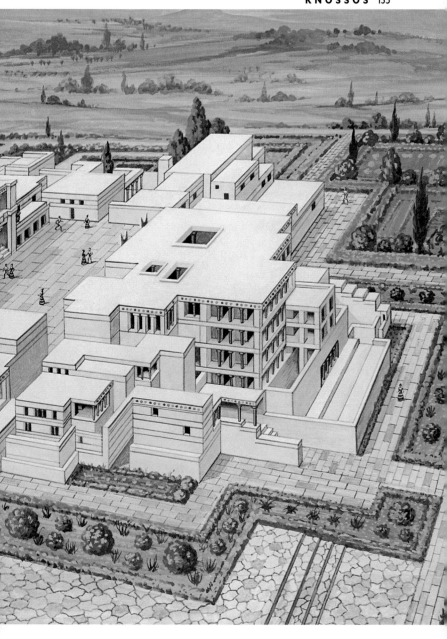

"Caravanserai" are closed to the public.

The imposing palace of Knossos is built on a hill, next to the river Kairatos. This area has been inhabited since Neolithic times (6000 B.C. and perhaps even earlier). Excavations have revealed that the Neolithic levels at Knossos are among the deepest in Europe. On the site of the Neolithic settlement an important Pre-Palace settlement developed in the 3rd millennium. The first palace was built on the Neolithic ruins sometime after 2000 B.C. and was destroyed in 1700 B.C. The second palace was erected on the same spot, even more magnificent and larger than the preceding one. Around 1600 B.C. a massive new earthquake caused severe damage to it but it was quickly repaired. During the same period other large structures were built around the palace such as the "Little Palace", the "Royal Villa", the "South House" etc., while Knossos developed into a large town with many thousands of inhabitants. Its size is shown by the extensive cemeteries which surrounded it. A new catastrophe occurred around 1450 B.C., which was probably connected with the great eruption of the volcano on Santorini. Nevertheless, as the finds demonstrate, the palace was repaired and

The north entrance of the palace of Knossos where the walkway to the "Customs House" began.

used again by an Achaean sovereign, until at least 1380 B.C. despite the fact that the other important centres in Crete had been destroyed. After the final destruction the palace was not used again except for the so-called "temple of Rhea" in historical times. Knossos continued its history as a great city-state throughout historical times till the first Byzantine period. In the Middle Ages it declined and turned into a village, known by the name Makrys Toichos ("Long Wall").

Excavations began in the area of Knossos at the end of the 19th century. In 1878 Minos Kalokairinos from Herakleion made trial sections in the area of the palace. Systematic excavations were begun by the Englishman Arthur Evans in 1900. The excavations undertook daring reconstruction work which, even though in terms of present-day excavation methodology appears excessive, proved vital for the ancient ruins and their preservation. Furthermore, the reconstruction helps us comprehend the size and the grandeur of the palace.

The present-day entrance leads along a picturesque path to the West Court of the palace (1). Two processional causeways, slightly elevated, traverse the flagstoned court. The right one leads to the entrance to the palace and the other to the Theatral Area.

In the left section of the courtyard, three deep walled pits, known as kouloures, were probably sacred depositories (or silos according to other exca-

The "Throne Room" with its unique stone throne and gypsum benches (Palace of Knossos).

vators). At the bottom of the central kouloura can be seen stairs which lead to the foundations of a room from a dwelling of the Pre-Palace period. Two altar bases lie close to the exterior west wall of the palace.

In the SE corner of the courtyard (2) is the entrance to the palace, from which begins the Corridor of the Procession, leading in a southerly di-' rection (3). The name is derived from the fresco of the Procession (Herakleion Museum) which adorned its walls. The floor of the corridor was made of gypsum slabs with a paving of green schist with red plaster at the interstices. It formed a U as it turned east and then north, joining another corridor which ends at the central court. Its S. section has been destroyed. At this point a visitor sees before him the "South House" (4). Turning left you encounter the enormous horns of poros limestone. Left is the South Propylon of the palace (5), partially restored, while on the west

Reconstruction of the central light-well which was surrounded on three sides by columns. On the walls hang copies of wall-paintings from the Hall of the Frescoes.

wall is a copy of part of the fresco of the Procession. A broad staircase leads to the upper floor – the "piano nobile" according to Evans – where there are large ceremonial halls and the Tripartite Shrine with three column bases and three pier bases. These areas have been reconstructed by Evans. A small narrow staircase leads to the Central Court (6).

We are now on the ground floor of the west wing of the palace. Immediately on the right is the Anteroom of the Throne Room (7) with a wooden throne (copy), benches and a stone basin which was transferred here from an adjacent corridor to the N. To the rear is the Throne Room with a unique stone throne, benches of gypsum and a lustral basin. The walls are decorated with depictions of griffins. Directly south of the anteroom is a stairway with 12 steps and two columns in the middle, which leads to the upper floor. South of the foot of the stairs is the Central Shrine of the palace which includes the Anteroom of the Pillar Crypts (8). Double axes are inscribed on the pillars. In the NW corner of the anteroom, a door leads to the Room of the Tall Pithos (9) with a giant pithos preserved in situ. Then a second door leads to a new space (10) where the Temple Repositories were. The Snake Goddesses were found there in one of the rectangular cists (Herakleion Museum). The Corri-

The South Propylon of the Palace of Knossos.

dor of the Procession (11) ends on the S. side of the Central Court where a relief copy depicts the Prince of the Lilies (Herakleion Museum).

The E. side of the palace, where the main royal chambers were, was built on a level area that had been fashioned on the side of the hill at a depth eight metres below the level of the Central Court. This building is also multi-storeyed with a broad stairway which was illuminated by a central light-well surrounded on three sides by colonnades. The two lowest flights were found intact while the rest have been rebuilt. There is a copy of fig-ure-of-eight shields on the E. wall of the first floor. At the end of the stairway, right, in the E. corridor (12) a door to the right leads to the "King's Megaron" a large, well-lighted room. Through a corridor you pass on to the "Queen's Megaron" (13) which is decorated with frescoes. To the W. is a small room (14) with a clay bathtub. On the SW side, a corridor leads to the Queen's Dressing Room (15) where there is a drainage system, and the next small space which was the Queen's Privy. Through a pas-sage you again arrive at the base of the stairway, from where another passage to the N. leads to the Royal Workshops for stone-carving, pottery etc. Further N. are the Magazines of the Giant Pithoi (16) with huge clay jars and the "Corri-dor of the Draughtboard" or "Gaming

Restored view of the Hall of the Double Axes.

Board" (17) (Herakleion Museum). Be-neath this passage can be seen a section of the aqueduct with clay pipes, which brought drinking water to the palace from Mount Juktas.

From the N. side of the Central Court an outdoor inclined corridor (18) leads out of the palace. To the W. one of the Bastions has been restored with a copy of a relief fresco of a bull (Herakleion Museum). N. of the Bastion are the foundations of the "Customs House" (19) with eight pillars. It was given this name because the road from the har-bour of Katsambas and Amnisos ended here. To the W. a processional way leads to the Theatral Area (20) with approxi-mately 500 seats which lies outside the palace. The theatre has two wings of seats and a dais, probably for the royal box. The Royal Road sets off from the Theatral Area and leads to the Small Palace, passing by the houses of the town which have been excavated here.

The sacred double horns on a special base on the Propylon ornamented the opening in the wall for the Processional Way.

HERAKLEION: Excursion 2

Turn off to Skalani (8.5 km.) - Varvari or Myrtia (Kazantzakis Museum) (21 km.) - Archanes (15 km.) - Vathypetro (20 km.) - Apanosiphis Monastery (31 km.).

Take the road to Knossos (Excursion 1) which is a good highway. Seven and a half km. west is a section of the arched aqueduct at Aghia Eirene which was built during the Egyptian occupation (1832-1840) to supply Herakleion with water. The region has many vineyards and olive trees. Eight and a half km. along turn off to the left for Skalani and Varvari and the Kazantzakis Museum. A good road with frequent signs for the museum leads to the village of Myrtia, better known as Varvari (21 km. from Herakleion), the birthplace of the father of Nikos Kazantzakis. This beautiful tidy village has streets lined with flower pots.

The Museum, in the central square, is housed in the renovated house of the Kazantzakis and Anemoyannis families. It contains personal effects of Nikos Kazantzakis, photographs, manuscripts and all the editions of his work in all languages. Of interest, in the central room, are small "dioramas" of scenes from the author's principal theatrical works, which were performed both in Greece and abroad. The display case with authentic costumes of some of the protagonists of the plays stands out. In another room, a 20-minute audiovisual programme in Greek, English, German and French, presents the life and work of Kazantzakis.

For scholars there are well-catalogued, extensive archives of his publications in many languages.

Returning on the public road to Herakleion you continue on to the crossroads right which leads to Archanes (15 km.), lying amid vineyards, a historical town with 3700 inhabitants (400 m.a.s.l.). The region produces a great deal of wine and an excellent table grape (*rozaki*).

The name Archanes has been retained since antiquity when the town flourished. In 1964 the archaeologists Yannis and Efi Sakellarakis began systematic excavations which have brought significant artefacts to light.

Archaeological Site of Archanes

So far three important archaeological sites have been excavated at Archanes: a section of the Minoan palace, the cemetery on Phourni hill and the Minoan sanctuary at Anemospilia. All these

Vine-growing region of Archanes with its large production of wine and table grapes.

The church of the Virgin at Archanes.

areas are still closed to the public as the excavations are ongoing.

The site of the palace is in Archanes itself, in the old Turkish quarter, and not far from the Church of the Virgin (Panaghia). The complex around the north entrance and a part of the east section of the palace, which was destroyed in 1450 B.C., have been found.

The excavations from 1966 to the present have brought to light the Minoan cemetery on Phourni hill, SW of the town (about 1.5 km.). The most important prehistoric cemetery in the Aegean, it was used for 1500 years and has three tholos tombs from the Pre-Palace and Old Palace periods, many square funeral buildings of roughly the same period and a Mycenaean grave circle – unique outside of Mycenae – with six shaft graves. Also important is a special building to service the needs of the cemetery. In tholos tomb A (1400-1350 B.C.), the first unplundered royal burial in Crete was found in a larnax with a host of gold, silver and ivory masterpieces. From the other tombs (Herakleion Museum) came important unique sealstones, figurines, jewellery made of precious metals (gold-silver), hundreds of clay vessels from all the periods and styles of the Minoan civilization.

The temple at Anemospilia is 5 km. SW of Archanes on the north side of Juktas. 200 metres after leaving the town take the turn left and 500 m. further on bear left again. It is an uphill road in only fair condition. Five km. later the archaeological site appears on the left bordering the road (it is fenced in).

The Minoan sanctuary consists of three main rooms and a long corridor to the north with three doors. The walls are of ashlared stone as in the palaces. Many artefacts were found in the area, namely pottery, amphoras, ewers, chalices and clay jars as well as a large stone basin. Two life-size clay feet were discovered in the central room; most probably they belonged to a wooden cult statue. In the east room there was an offering table and religious objects while in the west is a free-standing altar on which a human skeleton was found with a bronze knife in its chest. Two other skeletons were found in the same area while a fourth was located in the antechamber. Obviously this was a human sacrifice, the first to be excavated in the Aegean. The sanctuary was destroyed around 1700 B.C. at the same time as the first palaces of the other Minoan towns and by the same cause (earthquake).

Above Anemospilia, on the highest summit of Mount Juktas, is the very important Minoan peak sanctuary with an open-air altar, terraces and row of rooms.

The first turn left after Archanes (1 km.) goes through vineyards to the Byzantine church of the Archangel Michael (Asomatos - the Bodiless Saint) with frescoes from 1315.

Frescoes of the Pantocrator, the Crucifixion and the Assumption, as well as of the founder of the church, Michail

The Minoan cemetery at Phourni, the most important prehistoric cemetery in the Aegean.

Archanes. Tholos tomb (1400-1350 B.C.) found unplundered.

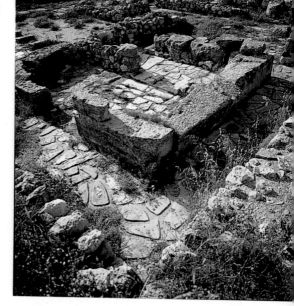

Three archaeological sites have been excavated in the region of Archanes. They are closed to the public. Right: part of the excavations

Patsidiotis with his wife, are well-preserved.

On Mount Juktas lies the peak sanctuary at Psili Korfi, very important to the Minoan centres at Knossos and Archanes.

Five km. south of Archanes, at the site Piso Leivadia (dirt road), the Minoan villa at Vathypetro was found. The site is not open to the public and may be visited after prior arrangement with the guards at Archanes.

The excavations were begun by Professor S. Marinates in 1949 and brought to light the ruins of a villa which was built around 1580-1550 B.C. The exterior walls are of hewn stone construction. The upper floor, which appears to have been in several sections, was of unbaked brick. The walls were faced with polychrome mortar. After its destruction, most likely by an earthquake around 1450 B.C., the villa was re-used as a farm. It contained a number of handicraft installations, wine and olive oil presses and a pottery kiln. The adjacent roofed area has 16 gigantic pithoi in situ.

Continuing south the dirt road leads to the village of Choudetsi. A paved road goes on for 5 km. toward Apanosiphis Monastery (31 km.) dedicated to Saint George. The monastery must have been built around 1600. The great earthquake of 1856 destroyed it. It was rebuilt in 1862 but destroyed again in the revolution of 1866 by the Turks because the monastery afforded assistance and refuge to the rebels of Korakas. The church and the other areas have been restored.

Anemospilia. The tripartite sanctuary made of ashlared stone. It was destroyed around 1700 B.C., perhaps by an earthquake. Below: details of the sanctuary walls.

Restoration drawing
of the Minoan
palace of Archanes.

The Minoan
mansion at Vathy-
petro in the area of
Piso Leivadia.

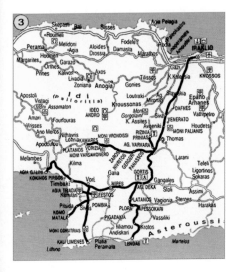

HERAKLEION: Excursion 3

Venerato (20 km.) - Paliani Convent (21 km.) - Aghia Varvara (29 km.) - (Turn-off north) Prinias (3.5 km.), west to Vrondisi Monastery (19 km.) - Varsamonero Monastery (26 km.) - Kamares (30 km.) - Aghioi Deka (45 km.) - (Lendas turn-off) Gortyn (46 km.) - Moires (53 km.) - (Turn off south to Kaloi Limenes) - Phaistos (59 km.) - Aghia Triada (61 km.) - Matala (70 km.) - Tymbaki (65 km.) - Aghia Galini (77 km.). Buses leave from the KTEL station outside the Chania Gate.

Take the road through the Chania Gate, heading toward Moires (sign at the 3rd km.). The road cuts through the richest raisin-producing area in Crete. At the 13th km. a turn-off to the left for Daphnes, source of the finest Malevizian wine. The village of Venerato is at the 20th km.

In the village the road left and then immediately right leads to the Convent of Paliani (1 km.), one of the oldest in Crete. It is mentioned in 668 by the names Palaia or Pala. Originally it belonged to the Patriarchate of Constantinople. In 1304 it was seized by the Roman Catholic Archbishopric. In 1821 the Turks destroyed it and killed all the nuns except one who restored' the convent. The Turks damaged it again in 1866. Today the church is triple-aisled, dedicated to the Dormition of the Virgin Mary (Koimisi tis Theotokou) and contains old Byzantine column capitals. There is a great festival on its feast day August 15.

To the rear of the convent is a myrtle bush, over a century old, in the trunk of which, according to tradition the miracle-working icon of the Panaghia Myrtidiotissa (feast day on September 24) was hidden. Fifty nuns, known for their hospitality, live at the convent.

Approaching Aghia Varvara (29 km.) to the right juts up the imposing hill "Patella tou Prinia". At the entrance to Aghia Varvara on a rock (after the third house) is a small chapel to Prophet Elijah (Profitis Ilias) which the locals believe to be the geographical centre of Crete.

A road passes through Aghia Varvara to the right leading to ancient Rizenia, just west of the village of Prinias (3.5

The Byzantine church of the Ten Saints (Aghioi Deka) in the village of the same name, where these early Christian martyrs were executed.

The Paliani Convent in the village of Venerato is one of the oldest in Crete (A.D. 688).

Vrondisi Monastery. At the entrance is a very beautiful Venetian fountain from the 15th-century.

The famous Varsamonero Monastery with well-preserved 14th- and 15th-century wall-paintings.

km.) where there are two carved cave-tombs. The ruins of ancient Rizenia, which were excavated by the Italian Archaeological School at the beginning of the century, are on the hill "Patella tou Prinia" (686 m. a.s.l.) from which there is a panoramic view. Rizenia occupied a strategic position between two large towns, Knossos and Gortyn, and flourished from 1600 B.C. to the Hellenistic period. The ruins of two temples from the 7th and 6th centuries B.C. were found there as well as the ruins of a fortress from the Hellenistic period. The excavations were resumed in 1966-1978. A large cemetery from the Geometric period was found at the base of the acropolis of Rizenia.

Back at Aghia Varvara a branch right, just before the south exit, leads to Zaro (17 km.). A difficult metalled road wends its way up through a fertile region of cherry, walnut and other fruit trees. Five km. along is the village of Panasos and near it the Barothiano cave with stalactites.

The road continues on traversing the villages Gergeri (plentiful water), Nivritos (pre-Greek name), Apano Zaro (340 m. a.s.l.) which also has abundant water and vegetation. Four km. from here, on the south side of Psiloreitis, is Vrondisi Monastery and 7 km. later the Monastery of Saint Phanourios, Varsamonero.

The exact date for the founding of Vrondisi Monastery is unknown but there is written testimony from 1400. During the Revolution of 1866 the leader Korakas organized the first armed band there and proclaimed the start of the revolution in central and eastern Crete. But the Turks burned the monastery to the ground. Today a few of its wall-paintings from the 14th century and a portable icon by the painter Angelos (1600) have been preserved in the church. There is a most beautiful Venetian fountain (15th century) at the entrance to the monastery.

Further west, at the village of Voriza, is the famous Varsamonero Monastery which during the Venetian occupation was an intellectual centre and distinguished for its clerics. Only the distinctive church is preserved. Various inscribed dates from 1332 to 1426 testify to the successive stages of the erection and the iconography. The wall-paintings from the 14th and 15th centuries have been preserved in good condition. The Head of Christ and the Divine Liturgy are works of the painter Rikos. The beautiful iconostasis is perhaps from the 16th century (the guard at Voriza has the keys to the church).

Four km. to the west is the village of Kamares (600 m. a.s.l.) from where, after a five-hour hike, one can reach the Kamares cave on the south side of Psiloreitis (1520 m. a.s.l.).

The first renowned Kamares style ware was found here. From the village of Kamares there is a better asphalt road, rather winding, which leads to the villages of Platanos and Apodoulou, Amariou.

Back at Aghia Varvara, the road south descends to the plain of Mesara, the granary of Crete.

Forty-four km. along is the village of Aghioi Deka, the place where ten early Cretan martys were executed. A Byzantine church was built near the site of the martyrdom in which are kept, in a glass case, beneath the iconostasis, the stone where they kneeled to be beheaded. In the church at Aghia Limni, outside the village to the left, are the tombs of the martyrs (follow the signs).

After Aghioi Deka a crossroads left leads north to the village of Platanos where two of the largest tholos tombs from the Prehistoric period were discovered with sealstones, tools and gold jewellery (Herakleion Museum). Continuing S. we reach the villages of Plora and Apesokari where two tholos tombs were also found. The road, recently completed, continues on to Miamou and Lenda, which are near ancient Lebena, the harbour of Gortyn. Here, in the 4th century B.C., the inhabitants dedicated a temple to Asklepios near hot springs which are still known today for their therapeutic properties. The Italian Archaeological School excavated the area in 1900 and 1910 to 1913 and found, 100 m. from the shore, between the headlands Lenda and Psamidomouri, the ruins of the sanctuary of Asklepios with a temple, a building from the Hellenistic period, stoas and a nymphaeum. Two reservoirs were found near the shore, probably for the ill to bathe in, and the ruins of a large structure, perhaps a hospice.

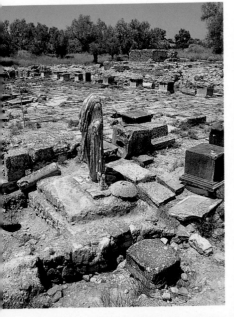

Headless statue from ancient Gortyn.

The altar and temple of Apollo in ancient Gortyn.

The Odeum of Gortyn on the walls of which are carved the texts of its famous laws.

More recent excavations (1958-60) by S. Alexiou uncovered tholos tombs from the Early Minoan period at the sites of Papoura and Yerokambos.

Back on the public road Herakleion-Phaistos, 1.5 km. from Aghioi Deka are the ruins of ancient Gortyn located on both sides of the road, scattered throughout the olive grove. During the Minoan period Gortyn did not play an important role but during the historical period (10th century B.C. and after) it gradually replaced Phaistos as the capital of Mesara. The Romans made it into the leading city of Crete.

To the right of the road are the ruins of the basilica of Saint Titus (6th century). It was an impressive building with thick walls made of large stone blocks. Architectural reliefs from the church are in the Historical Museum of Herakleion. A path leads to the Odeum (1st century B.C.). It was built of material from an older monument. On one of its walls are inscribed the texts of the famous Law Code of Gortyn (5th century B.C.). The Odeum was restored in A.D. 100. Behind the Odeum is an evergreen plane tree under which, according to tradition, Minos, Rhadamanthys and Sarpedon were born from Zeus and Europa.

On the S. side of the public road are the ruins of a temple dedicated to Isis and Sarapis, as well as a sanctuary dedicated to Pythian Apollo. A little further east is the complex of the Praetorium and the baths. Just before the village of Metropolis is an Early Byzantine church with marvellous mosaic floors.

Gortyn was the capital of Roman and Early Byzantine Crete and was one of the largest towns in the eastern Mediterranean.

At the 53rd km. you enter the modern market town of Moires, a communications and commercial centre, with many rooms for rent, tavernas and restaurants. A fork to the left leads to Pombia, Pigadakia, the Hodegetria Monastery and the beach at Kaloi Limenes (the road is under construction). The

The ruins of the basilica of Saint Titus (6th cen-tury A. D.).

church of the Hodegetria Monastery is double-aisled with interesting portable icons. On the convent's north gate is the date 1568. Excavations in 1981 brought to light a tomb complex from the Early Minoan period in the environs of the convent, with five rooms, two tholos tombs, and a paved court. Hundreds of clay vases, dozens of stone ones, sealstones, gold jewellery and bronze tools were among the finds.

According to tradition, the Apostle Paul landed at Kaloi Limenes when he was being taken to Rome. A short distance to the E. is the ancient town of Lasaia, harbour of Gortyn. There are some ruins from the Roman period, and Early Minoan tholos tombs.

Across from Kaloi Limenes are the Megalo and Mikro islands.

The public road continues on from Moires. A branch to the right leads to Phaistos (63 km. from Herakleion). The palace of Phaistos on top of a small hill (elev. 100 m.) dominates the plain and the surrounding mountains: to the N. Psiloreitis and to the S. Asterousia. The palace is smaller than Knossos but it was built with care and high quality materials. Unlike Knossos there has been no restoration work here.

Archaeological Site of Phaistos

Phaistos, one of the most ancient Cretan towns, was second in importance to Knossos. Its dominion, at its peak, stretched from Lithinon to Psychion (Melissa) and included the Paximadia

islands (Letoai islands). It was the principal town of Mesara, with two harbours, Matala and Kommos. According to mythology, the dynasty of the son of Zeus, Rhadamanthys, ruled at Phaistos.

The region around Phaistos was inhabited from the Neolithic period (3000 B.C.), as is revealed by the foundations of houses and Neolithic tools. The first palace was built in approximately 1900 B.C. and was destroyed by a great earthquake in 1700 B.C. But it was quickly rebuilt, on a more majestic scale than the first one. Most of the buildings we see today belong to the second palace. During the Archaic, Classical and Hellenistic periods Phaistos was independent and autonomous. It was the birthplace of important men, among whom was Epimenides, one of the seven wise men of antiquity. It was frequently at war with Gortyn, which destroyed it at the end of the 3rd century B.C.

The excavations at Phaistos were begun in 1900 by the Italian Archaeological Mission headed by F. Halbherr and were continued by L. Pernier and D. Levi.

The visit to the site begins at the present-day entrance (NW of the palace) where there is a paved Upper Court (I), which is traversed by a slightly elevated "processional way". This court was used during both the Old and the New Palace periods. To the SE, a stairway (2) leads to the large West Court (3) which is 6 m. lower. This is also stone-paved and contemporary with the previous

The shore at Kaloi Limenes from where, according to tradition, the Apostle Paul landed when he was being taken to Rome.

one. On the N. side of the court eight well-preserved tiered rows of seats 22 m. long were used as theatre seats. The "processional way" continues through the Theatral Area and proceeds on through the West Court to the palace. In the middle of the court it turns W. toward circular wells (4), similar to the "kouloures" at Knossos.

On the E. side of the West Court the façade of the new palace has been located approximately seven metres further back than the old palace. Toward the E. there is the Grand Staircase (5) (14 m. wide), a unique achievement of Minoan architecture, with stairs that are slightly convex (like the Parthenon) so the rain water will flow away.

The Grand Staircase (5) leads to the Propylon (6) behind which is a light-well (7) with three columns.

A narrow stairway right (8) leads to the flagstoned Antechamber of the Storerooms (9) where a large number of sealstones were found. A corridor begins (10) to the W. with a pillar in the middle. Right and left of the corridor are many storerooms. In the final one right (11) (covered today) are giant clay jars (pithoi) and a built-in receptacle in the floor to collect liquids.

From the antechamber (9) you exit into the Central Court (12), also a remnant of the old palace.

Aerial view of Phaistos.

Restoration drawing of the propylon of Phaistos.

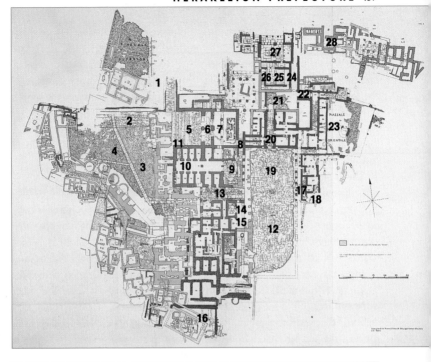

PHAISTOS
Plan of the Palace of Phaistos.

1. Paved Upper Court
2. Kerkides
3. West Court
4. Wells
5. Grand Staircase
6. Propylaeum
7. Light-well
8. Narrow stairway
9. Antechamber of the Storerooms
10. Corridor between storerooms
11. Storeroom with pithoi
12. Central Court
13. Corridor
14. 15. Rooms with benches
16. Temple of Rhea (outside palace grounds)
17. Lustral basin
18. Lavatory
19. Entrance to Royal Apartments
20. Corridor to North Court
21. North Court
22. Corridor to East Court
23. Horseshoe-shaped smelting furance
24. Corridor to Royal Apartments
25. «Queen's Megaron»
26. Narrow staircase
27. «King's Megaron»
28. Room where «Phaistos disc» was found

To E. and W. piers and columns create porticos.

The W. wing of the palace is divided into two sections by a corridor (13). On the S. side of the corridor is the main shrine with connected rooms containing stone ledges (14 and 15). There is a low table in room (14). Outside, S. of the palace, is the Archaic temple of Rhea (16).

The E. wing of the palace, with its small dimensions (a part has collapsed) gives the impression of having been a prince's apartment. Here were found small cisterns, a lustral basin with stairs (17) as well as another small space, probably a lavatory (18).

On the N. side of the Central Court is the entrance (19) to the Royal Apartments. The outdoor corridor (20) with rooms right and left starts from this exit. The corridor (20) leads to the North Court (21). Another corridor (22) ends at the East Court in the centre of which is a horseshoe-shaped furnace (23), probably for smelting copper.

The western rooms must have been workshops.

Returning to the North Court, the corridor (24) leads to the Royal Apartments. To the W. is the "Queen's Megaron" (25) on a lower level with a light-well. Alabaster tiles covered the floor repaired today with interstices of red plaster and benches lined with slabs of the same stone. A narrow staircase (26) leads to the upper floor; to the N. is the "King's Megaron" (27) with its pier-and-door arrangement. The floor is of alabaster while the walls were decorated with frescoes.

To the NE of the palace spreads out a complex of Old Palace buildings. In one of these (28) was found the famous Phaistos Disc (Herakleion Museum).

A well-paved road leads to the ruins of the Minoan villa of Aghia Triada, 3 km. W. of Phaistos.

Archaeological Site of Aghia Triada

The ancient place name is not known. The area takes its name from the nearby double-nave church of the Holy Trinity (Aghia Triada) from the 14th century which is on a hill, 250 m. SW of the villa. The church amid the ruins is of Saint George Galatas, a single-aisled tile-roofed church with wall-paintings from the 14th century.

The excavations of the Italian Archaeological School, which were begun around Aghia Triada in 1902 continued until 1944 and were renewed in 1976, have brought to light a Minoan building, the "palace", with a wealth of archaeological material (Herakleion Museum). The region has been inhabited since the Neolithic period. Tholos tombs were found from the Pre-Palace and the Old Palace periods, as well as remains of dwellings on top of which the palace was built in 1600 B.C.; it was destroyed by fire around 1450 B.C. During the Post-Palace period the region was re-occupied, as is shown by the settlement to the NE. A Mycenaean megaron was built on the site of the Minoan palace.

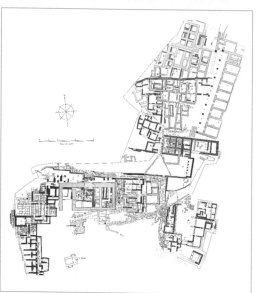

The archaeological site of Aghia Triada which took its name from the neighbouring church. Excavations have brought to light a Minoan building with a great wealth of archaeological material.

Plan of the palace of Aghia Triada.

The visit to the archaeological site should preferably begin on the west side of the church of Saint George.

The villa of Aghia Triada was built in two principal wings: one on a north-south axis, the other on an east-west axis. The row of apartments in the N-S wing, with floor of beaten earth, probably belonged to the servants. In one of these was found the famous "Chieftain's Cup" (Herakleion Museum). The main apartments were found in the NW corner with flagstoned floors and pier-and-door arrangements. One room, now roofed, has a restored bench around the walls which is covered with a gypsum dado. The northern door leads to a small room with a slightly raised gypsum slab that was probably used as a bed. Further north of this room were found the 19 copper talants (Herakleion Museum). A little further east a noteworthy collection of clay sealings was discovered, as well as famous frescoes, such as the wildcat hunting pheasant (Herakleion Museum).

Along the entire N. wing are the traces of a stepped, paved road. The storerooms are on a lower level and E. of them are other rooms that were used as dwellings. A road that starts in the E. must have ended at Phaistos. The drainage system remains in excellent condition. In the South Court was an open-air sanctuary from which came a series of bronze figurines.

To the NE a stairway leads to the square of the Post-Palace settlement,

Matala. The combination of caves carved out of the rock and the sandy beach attract a large number of tourists.

the Agora. Descending right you find a building arranged in a manner which is reminiscent of a Hellenistic stoa with columns and pillars on the facade and a row of eight rooms to the back.

N. of the agora (150 m.) two tholos tombs from the 3rd and 2nd millennium were found. The E. one has a diameter of 9 m. and the walls are 2 m. thick. The famous painted sarcophagus (Herakleion Museum) from a later burial (1400 B.C.) was found in a square tomb.

From Aghia Triada you return via the Phais-tos-Matala road, which is a pleasant journey. At the village of Aghios Ioannis there is a small Byzantine church of Saint Paul. At the 7th km. (from the Phaistos crossroads) is the village of Pitsidia, where there are rooms to rent. To the right is the Libyan Sea. One and a half kilometres after Pitsidia a branch of the road leads to Kommos, the ancient port of Phaistos, at which excavations where begun in 1976 by a professor of the University of Toronto, J. Shaw (the archaeological site is not open to the public). The high point of the settlement was during the Middle and Late Minoan period but it continued to be inhabited

*Aghia Galini.
Summer resort west of Matala.*

till the Roman period. The sanctuary complex from historical times, with a temple, a prytaneum, a circular building and a court with four square altars is very important. Under the sanctuary were discovered large buildings with porticoes from the Post-Palace period, which were perhaps storerooms.

The public road continues on another 2 km. to Matala, the second port of Phaistos and later a port of Gortyn during the Roman period. The houses from the ancient settlement are a part of the modern settlement.

The artificial caves, carved into the north face of the coast, which are tombs from the 1st and 2nd centuries A.D., are quite impressive. These caves, in combination with the sandy beach, form a semi-circle on both sides of which jut up towering rocks; they act as a magnet for many people, usually young tourists from all over the world. The beauty of the coast continues beyond this semi-circle where following a path along the rock you reach the enchanting "red sand", beach, a place for those who are young and daring. Today, the tomb-caves of Matala are protected by the Archaeological Service.

The rapid increase of tourist trade led to the unprogrammed and hasty erection of temporary structures near the coast that have altered the surroundings. Now an effort is being made to construct further inland fine houses and hotels with the most modern conveniences. Camping sites have also been developed.

Back at Phaistos the road left continues on to Tymbaki (3 km.), a rich agricultural centre. During the summer there are a number of rooms to rent in the village and the adjacent beach, one of the most beautiful in Crete – with the settlement Kokkinos Pyrgos – attracts many visitors.

The road from Tymbaki goes uphill to the border of the prefectures of Herakleion and Rethymnon and then down to the picturesque tourist village of Aghia Galini (12 km. from Tymbaki and 77 km. from Herakleion).

The finest hotels and pensions, as well as all sorts of restaurants, tavernas and night clubs, in combination with the beautiful beaches here, have turned Aghia Galini into one of the most popular summer resorts on the Libyan Sea. There are car and motorbike rental agencies, as well as agencies which organize tours to the archaeological sites.

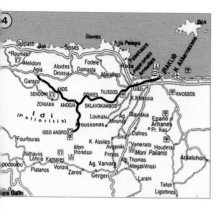

HERAKLEION: Excursion 4

Tylissos (14 km.) - Sklavokambos (22 km.) - Gonies (26 km.) - Turn-off Idaian Cave (55 km.) - Anogeia (36 km.) - Axos (45 km.).

You leave via the Chania Gate toward Rethymnon along the old national road. At the 10th km. a crossroads left leads to Tylissos and Anogeia. The large village of Tylissos is on a small plain, densely planted with vineyards and olive groves at the foot of Psiloreitis (Ida), 14 km. from Herakleion; there is a tourist guest house in the village. It has kept its name since antiquity, something quite rare. Its fame increased after the excavations by Joseph Chatzidakis (1902-1913), which brought to light three Minoan villas from the New Palace period, which were inhabited till around 1450 B.C. During the Post-Palace period a Mycenaean megaron was erected on the site of the north villa. During the Classical period

Tylissos was an autonomous city and minted its own coins.

The archaeological site is on the north side of the village.

Archaeological Site of Tylissos

The three villas have a great deal of similarity in the way their spaces are arranged. The walls are of isodomic ashlar masonry and mortar with vertical wooden supports (the traces can be seen) for protection against earthquakes. The external walls are thicker and the corners made with care. The floors were stone paved and covered with a mixture of slaked lime and sand and painted red. The roof must have been earthen and covered with schist slabs.

The three dwellings appear to have consisted of separate apartments of 3-4 rooms which could be isolated from each other by a door. The ground floor was primarily taken up by the servants' quarters, the storerooms and the workshops. The main living quarters were on the upper floor. The water came via an aqueduct from Aghios Mamas (2 km. away); the village continues to get its water from there even today. A plumbing system was found in good condition as well as a circular reservoir with a staircase, which belong to the Post-Palace phase of the north villa. The water reached the reservoir through a stone pipe after first passing through a sump where impurities settled out.

The most important find is a cast

bronze statuette of a man in a votary position. In the second dwelling is a stone for grinding olives, while small clay vases, axes and votive objects were found in other areas. In the so-called House A were found three great bronze cauldrons (4) (Herakleion Museum), the largest of which weighs 52.5 kilos. There were also clay jars in which were found various pigments, red, ochre, yellow, black, blue and white.

From Tylissos the road winds on toward Anogeia where, at the 17th km., there is a monument at the edge of the town to those executed by the Nazis during World War II. The landscape changes, becoming rocky and barren. But then a long, narrow valley begins, known as Sklavokampos ("Slave plain") because according to tradition the Cretans incarcerated seven Turkish Pashas there. Twenty-two km. along a sign points to the site where in 1930 a Minoan megaron from 1500 B.C. was discovered; it was destroyed by a fire so intense that the stones of the dwelling were calcined. The structure is divided into three apartments with floors at different levels.

Twenty-six km. along you reach the mountain village of Gonies (620 m. a.s.L), built amphi-theatrically. The view is lovely as is the background with the imposing peaks of Psiloreitis (2456 m. a.S.l.).

At the 34th km. you reach the entrance to the market town of Anogeia. A crossroads left leads to the Ida-ian Cave, at the foot of Psiloreitis. The road (21 km. long) is quite good, paved most of the way. Before beginning the final ascent you cross the Nida plateau.

According to mythology, Rhea hid her son Zeus in the Idaian Cave so he would not be eaten by his father Kronos, while the Kouretes banged on their bronze shields to drown out the crying of the young god.

This was the most famous religious cave in antiquity, mentioned by a host of ancient writers including Pindar, Plato and Theophrastes, who said it was visited by such people as Epimenides and Pythagoras.

The Idaian Cave is a vast cave located at height of 1540 m. a.s.l. on the central mass of Psiloreitis above the beautiful Nida plateau. It was identified in 1885 when the first excavations also took place producing important finds such as the large bronze shields (Herakleion Museum). In 1982 Yannis Sakellarakis began new excavations inside the cave under extremely difficult conditions given that some years there is still snow in the cave in summer. The new excavations brought to light a very large number of finds from various periods, of precious and semiprecious materials: vases and utensils, figurines and rings, sealstones and pieces of jewellery. The finds reveal the presence of human beings in the cave since the end of the Neolithic period in Crete with an uninterrupted religious tradition stretching from the Late Minoan period to the 5th

Aerial view of Tyiissos. The excavations which uncovered three Minoan villas from the New Palace period can be seen.

century A.D. During the Minoan period the Vegetation god, who died and was reborn every year, was worshipped in the Idaian Cave; he was succeeded by Zeus in the form of Cretan-born Zeus who, for the Cretans, is not immortal, but is born and dies every year.

A religious tradition stretching across millennia is continued up to the present at the small church of the Ascension of Christ. The inhabitants of Anogeia who come to partake in the festival, among other ceremonies make offerings to their dead.

Midway between Anogeia and the Idaian Cave Dr. Yannis Sakellarakis discovered and partially excavated a large, very important Late Minoan building at Zominthos, a site which still preserves its Pre-Greek name.

The area attracts many visitors during the summer months. Since 1986 a ski centre has been operating near the cave.

Back on the main road, from which you turned off to the Idaian Cave, you arrive at the market town of Anogeia (740 m. a.s.l.), which is 36 km. from Herakleion and 54 km. from Rethymnon. Without question it is the most touristically developed mountain town in Crete, with two small hotels, rooms to rent and restaurants.

The villagers are mainly employed in stock-raising while the women carry on the long tradition of weaving for which Anogeia is famed.

Because this area is difficult to reach, the inhabitants developed a sense of independence and love of liberty which, however, was not able to protect them from calamity.

Anogeia was often a centre for revolutionary movements during the Turkish and German occupations. In August 1944, in reprisal for the resistance activity of its inhabitants, the village was flattened and many of its residents executed by Hitler's forces.

Of late Anogeia has become noted for its cultural events; during the summer months there is a cultural festival to which foreign and Greek visitors are attracted from all of Crete.

Northwest of Anogeia, at a distance of 9 km. is the village of Axos (510 m. a.s.l.), tucked into a valley of fruit trees through which the Oaxos river flows. At the entrance to the village is the tiny church of Saint Irene (14th-15th century). Above the church a sign points to the site of ancient Axos on a hill 400 m. high. It was built on terraces down the slopes, while on the peak was a fortified acropolis.

The most reasonable explanation

The remote country town of Anogeia which has recently experienced some noteworthy cultural activity.

for Axos is that it was founded after 1100 B.C., like other towns, when many Cretans sought refuge in the mountains. Archaeological, excavations have uncovered the ruins of a sanctuary from Archaic times and clay figurines (Chania Musuem), as well as ruins of structures from the Hellenistic period. It was the only town of ancient Crete which in the 7th century B.C. still had a king – Etearchos mentions him.

Axos continued to be a powerful town in both the Roman and Byzantine periods. Various sources relate that there were 46 churches in Axos of which only nine remain.

East of the village, in the middle of the valley. is a wall eight metres high which is obviously the ruins of an aqueduct from the Venetian occupation. To the west of Axos is one of Crete's most interesting caves – that of Sedoni.

The winding road from Axos leads NW until it joins the old Herakleion-Rethymnon national road 10 km. east of Perama.

Anogeia. The village square.

THE SEDONI CAVE

It lies near the village of Zoniana (Prefecture of Rethymnon) in a region framed by a majestic rocky complex, an extension of Mount Ida. The spring near there and the immense vistas which open out on the other sides complete the perfection of the site. A small girl, influenced by the idyllic surroundings, wanted to find out what was hidden in a small hole near there. Entranced by the gorgeous things she saw she wandered heedlessly deeper and deeper till she was lost in its vastness (3400 sq. m.). They found her eight days later, dead, at the end of the cave with a sweet smile on her face and the locals said she had been "lured away by the neraids". Recent excavations in the cave prove it was used during antiquity.

Impressive columns divide the cave into chambers.

THE IDAIAN CAVE

It is located on the eastern slopes of Mount Ida (1540 m., a.s.l., 21 km. from Anogeia (Prefecture of Rethymnon). It is one of the two Cretan caves which claims to be the birthplace of Cretan Zeus. The other is the Diktaian cave on Mount Dikte. According to mythology, Zeus's parents were Rhea and Kronos, children of Gaia (Earth) and Uranos (Sky). Kronos wanted to devour Zeus to preserve his heavenly kingdom. To fool him Rhea wrapped a stone in swaddling clothes which Kronos unsuspectingly swallowed.

The Nymphs Adrasteia and Ida fed him milk from the goat Amaltheia and wild honey. When he cried the Kouretes protected him by banging their swords against their shields.

From the finds of the excavations (shields, weapons, tools, gold, ivory and bone objects, clay tablets with various depictions, figurines, lamps, bones of herbivores, ash, etc.) it is evident that the cave was sacred and that secret rites of inflation and propitiation were performed there. Beginning in the Minoan period it was also a cult centre.

Excavations being carried out near the back of the cave.

Ano Viannos. Mountain village with a long and heroic history of participation in Cretan struggles for liberation.

village. There was formerly a Venetian fortress where the high school is now located. West of Kastelli is the village of Sklaverochori where there is a beautiful church of the Presentation of the Virgin (Eisodeia tis Theotokou).

Four km. east of Kastelli is the village of Xidas, site of ancient Lyttos an important town in the Archaic and Hellenistic periods. It was built amphitheatrically on a fortified site (650 m. a.s.l.), precisely when has not been determined because there have been no systematic excavations yet.

However it is certain it reached its peak in historical times and that it was continually at war with Knossos. Finally, with the assistance of Gortyn, Knossos managed to destroy it (219 B.C.). The town was rebuilt with the backing of the Spartans but was never able to regain its old power.

From Kastelli a road straight south meets the main road Herakleion-Arka-

HERAKLEION: Excursion 5

Peza (18 km.) - Kastelli (36 km.) - Arkalochori (32 km.) - Aphrati (46 km.) - Ano Viannos (65 km.) - (Turn-off for Arvi 82 km.) - Pefkos (76 km.) - Myrtos.

You exit on the road to Knossos in the direction of Archanes (see Excursion 2). Passing the turn-off right to Archanes you reach the village of Kounavoi at the 15th km. where there is a three-aisled Byzantine church dedicated to Christ the Master (Aphendi Christou), Saint Nicholas and Saint Dimitrios. After the village of Peza (18 km.) the road forks right to Kalloni - Aghios Vasileios - Apanosiphis Monastery (see Excursion 2), but you follow the road left for Kastelli Pediados, through the villages of Aghies Paraskies, Sambas and Aghioi Apostoloi.

Kastelli is built on a hill on the east side of a small vallery. A Roman cemetery was found at the entrance to the

The village of Peza, 18 km. outside Herakleion.

Kastelli. Finds from the Minoan period. To the rear ruins of a Venetian fortress on the site of the present-day high school.

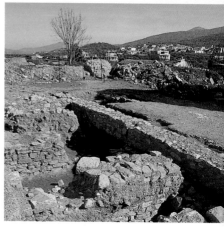

lochori at the 38th km. Returning to the 32nd km. you reach Arkalochori where every Saturday there is a trade fair in grain and livestock which attracts a lot of people from the Prefectures of Herakleion and Lasithi.

Right next to the village is a sacred cave on the Profitis Ilias hill, where important artefacts from the Minoan period were found. In 1932 the archaeologists S. Marinates and Nikolaos Platon found small gold axes and a gold handle there. Some of them are decorated. A bronze axe has an inscription with fifteen hieroglyphs (similar to the ones on the Phaistos Disc) (Herakleion Museum) while another has a Minoan inscription in Linear A. Hundreds of knives, rapier blades and bronze double axes were found in this cave. Some of them still have their wooden hilts. One of the finds was a sword one metre long, the longest bronze sword of prehistoric Greece. The finds reveal that the cave was used as a religious site from 2500 B.C. It was destroyed around 1450 B.C., obviously by an earthquake. However, the inhabitants continued to bring dedications, which were placed at the entrance to the sealed cave.

At the 46thr km., right, is the village of Afrati where the large, ancient town of Arkadia or Arkades is located at the site of Profitis Ilias. The Hellenistic acropolis, a sanctuary from the Geometric-Archaic period, houses from the same period and tombs (tholos as well as jar burials) have been found there. The excavations were carried out in 1924 by the Italian D. Levi and more recently by A. Lembesi.

The church of Saint George, with wall-paintings by Emmanouil Phokas (1436-37), is located at the village of Embaros (50 km.).

About fifty-five km. along, this road meets the southern National Road which is under construction. Continuing east you reach Kato Viannos and then Ano Viannos (65 km.) (500 m. a.s.l.). The village is built amphitheatrically on the SW slopes of Mount Dikte amid dense vegetation and running water. Like nearly all the mountain villages in Crete, Viannos has a long and heroic history of participation in the island's struggles for liberation from both the Turks and the Germans in World War II. It also had to make the same sacrifices. In 1822 it was destroyed by Hasan Pasha, while during the Great Cretan Revolution in 1866 it was levelled once more by Omar Pasha. In 1943 powerful German forces burned many of the surrounding villages and executed 820 people.

The church of Saint Pelagia with well-preserved frescoes from the 14th century and the church of Saint George with frescoes from 1401 are both at Plaka in Ano Viannos.

The present village is built on the ruins of the ancient town of Viannos, which was autonomous, as its coins reveal. In 1954 N. Platon excavated the site of Galana Charakia and discovered two large tombs in hollows in the rocks

The village of Amira, 7 km. east of Ano Viannos.

which contained thirty burial jars, clay vessels from the Early Minoan and Middle Minoan period. A large Minoan dwelling with four rooms was excavated in the same region at the site of Kephala Chondrou. In 1956-1959 the same archaeologist excavated a large settlement from the Late Minoan period.

Seven kilometres east of Ano Viannos, at the village of Amira a turn-off right leads, after 14.6 km., through a small valley planted with banana trees, to the beautiful beach at the settlement of Arvi.

Above the village of Symi, at the site Krya Vrysi, an important temple to Hermes and Aphrodite, which was used from 1600 B.C. to A.D. 300, was recently excavated. It reached its peak during the Archaic period. In the centre is a square outdoor altar where the offerings were placed on a pyre. Three terraces were fashioned S. and E. of the altar, while small rooms used for worship were erected north of it. The finds from Symi are exhibited in Gallery XII of the Herakleion Museum.

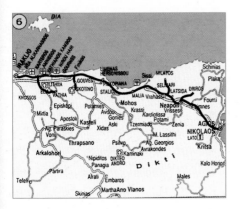

HERAKLEION: Excursion 6

Amnisos (8 km.) - Eileithyia Cave - Nirou Hani (13 km.) - (Turn-off for Gouves, Skoteino Cave 18 km.) - Chersonisos (26 km.) - Malia (34 km.) - Neapolis (55 km.) - Diros - Aghios Nikolaos (70 km.).

The north coast, between the two largest tourist centres on the island, Herakleion and Aghios Nikolaos, has the most complete tourist facilities. Large, touristic units of international standard alternate with a host of hotels of all categories and camping sites that will satisfy even the most demanding visitor. The sandy beaches are succeeded by dramatic, rocky shores which are split by isolated coves. An excellent road network with two parallel national roads (the one a modern highway) allows for high speeds and ease of movement. A number of the most noteworthy archaeological sites are found in the vicinity of

this road axis. For the traveller who is in a hurry to reach his destination in eastern Crete, the new national road is recommended (70 km.). The old national road, narrower and winding, is recommended for touring as it passes through villages and allows one to enjoy the landscape and the comforts afforded by the numerous seaside restaurants, tavernas and cafeterias.

You leave Herakleion to the east, through the neighbourhoods of Poros and Nea Alikarnassos, along the old national road, passing through a built-up area developed for tourists.

Six km. along, to the right, is a small church with a cave dedicated to Saint John the Baptist.

At the 7th km. is the popular public beach of Karteros where in 826 the Byzantine General Karteros landed to liberate Crete from the Saracens.

At the 8th km., to the left, is the hill Paliochora or Mesovouni around which ancient Amnisos was located, the harbour of Knossos where there are Minoan ruins. The ruins at the top of the hill belong to a Venetian village from the 16th century. A Minoan villa from 1600 B.C. (fenced in today) lies at the eastern base of the hill; it is contemporary with the new palace at Knossos and was excavated by S. Marinatos in 1930. It is here that the well-known frescoes with the lilies were found (Herakleion Museum). At the north base of the hill is a small dwelling that was called the "Limenarcheion" (Harbour-master's Office).

Ancient Amnisos, harbour of Knossos. It was here that the villa from 1600 B.C. with the famous wall-paintings with the lilies (Herakleion Museum) was excavated.

Marinatos found pumice which reinforced his theory that Minoan Crete was destroyed by the explosion on Santorini.

On the NW side of the hill a sanctuary to Zeus Thenatas was discovered.

From the top of the hill there is a magnificent view of the expanse of sandy beach with its well-appointed hotels, rooms to rent, outdoor restaurants and camping sites. The islet opposite is Dias.

To the right, a turn-off leads to Elia and Kato and Ano Vatheia. At the first turn is the Eileithyia Cave (goddess of fertility and childbirth), which was a place of worship from the Neolithic period to the 5th century A.D. At its centre are two cylindrical stalagmites which were obviously worshipped in antiquity.

Thirteen km. along we reach Vathiano Kambo with many tavernas and restaurants.

Right (next to the Demetra hotel) is an archaeological site known as Nirou Hani. This had to be a Minoan structure, one of the better preserved, with walls that are still one metre high. It most probably was a country house but archaeologists frequently refer to it as the "House of the High Priest" because of the religious objects found there, such as approximately 40 tripod offering tables and the four enormous bronze double axes (Herakleion Museum). Clay jars, vases, lamps and drinking cups were also found. The dwelling has a square shape and occupies about 1000 sq. m.

Ground floor rooms have been preserved with benches and two courts laid with slate tiles. It was destroyed by fire. On the beach NW of the villa is the Minoan harbour, near the church of Saints Theodore (Aghioi Theodoroi).

Passing Gournia on the left the road continues on and reaches a turn-off (17.7 km.) for the village of Gouves followed by the village of Skoteino where there are signs to the large cave of Skoteino. This is one of the most important sacred caves in Crete with a depth of 160 m. and four levels. In 1962 K. Davaras carried out a systematic excavation and found in a layer of ash, parts of vases, bone needles and Late Minoan bronze figurines in a votary stance (Herakleion Museum).

Back on the old national road a turn-off right at the 23rd km. leads to Lagada and the Lasithi plateau (see Excursion 7).

At the 26th km. you reach Chersonisos, a summer resort with large and luxurious hotels and tourist shops. At the entrance left an arrow points to the harbour, while practically opposite a narrow road leads to the village of Piskopiana (2 km.) where an agricultural museum will soon open in an old olive press that has been restored.

During the Hellenistic and Roman periods Chersonisos was an important town. Originally it was the harbour of Lyttos but it must have gained its autonomy during the 4th century B.C. and minted its own coins. The historian

Strabo mentions a temple dedicated to Britomartis Artemis at Chersonisos. During the Roman period a large aqueduct was built there (1st-2nd century A.D.), the ruins of which can be seen at Lagada, at the site Xerokamares, on the road to Lasithi. On the east side of the harbour the moles and other installations from the Roman harbour are visible. To the west, on the imposing height of Kastri, which protected the harbour from this side, a triple-aisled basilica (first built at the end of the 5th century), which is considered to be one of the largest in Crete and probably the seat of a bishopric, has been excavated. Another basilica, dated to the 6th century, nearly as large, lies east of the town at the church of Saint Nicholas. A theatre and a fountain with lovely mosaics still survive from the ancient town. East of Chersonisos the bay of Malia begins.

At the 34th km. you reach the modern town of Mala on a gorgeous sandy beach with many hotels, restaurants and folk art shops serving thousands of visitors every year.

The surrounding region is fertile with fruit, vegetables and bananas. East of the village (3 km.) is the archaeological site of Malia.

Anthropomorphic stalagmites which were worshipped as representations of the divine Mother.

THE EILEITHYIA CAVE

It is located at the site of Koprana or Mefeze Pediados at a distance of 9 km. from Herakleion going toward Episkopi. Its total dimensions are 64 x 19 x 4.5 m. and it is adorned with stalagmites, columns and small lakes. The goddess Eileithyia, daughter of Zeus and Hera and mother of Eros, was worshipped here for many centuries. She was the goddess of childbirth and motherhood. The finds (Neolithic, Early Minoan, Middle Minoan, Late Minoan, Roman, etc.) brought to light by J. Chatzidakis in 1884 prove this.

Archaeological Site of Malia

The excavations at Malia were begun in 1915 by J. Chatzidakis and were continued by the French Archaeological School. The palace, houses in the town and the cemetery at Chrysolakkos have already been excavated.

According to tradition the third son of Zeus and Europa, Sarpedon, ruled here. The area was inhabited during the Neolithic period. The first palace was built in 1900 B.C. and destroyed in 1700 B.C. when a new palace was built. Following the fate of the other palaces in Crete, it was also destroyed in 1450 B.C. The present ruins are mainly those of the new palace.

In comparison with Knossos and Phaistos, the palace at Malia (its ancient name is not known) is poorer and more provincial, despite the fact that it is about the same size as that of Phaistos. Local materials, such as sandstone for the exterior walls and several of the interior walls, were used in its construction. No frescoes were found.

Today the entrance to the site is through the West Court where there are the customary raised processional walkways. Right and to the south of the ruins are eight deep man-made holes which are called "silos" (grain storage areas). Their roof was vaulted and supported on a central column. The Central Court is similar to the one at Phaistos with porticoes N. and E. with pillars and columns which supported a gallery on the first floor. To the W. of the Cen-

tral Court lie the most important areas of the building and the Grand Staircase (1). In the middle of the staircase was a column to support the roof. To the rear is another smaller staircase (2) with columns on both sides which leads to a small room (3). A ceremonial stone mace head in the shape of a panther was found in a jar here while outside this

Chersonisos. Summer resort with luxurious hotels and tourist shops.

was a dagger and a long sword (Herakleion Museum). S. is another stairway (4) which led to the upper floor. The space directly to the south (5) is important, with a crypt and benches. On the pillars of the crypt were incised symbols: tridents, star and double axe. In the middle of the Central Court the four supports of an altar (6) were found. On the SW side a broad stepped structure (7) has been uncovered which was probably used like the kerkides of a theatre. Near this spot a kernos was found, a stone object with small cavities on the circumference and a larger one in the centre – probably for offerings. To

Malia. Aerial view of the palace.

the E. of the Court, behind the portico there are long, narrow store-rooms with clay jars in two rows. In the middle there is a trench with a receptacle sunk in the floor (in order to protect it the best-preserved storeroom is kept closed). On the N. side, behind the portico, was a room with six columns in two rows (8). Further west is an apartment with a paved floor, perhaps a royal dwelling. In the southern part of this space, a light-well communicated with this area where there was a cult pillar (9). Clay tablets, discs and staffs with hieroglyphic inscriptions were found here. Next to it was a lustral basin (10).

Various quarters developed around the palace. It is obvious that the wealthier ones were located on the NE side where a marvellous example of a Minoan house was excavated. In general, the private houses of Malia with their courtyards and baths have illuminated archaeologists concerning the evolution of the architecture of the private dwelling.

At a distance of 500 m. N. of the palace, facing the sea, is the cemetery of Malia, at the site Chrysolakkos, a complex of rectangular burial rooms of the Old Palace period. Excavations have brought to light an altar and offering tables used in the cult of the dead. Among the impressive finds from this cemetery is the unique bee pendant (Herakleion Museum).

At Malia we turn right from the new national road and continue to Latsida, Neapolis. A little before Latsida a road to the left leads after 7.5 km. to the village of Milatos. NW of the village is the cave of Milatos. At Latsida, a short distance before Neapolis, are the churches of the Virgin and Saint Paraskevi with frescoes from the 14th and 15th centuries.

At the 55th km. the new national road bypasses Neapolis, a commercial town in the middle of a fertile plain, which once fed the inhabitants of ancient Dreros. Dreros has two hills each with an acropolis. Between them were discovered the ruins of an ancient agora and temple from the Geometric period, dedicated to Apollo. From this temple came the unique statues of Apollo, Artemis and Leto (Herakleion Museum) made by the technique of hammering bronze plates over a wooden core. In 1855 a rectangular stone was found in this region on which was inscribed in the Dorian dialect an oath of loyalty sworn by the young men of ancient Dreros (Istanbul Museum). From Neapolis an asphalt road leads to Aghios Nikolaos.

THE MILATOS CAVE

It is located on a deep and precipitous ravine, at a distance of 3 km. from Milatos by road and then a twenty-minute walk on a path. Here, according to tradition and an inscription carved above the left-hand entrance, the hordes of General Hasan slaughtered 3600 men, women and children in 1823. Later the bones that were left were gathered in a "Heroon" in the cave. The Sunday of Saint Thomas has been deemed a local holiday and is celebrated in the cave with an official ceremony.

The cave has eight entrances in a row covering a total space of 40 m. with a platform overlooking the ravine and it covers an area of 2000 sq. m.

In the Milatos cave a small church next to the "Heroon". On the Sunday after Orthodox Easter (feast of Saint Thomas) a Mass is held in memory of the slaughter of 3600 Cretans by the Turks in 1823.

HERAKLEION: Excursion 7

Ardou (39 km.) - Gonies - Lasithi Plateau - Tzermiado (57 km.) - Psychro (70 km.) - Diktaian Cave (72 km.).

The visit to the Lasithi Plateau, with its 10,000 windmills and the impressive Diktaian Cave, can be made either from Herakleion or Aghios Nikolaos. The eastern approach via Neapolis is certainly more difficult than the NW one which sets off west of Chersonisos. Recently (1986) a fine, wide asphalt road opened from Stalida (30 km. east of Herakleion between Chersonisos and Malia) which, by way of Mochos, meets the main road to Lasithi between Avdou and the Kera Kardiotissa Monastery.

The route follows the national road Herakleion - Aghios Nikolaos (Excursion 6) till the 23rd km. A turn-off right leads to Lagada and the Lasithi plateau. The road passes among greenhouses of flowers and then traverses a valley dense

with olive trees. At the 29th km. there is a crossroad right for Kasteli Pediados and immediately after, on the right, are the ruins of a Roman aqueduct which brought water from the springs of Dikte to Chersonisos. At the 32nd km., a little before the entrance to the village of Potamies, left, on a slope, is the church of the Virgin, the only building left from the Gouverniotissa Monastery, with well-preserved wall-paintings from the 14th century on the west side and the Pantocrator in the dome.

At the 39th km., just before the long ascent to the Lasithi plateau, is the picturesque village of Avdou with small Byzantine churches – Saint Anthony with wall-paintings from the 14th century, Saint George, the Annunciation and Saint Constantine. Avdou is a village with a long revolutionary tradition during the struggle against the Turks. There are interesting caves in the region at a height of 1000-1100 m. a.s.L, Phaneromenis and Aghia Photeini with a chapel.

The ascent begins at the village of Gonies on a well-paved asphalt road with a fair number of bends. At the 41st km. there is a turn-off left to Mochos. At 48.5 km., among walnut and plane trees, the renovated and well-cared for convent of Kera Kardiotissa (560 m. a.s.l.) looms up; it is dedicated to the Nativity of the Virgin (festival on September 8). The view from the terrace of its courtyard is magnificent.

The unusual form of this church is the result of four successive building

The Lasithi plateau which is surrounded by sheer mountain masses. The village of Gomes in the background.

phases. The oldest is the little church to the east which is used as a bema today with wall-paintings from the 14th century. On the iconostasis of the church is the miracle-working icon of the "Panaghia Alyssodemenis" ("The Virgin Chained"), According to tradition, this icon had been transferred to Constantinople but returned to the monastery. It was stolen again and chained to a column so it could not be taken away. But the icon uprooted the column (it is fenced in the courtyard of the monastery) and returned here with it.

After the village of Apano Kera (680 m. a.s.l.) the road continues to climb till the 52nd km. up to the defile of Ambelou (900 m. a.s.l.) where right and left of

Half-ruined, stone-built windmill, where the inhabitants ground their wheat till the beginning of the present century.

Saint Constantine. Small Byzantine church in the village of Avdou, which has a long history of struggle for the liberation of Crete from the Turks.

the road, like vigilant guards, rise up half-ruined stone-built windmills which ground wheat till the beginning of the century. At this point it is worth taking a break from the arduous driving (there is a restaurant) to admire the marvellous panoramic view. To the N. (behind) can be seen the Cretan Sea and the north coast of Crete. South, to the rear, rises up the mountain mass of Dikte (2148 m. a.s.l.), while before you spreads out the acclaimed Lasithi plateau, the only plateau in Crete that is inhabited all year around. To the E., after the windmills, left, a steep path leads to the peak Karphi (1100 m.) where the British

Archaeological School, in 1934-1935, excavated a settlement of Eteo-Cretans who took refuge and lived at this fortified site.

There is an easier path from the village of Tzermiado (one hour journey). During the excavations, buildings and figurines of deities with the traditional cylindrical garment were found. One goddess, about one metre tall, has birds adorning her hair (Herakleion Museum).

Lasithi is a plateau surrounded by mountains with eight natural entrances. It has always been a refuge for the persecuted and a place where revolutions started. During the Venetian occupa-

The Lasithi plateau where 10,000 windmills operate during the summer.

tion, after the suppression of a large uprising, the inhabitants were forced to leave Lasithi for nearly two centuries. Finds reveal that the region was inhabited during Neolithic and Minoan times. During the Hellenistic and Roman periods it belonged to the city-state of Lyttos. There were important sanctuaries and religious centres at the Trapeza Cave, at the exit from the village of Tzermiado, and at the Diktaian Cave at Psychro. Today there are around 20 small villages on the plateau. During the summer months the area is irrigated by wells run by the 10,000 windmills. The spectacle of the mills with their sails

open is truly incredible. The main product of the plateau is a potato of exceptional quality.

After the descent from the defile of Ambelou you meet up with the ring road that goes around the entire plateau. From east to west the road passes through the villages of Pinakiano, Lagou and Tzermiado (830 m a.s.L), which is the largest village on the plateau with small hotels and rooms to rent. At the exit from the village a sign points left for the Kronio Cave (Trapeza Cave). A short path left leads to the entrance to the cave which was used from the Neolithic period (5000 B.C.) as a re-

The coast at Malia.

fuge, while in the Pre-Palace period it was used for burials and then after 2000 B.C. as a religious site. On the neighbouring mountain Kastellos were found the ruins of a Neolithic and Minoan settlement. The road continues on passing through the villages of Pharsaro, Marmaketo, the Kroustallenia Monastery (it has a hostel), Aghios Konstantinos and Aghios Yorgios.

At Aghios Yorgios it is worth visiting the Folk Museum which is housed in the D. Kasapakis residence built in 1800.

This is a genuine farmhouse which in its single space has all the features and equipment for the self-sufficient life of the farmer: loom, oven, wine-press (which was also used as a bed) kitchen and washroom. To the rear is the cellar and the stable is in an adjoining space. The tools of the various professions such as basket-weaver, raki distiller, cheese-maker, ironmonger, barber, etc., are exhibited in quite a marvellous fashion in another space. There are also small, good tavernas in the village.

At the 71st km. you reach the village of Psychro (840 m a.s.L.). At the end of the village is a sign left for Spilia (Diktaian Cave, 2 km.). A paved road leads to the tourist pavilion and a car park.

From there a path about one km. long (15 minutes on foot) takes you to the entrance of the cave (1051 m. a.s.L.).

In the summer there are donkeys for hire.

According to one tradition Rhea brought Zeus here and not to the Idaian Cave. Another account says that Zeus brought Europa to the Diktaian Cave and not Gortyn.

In any case the fact is that the cave was a religious site for the Minoan divinity. This was proven by the excavations carried out by the English archaeologist D. Hogarth in 1900, which brought to light clay vases, offering tables, bronze figurines, tools, double axes, etc.

On your return, after completing the circuit of the plateau, you can choose the steep, mountainous road, which sets off left from the village of Marmaketo (east side of the plateau) for Mesa Lasithi - Potamoi - Zenda - Vryses - Neapolis or you can return via Avchena - Mochos to the coast at Malia. This excursion is worth taking if only to see the incomparable view, 2 km. after Mochos, of the entire bay and plain of Malia.

THE DIKTAIAN CAVE

It is on the north side of Mount Dikte (1000 m. a.s.L). To reach the cave there are uphill paths which start at the tourist pavilion at Psychro and reach the enormous mouth 20 minutes later.

It consists of a vast cavern (85 x 37 x 15 m.) which at its end is divided into four chambers by beautiful columns and stalagmites all in a row. In the last cham-

ber Rhea gave birth to Cretan-born Zeus. To protect him from his father Kronos, who wanted to devour him so as not to lose his kingdom, she entrusted him to the Kouretes who took him to the Idaian Cave. There he was fed by the Nymphs on milk from the goat Amaltheia and wild honey.

Excavations brought to light numerous and remarkable finds which testify to the worship of Zeus from the Middle Minoan to the end of the Late Minoan period: gold fibulae, pins, double axes (symbols of Zeus), bronze fig-urines of men, clay vessels and the like.

Wall of columns which divides the small lake from the chamber of "Zeus's Mantle".

AGHIOS NIKOLAOS

Aghios Nikolaos (8500 inhabitants), capital of the Prefecture of Lasithi. is without a doubt the most picturesque harbour in Crete. Built on the west recess of Mirabello bay, it is considered to be one of the most highly developed tourist towns in Greece. The good road network permits easy communication with the other centres of central and eastern Crete, Herakleion (65 km.), Siteia (70 km.) and Hierapetra (36 km.). There is no airport but the trip from Herakleion airport by car or taxi takes no more than one hour. There is a frequent bus sevice from Herakleion and Aghios Nikolaos is connected to Piraeus by a boat which leaves Siteia and makes a stop at Melos. During the summer Aghios Nikolaos is serviced by a boat of the Piraeus-Rhodes line with intermediary stops in the Cyclades and at Kassos-Karpathos-Kos in the Dodecanese.

Every summer the Municipality of Aghios Nikolaos organizes cultural events under the name "Lato". Music and dance groups, folkloric and modern ensembles, Greeks and foreigners participate in these. Theatrical perfomances, exhibitions, artistic swimming contests and shows are organized. Every other year, during the festivities surrounding Naval Week, swimming contests, wind-surfing, water-skiing etc. are held. Moreover, during Easter there are interesting local customs, such as on the night of the Resurrection when Judas is burned on a special stand in the

centre of the harbour. Another interesting event is connected with New Year and involves two decorated caiques; one of them leaves the harbour symbolizing the Old Year and the other one comes in bringing the New Year and Saint Basil.

History of the Town

The history of the town begins in historical times, when it was the harbour of "Lato Etera" and called "Lato pros

Kamara". It was also used as a harbour during Roman times and the First Byzantine period. During the Venetian occupation a fortress was built on the site where the

Prefecture office is today, called "Mirabello" because of the beautiful view. Nevertheless, the importance of the harbour lessened as the Venetians built another one in the region of Eloun-da (NW) more protected, the "Port di San Nicolo". The name Aghios

Aghios Nikolaos.
Partial view of the town.

Nikolaos is that of the small Byzantine church with frescoes from the 8th, 10th and 11th centuries, located on the peninsula of Limena.

Despite the fact that the centre of the town is considered to be Eleftheria Square – where some of the oldest hotels are – the vital, tourist centre of

Seaside area with villas near Aghios Nikolaos.

"Aghios" are the wharves around the harbour and the small lake Voulismeni (64 m. deep), which are connected to each other by a small canal.

Some of the most frequented coffee houses and restaurants are there and the entire area has been inundated with tourist shops.

Small boats leave the harbour to visit the Venetian fortress of Spinalonga, opposite Elounda (Excursion 8).

What is particularly impressive is the host of hotel units – around 100 – which have been erected of late, not only in the town but along the entire developed coast, mainly to the north. .

Aghios Nikolaos possesses the second finest Archaeological Museum in Crete (68 K. Palaiologou St.) which was opened in 1970. Splendid archaeological finds from throughout the Prefecture of Lasithi are displayed in its eight galleries.

THE ARCHAEOLOGICAL
MUSEUM OF AGHIOS NIKOLAOS

Gallery I. In the centre *Case 2:* a unique "idol" from the Peleketo Cave at Zakros, phallusshaped, anthropomorphic (Neolithic period). Perhaps it is an abstract depiction of the deity of fertility. In the other cases are a collection of grave goods (3000-2300 B.C.) from the ce-metery at Aghia Photia near Siteia. *Case 5:* The chalice, Pyrgos type, with incised decoration, has a typical Cretan shape. Impressive vases in *Case 4:* the large *pyxis* with a conical stopper like the Cycladic prototypes. In *Case 46:* twin *pyxis-kernos,* the bird-shaped vase with a thin neck, tail and three legs for a base and linear decoration as well as the Early Minoan vessel with triangular openings which form grills (probably a censer or a brazier). *Case I:* beautiful examples of vases in the Vasiliki style from the EM II settlement of Myrtos, Hierapetra and in *Case 3:* bronze burial offerings among which are fish hooks, tools and weapons.

Gallery 2. *Case 16:* Anthropomorphic libation vase, the "Goddess of Myrtos", one of the masterpieces of the Early Minoan period. The small head on the thin neck is a marvel. The goddess is holding an ewer, the mouth of which is also the only opening on the entire vessel. *Case II:* Early Minoan cup with a cylindrical handle and lavish decoration, from the Mochlos cemetery. A collection of stone vessels; the small ones were probably used to keep cosmetics in. *Case 9:* important gold jewellery of Pre-Palace Crete from Mochlos, such as the hairpin in the shape of a daisy and the diadem with three double horns decorated in the dot-repousse technique. *Cases 14, 15:* collection of Middle Minoan votive offerings, clay figurines of people and animals. The human ones, which are obviously models of the faithful with their arms raised in an attitude of worship, show the dress and the hairstyles of the men and women. There are a variety of head coverings.

Gallery 3. *Case 27:* a rare example of a clay staff, Middle Minoan period, with a text in Linear A on four sides, from Malia. Also a gold pin which on its reverse side bears a large inscription with 17 Linear A symbols, perhaps from Malia. *Central Case:* figurine of a priestess from Myrsini, Siteia, of the Post-Palace period with her hands joined between here breasts in an at-titude of prayer. Collection of Late Minoan larnakes from Tourloti, Praisos, etc.

Other interesting objects include ivories from the palace of Malia, and the unique relief stone rhyton in the form of a triton shell.

Gallery 4. *Case 28*: Late Minoan *kylix* with a high base from the cemetery of Kritsa and a stirrup jar with a representation of an octopus. *Case 30*: Triple religious object with sculpted birds, from the Myrsini cemetery. In the centre of the room a rare example of an infant burial in a jar, placed in a tiny tholos tomb (end of the Late Minoan period). It is displayed in exactly the way it was found at Krya, Siteia.

Gallery 5. In this room are exhibited a host of figurines from Dedalic workshops (7th century B.C.) of eastern Crete, with little Minoan influence. In the centre of the room, head of an Archaic clay statue from a repository at Siteia, considered to be one of the masterpieces of Greek art. Little has been preserved of the painted decoration while the mouth still shows the famous Archaic smile.

Votive offerings from the Minoan peak sanctuary at Xerokambos, Siteia. Typical headdress and high collar. Old Palace period, 2000-1600 B.C.

The "Goddess of Myrtos". One of the most important finds of Minoan art. The painted decoration and the vessel (an ewer) she is holding are distinctive. Early Minoan II period, 2500-2300 B.C.

Gallery 6. *Case 59*: large female protomes with the Archaic smile, rich hairstyle and large, open eyes. They come from a repository in Olous. *Case 47*: Siren in the form of a bird with a human head.

Gallery 7. *Case 44*: clay masks of the Ist century A.D., from the Potamos cemetery (Aghios Nikolaos) and glass perfume flasks. In the case at the back of the room, the skull with a wreath of gold olive leaves in considered to be unique because the wreath was found stuck to it. In the mouth of the dead person was a silver coin from Polyrrhenia, which had oxidized the jawbone that it had lain in for 1900 years.

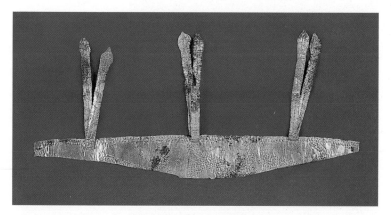

Pointed gold diadem with dot-repousse representations of Cretan ibexes in relief. From Mochlos, Siteia. Early Minoan II period, 2500-2300 B.C.

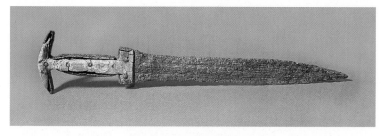

Minoan bronze dagger with an ivory handle. From the Chamezi tomb, Siteia. Late Minoan IIIC - Subminoan period, 1100-950 B.C.

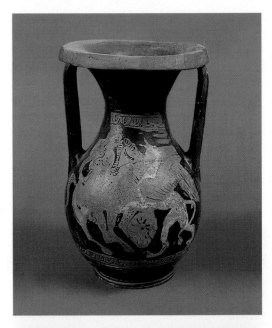

Red-figure pelike depicting a horseman batting a winged monster. 4th c. B.C.

Beak-spouted ewer from the Minoan settlement at Myrtos (EMII). Its exterior painting, done in the so-called Vasiliki style, is impressive.

Incised vessel of the
Cycladic type known as
"frying pan". From the
Minoan cemetery of
Aghia Photia, Siteia.

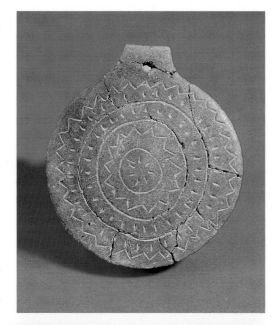

Large lamp with a leaf-
shaped ornament on
the handle. From Siteia,
Roman period.

Clay mask from the Roman cemetery at Aghios Nikolaos.

Late Archaic female protome from Elounda (ancient Olous).

An Archaic ceramic .
tile from Aghios Yorgios,
Siteia. A warrior and
a small child, perhaps
Achilles and Troilos,
are depicted.

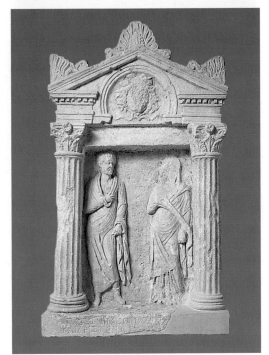

Tombstone in the shape
of the facade of a
house, perhaps
a cemetery building.
It depicts the dead
Pagon and a female
figure. From Siteia,
Roman period.

AGHIOS NIKOLAOS: Excursion 8

Olous-Elounda (II km.) - Spinalonga islet (frequent daily connections).

The road to Elounda is along the shore. As the road gains height, the coast, with its small coves, presents an alluring sight. The entire length of this coastal excursion is covered with tourist villages, done in a traditional island style, as well as many hotels, both small and large, which are filled each summer by visitors from every part of the world. Near the shore is the islet of Aghioi Pandes.

After 5 km. a sign points left to Aphrodisia where a few ruins from a temple of the 2nd century B.C. (400 m. from the road) have been preserved (dedicated to Ares and Aphrodite).

At the 6th km. right, is a parking area where it is worth stopping for a few moments to enjoy the view.

This region is not noted for its sandy beaches but for its coves and rocky coastline. To the rear the commanding peninsula of Spinalonga projects into the sea. Today this peninsula is separated from the mainland by the channel dug through the isthmus by French sailors at the end of the past century.

The area of Elounda with its hotels, large and small, which are filled every summer with visitors from around the world.

A narrow bridge joins the peninsula to the mainland near a renovated windmill (a coffee house today). Here is the ancient Greek town of Olous which has noteworthy monuments and temples. Very little has been excavated. Near the isthmus and SW of a small white church, the foundations and the mosaic floor of an early Byzantine basilica church were found; one of the walls contained sections of an inscription in the Doric dialect which testifies to the end to the alliance between Oloundians and Rhodians (Aghios Nikolaos Museum).

The village of Elounda (11 km. from Aghios Nikolaos) is touristically developed with many coffee houses and restaurants on the shore and several hotels famed for their comforts. The community office, at the right end of the central harbour, has useful information about the village and the various activities that take place there during the summer.

In the summer caiques and motorboats leave the harbour every hour, transporting visitors to the small islet of Spinalonga where, since antiquity, the fortress has protected the harbour of ancient Olous.

The name Spinalonga is Venetian (*Spina* = thorn, *longa* = long). The Venetians built a fortress here in 1579 to protect the harbour of Elounda, one of the most important and finest fortresses built on Crete. In 1630 it had 35 cannon and was thought to be impregnable. For half a century after the Turkish conquest of Crete, Spinalonga remained in the hands of the Venetians and was a refuge for many Christians who fled there to escape the Turks. Finally in 1715, the fortress was handed over to the Turks by treaty; they settled Ottoman families there. In 1903, after the last of these had left, the Cretan Republic made Spinalonga into a colony for the lepers of Crete. They were housed on this rock for nearly half a century. Today the fortress of Spinalonga has opened its gates to a host of Greek and foreign visitors who are attracted by its history and architecture.

AGHIOS NIKOLAOS: Excursion 9

Kritsa (11 km.) - Lato (14 km.). (A short excursion, served by a frequent bus service).

After 1.5 km. on the road to Siteia a turn-off to the right goes to Kritsa and Lato (14 km.). One hundred metres to the right is a road for the Lasithi plateau (Excursion 7). The road to Kritsa is paved, with few bends, and cuts through pleasant olive groves. One and a half km. before the village, to the right (100 m. from the road), is the church of Our Lady of Kera (Panaghia Kera), which is famed for its Byzantine wall-paintings. It is triple-aisled with a dome. The central aisle is dedicated to the Assumption of the Virgin, the south to Saint Ann and the north to Saint Anthony. The south section is the oldest, with wall-paintings from the 14th century. All the interior surfaces of the monument are covered with wall-paintings in excellent condition. They are considered interesting both for their technique (they are related to ones at Mystras, those of the Macedonian School and those at Mount Athos) and for their rare iconographic subject matter, especially the scenes from the Life of the Virgin.

The village of Kritsa is very picturesque and is known for its weaving, but it is very difficult to find a place to park there. A dirt road from Kritsa north (3 km.) leads to ancient Lato, the "Lato Etera" (the "Other" Lato) as it was called

The islet of Spinalonga, with the Venetian fortress which protected the harbour of Elounda.

The village of Kritsa, known for its weaving.

because there was also "Lato pros Kamares" at the site of the present-day town of Aghios Nikolaos. "Lato Etera" must have been built during the Archaic period (7th century B.C.). It was famous as one of the most powerful towns in Crete with two acropolei. The view from this spot is unique. The archaeological site was excavated by the French Archaeological School at the beginning of the century; it resumed work in 1967. The city wall still preserves its main entrance from which a road – really a stairway with 80 steps – sets off for the agora. On its right are workshops and other shops. The third house, as you ascend, contains a tub, basin and cistern which suggest this was a dye-works. In the centre of the square is a small sanctuary and a reservoir. To the north are flights of steps-seats for citizens' gatherings and behind them the prytaneum and the nobles' dining-hall. SE of the agora are a large temple and the seats of a theatre. Besides the agora and the civic buildings many houses of the period (7th-3rd c. B.C.) have been excavated.

West facade of the Church of Panaghia Kera at Kritsa, Mirabello. A tile-roofed, three-aisled church with a dome over the nave.

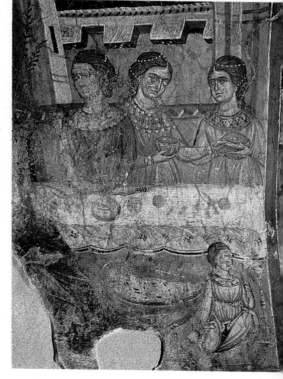

Birth of the Holy Virgin. Wall-painting in the south aisle of Saint Ann in the church of the Panaghia Kera at Kritsa. Detail showing servants placing plates of food on the table for Saint Ann in childbed. Middle of the 14th century.

The Nativity. Wall-painting in the nave of the Panaghia Kera at Kritsa. Archaicizing linear style from the 13th century.

The Water of Verification. Wall-painting in the south side of Saint Ann of the Panaghia Kera at Kritsa. Scene inspired by the Apocryphal Protoevangelio of James. Middle of the 14th century.

Personification of Earth. Detail of wall-painting in the north aisle of Saint Anthony in Panaghia Kera at Kritsa. The female form with the coiled snake personifies the Earth in the depiction of the Second Coming. Palaeologan style of the second half of the 14th century.

Journey to Bethlehem. Wall-painting in the south aisle of Saint Ann of the Panaghia Kera at Kritsa. Palaeologan style from the middle of the 14th century.

*Paradise.
Wall-painting in
the nave of the
Panaghia Kera at
Kritsa. The children
in the embrace of
the Patriarchs
symbolize the souls
of the Just, Archai-
cizing linear style
from the 13th
century.*

*The Last Supper.
Wall-painting in the
nave of the
Panaghia Kera at
Kritsa. Archaicizing
linear style from
the 13th century.*

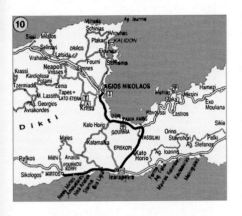

AGHIOS NIKOLAOS: Excursion 10

Gournia (18 km.) - Vasiliki (24 km.) - Hierapetra (36 km.) - Myrtos (50 km.).

Leave Aghios Nikolaos on the road to Siteia. The road is paved, picturesque and coastal (until the 21st km.). From the 4th to the 6th km. is a small tourist settlement on a beautiful beach with hotels and pensions in the Aegean island architectural style.

Archaeological Site of Gournia

At the 18th km. right, you reach the archaeological site of Gournia, set on a hill which commands the surrounding area. The Minoan name of this village, which was built in such an advantageous location, is not known. It is called Gournia today because of the small, ancient basins (*gournes*) that were found at the archaeological site. The excavations, which were conducted by the American woman H. Boyd between 1901-1904,

brought to light an entire Minoan town which flourished during the Late Minoan period (1550-1400 B.C.). It was destroyed by fire at the end of the Minoan period (12th century B.C.) and was not rebuilt. Agriculture, stock-raising and handicrafts were the main occupations of its inhabitants. The town is crossed by stone-paved roads, 1.5 to 2 m. wide, often uphill. The houses usually have one door facing the street with a stone threshold through which the residents entered an antechamber and the ground floor rooms, while stairs led to the upper floor. The walls were built with irregular stones and mud, plastered and painted, while plaster mixed with grog was used for the floor. The roof was supported on wooden beams and columns.

A large structure, the "palace" obviously the residence of the local ruler, was excavated at the highest point of the hill. North of this dwelling is a sanctuary in which were found religious objects. Utensils and tools, moulds for the casting of metal tools etc., were found in the private dwellings.

At the 21st km. is the marvellous beach of Pachia Ammos. Immediately after, a turn-off right leads to Hierapetra. This is the narrowest part of the island, only 12 km. from the Cretan to the Libyan Sea. The road is straight.

At the 24th km., a turn off right leads to Vasiliki, an important settlement during the Pre-Palace period (2600-2000 B.C.). The excavations, which have been recently carried out by Professor A.

Gournia. Aerial view of the archaeological site.

Zois, were begun in 1906 by the American R. Seager. Leaving the guard hut on the right, a path leads to the first level of the latest excavations (the finds have not yet been catalogued). A little higher up houses of the Pre-Palace period were found, such as the "House on the Hill", as well as other dwellings from all the Minoan periods. The walls have been preserved to a height of around 1.5 m.

and in parts are covered with red lime plaster. Here were found a large number of distinctive clay vases in the "Vasiliki" style of the EMU period (2500-2000 B.C.) (Herakleion Museum and Aghios Nikolaos Museum).

Continuing on the road to Hierapetra, at the 28th km. is the village of Episkopi. At the 36th km. is Hierapetra, the southernmost town in Greece and

the fourth largest in Crete (9,000 inhabitants). It has wonderful beaches both E. and W., abundant fish, vegetables and fruit. It is a holiday centre in both winter and summer and the temperature rarely falls below 12° C. There are many hotels, restaurants, bars and cafeterias but its shores are not crowded like those in northern Crete.

In the centre of the town, not far from the harbour is a small archaeological museum in which are exhibited Greek and Roman statues, among which the best-known is that of the goddess Demeter, which the museum acquired recently and the clay larnax (LM III) from Episkopi, unique for the richness and significance of its representations.

Ancient Hierapetra was built near the site of ancient Hierapytna. There has of yet been no systematic excavation but it is known that Hierapytna reached its peak in the 2nd century B.C. and that it was in a state of nearly continual war with the towns of Praisos and Itanos, at the eastern end of the island. It resisted the Roman invasion as few Cretan towns did but finally capitulated in 66 B.C. During the Roman period it was rebuilt and flourished but nothing can be seen today of its theatres, temples, baths and aqueduct.

The Venetians built a strong fortress at the harbour which was enlarged and

reinforced in 1626 and has recently been restored. There is probably little truth in the tale that Napoleon landed in Hierapetra in 1798 during his Egyptian campaign.

From the west exit a good road – it makes up part of the south national road – goes along the south coast to Myrtos (14 km.). The entire coastal plain, almost 8 km. long, contains many greenhouses for early fruits and vegetables.

At 10.5 km., right next to road on a knoll 66 m. high, known as "Phournou Korifi" (you go up by a path on the west side), the English archaeologist, Professor P. Warren discovered a settlement of the Early Minoan period (2500-2000 B.C.). Approximately 90 rooms were excavated in which were found many vases in the Vasiliki and Myrtos styles (Aghios Nikolaos Museum) as well as sealstones, large daggers, loom weights, stone vessels and tools, etc.

A short distance before the entrance to Myrtos, a sign points to a path right which leads to a second Minoan settlement at the site of "Pyrgos". The site was excavated by the English Professor G. Cadogan. It was first founded during Early Minoan times. At the top of the hill a large two or three-storey megaron from the New Palace period (1600 B.C.) was excavated.

Today, Myrtos is a relatively small coastal village built on top of a Roman settlement with a few cozy hotels and houses with rooms to rent.

After Myrtos the road becomes mountainous and heads for Viannos-Herakleion (Excursion 5).

AGHIOS NIKOLAOS: Excursion II

Pachia Ammos (21 km.) - Kavousi (26 km.) - Sphaka (40.5 km.) - (Crossroads Mochlos - Pseira islet) - Chamezi (59 km.) - Siteia (70 km.).

The eastern end of Crete has a large variety of archaeological sites. In order to visit them leisurely an overnight stay in Siteia is recommended.

Aghios Nikolaos - Pachia Ammos (21 km.) (See Excursion 10). From Pachia Ammos the road continues on to Kavousi (26 km.) which lies at the base of Mount Kapsas (1002 m. a.s.l.). The road, which is paved and easy to drive on, begins to climb after Kavousi and at the 31st km. there is a country taverna next to a spring where there is a gorgeous view of the Gulf of Mirabello with the islets of Pseira, Konida and Mochlos.

At the 40th km. is the village of Sphaka. A narrow road to the left (6.5 km.) leads to the lovely little seaside settlement of Mochlos. Exactly opposite, 150 metres from the land, is the islet of Mochlos which during Minoan times was connected to it forming a peninsula.

In 1908 the American R. Seager carried out some excavations there. He uncovered a settlement and many collective house-tombs from the Early Minoan period on the west side of the island. If one judges by the gold jewellery and the diadems found there (Herakleion and Aghios Nikolaos Museums), these tombs certainly belonged to wealthy families. The collection of stone vases from Mochlos is considered to be one of the most important. Supplementary excavations were carried out in 1971 by the Greek archaeologist K. Davaras, which brought to light finds such as the silver pyxis and the famous gold diadem with horns (Aghios Nikolaos Museum). During the summer boatmen from the village of Mochlos take visitors to the island.

Northwest of Mochlos is the island of Pseira, which is today uninhabited and barren. It can be visited by renting a boat from Aghios Nikolaos or the small village of Mochlos.

R. Seager carried out excavations on Pseira in 1906-7 and brought to light a settlement, built amphitheatrically on the east side of the island protected from the winds. The houses are simple in design, densely built with narrow lanes and cover an area of approximately 15,000 sq. m. There are remains from all periods till 1450 B.C. when the settlement was completely destroyed. One of the houses of the settlement was found decorated with relief frescoes (Herakleion Museum). All indications lead to the conclusion that the inhabitants of the island were merchants, sailors, fishermen and artisans who processed sponges and porphyry. In 1985 excavations were resumed under a joint Greek-American mission.

From Sphaka the road continues along the foot of Mount Ornos, passing through lovely little villages.

At the 46th km., after the village of Myrsini, there is a beautiful view of the north coast and the islets of Pseira and Mochlos. At the 54th km. is the amphitheatrically built village of Mouliana known for its wine. Here S. Xanthoudidis excavated two tholos tombs from the Late Minoan period.

At 58.5 km., a sign right points to the large Minoan house which was originally excavated in 1903 by S. Xanthoudidis on the hill of Souvloto Mouri (1.5 km.), near the village of Chamezi. The building complex, which is like a fortress, consists of an elliptical house from the beginning of the Middle Minoan period, which is an unusual type of dwelling, unique in Greece. (Recent excavations of K. Davaras).

From the centre of the village of Chamezi a signpost points to the Folk Museum with notable collections of folk objects. Of particular interest is the "workshop-house" with a rare kind of loom and all its accessories. From Chamezi the road continues on to Siteia with a gorgeous view all the way.

SITEIA

Siteia (70 km.) is a harbour town with 8500 inhabitants which can be used as a base for a visit to the eastern end of Crete. It is maintained that ancient Iteia, homeland of Mysonas, one of the seven wise men of antiquity, was on the site of present-day Siteia. Regardless, Siteia has been inhabited since the Minoan period. At Petra, to the east of the town, a section of a settlement from the Minoan period has been excavated. This was evidently one of the largest harbours in Crete in the New Palace period. A large central building (palace?) has been revealed, storage areas and Linear A inscriptions.

Unique in Crete is the "Cyclopean" wall at the foot of the hill. It developed significantly during the Venetian occupation when the town was powerfully fortified with walls and towers. Nevertheless, first earthquakes, then the attacks of the Turks and finally its capture by them turned it into a heap of ruins and its inhabitants deserted it. Only during the 19th century was it rebuilt, and became the capital of the province.

It has a good number of hotels, pensions and houses with rooms for rent, as well as a youth hostel.

It has a regular bus service to all eastern Crete and acquired an airport in 1984 (10 minutes from the centre). For the present it is connected by air to the islands of Karpathos, Kassos and Rhodes as well as by a boat of the Piraeus-Dodecanese line. It is also connected to Piraeus by ship which stops at Aghios Nikolaos and Melos. Useful information can be obtained from the Tourist Police and the Public Relations Office of the Municipality.

During the summer cultural events take place in the theatre which operates in the town's restored Venetian government house.

THE ARCHAEOLOGICAL MUSEUM OF SITEIA

The Archaeogical Museum of Siteia began to operate in 1984.

The museum's collection, one of the most interesting in Crete, is exhibited in one large room around a courtyard and contains antiquities from the province of Siteia. It is divided into four sec-

Siteia. Partial view of the harbour.

tions. At the beginning of each section is a chart with an explanatory note, photographs and drawings and a relief map showing the excavation site.

We begin on the left with the section on Minoan finds.

Cases I and 2: Early Minoan vases (3000-2500 B.C.) from Aghia Photia, Siteia, with Cycladic influences.

Case 3: Votive figurines from peak sanctuaries of the region, principally from the Petsophas Sanctuary at Palaikastro.

Case 8: (in the centre): Stone lamp from the Minoan settlement of Pseira.

Case 5: Double stone horns, rhyta, tripods and kernoi from Palaikastro.

Case 9: An impressive find is a burial from the Minoan cemetery at Tourlotis.

The next section contains finds from the palace and a house at Zakros. The wine-press from the New Palace period is of interest.

Case II: Remains of animal feed in a pithos of the Late Minoan period. Giant pithoi which were used for food storage are also on display.

Case 16 (Centre): Clay tablets with texts in Linear A, from Zakros.

Case 13, 14, 17: Collection of vases from Zakros.

Case 18: Noteworthy is a clay brazier, most probably used for cooking, as well as a fragment of bone with a text in Linear A. The lids of large pithoi are arranged on the walls. The third section includes examples of Eteo-Cretan pottery, (from the Subminoan phase to Early Orientalizing).

Case 19, 21: Finds from the Geometric period.

Case 22: Dedalic heads and clay figurines that were found in the centre of Siteia.

The final section is dedicated to the Hellenistic and Roman periods. Of particular interest is the Hellenistic grain mill from Krya.

Case 24: Graeco-Roman vases from Petra, Makryyalos and other regions.

Case 25: Among other finds, Graeco-Roman lamps and a collection of shells from Kouphonisi (including some like those from which the Minoans extracted porphyry). Before the exit is an impressive mass of vases from a shipwreck in Roman times, which are kept in a water tank; also from Kouphonisi, opposite the SE coast of Crete. At the exit a burial inscription of the Ist century B.C., from Itanos.

Siteia also has a noteworthy Folk Museum with collections of embroideries, weaving, furniture, local costumes and household ware. The embroidered bed hangings and the loom with all its accessories are of interest.

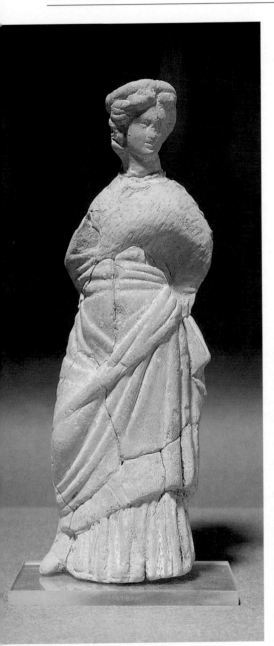

Clay "Tanagraia" figurine from the Hellenistic town of Xero-kambos. She wears a himation, chiton and headdress. Her weight is on her left leg and her head tilted to the left.

Clay statuette of a woman nursing an infant. Her high cylindrical headdress, official garments and "Egyptian" coif-fure indicate that this repre-sents a goddess. From the Dedalic repository in Siteia.

A pithamphora with highly stylized decoration. From the palace of Zakros.

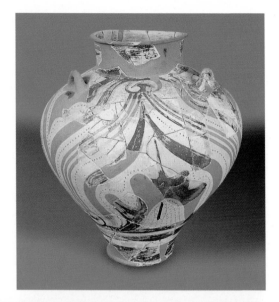

Middle Minoan I bull-shaped rhyton (ritual vessel) from the excavation at Mochlos.

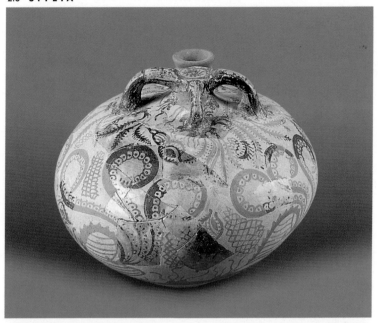

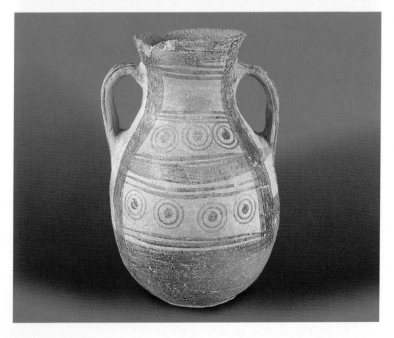

Stirrup jar from the excavations at the Minoan settlement on the islet of Pseira. Superbly decorated in the so-called "Marine" style. Late Minoan IB period, 1500-1450 B.C.

Clay tile with two relief forms, one male and one female, on a chariot. Probably depicts the abduction of Persephone by Pluto. From the Dedalic repository in Siteia.

Handmade Geometric amphora with panel-decoration of concentric circles. Unpublished. Printed by kind permission of the excavator M.Tsipopoulou. From a grave at Aghios Georgios.

SITEIA: Excursion 12

Aghia Photia (6 km.) - Turn-off Toplou Monastery (18.5 km.) - Vaï (Palm forest) (27 km.) - Palaikastro (20 km.) - Kato Zakros (41 km.).

Exit east from Siteia toward Zakros. At the 6th km. the village of Aghia Photia where the archaeologist K. Davaras excavated an important Early Minoan cemetery with more than 250 tombs. It is the largest cemetery from that period. In the small chamber tombs and cist graves were found around 1800 vases, stone and bronze artefacts (fish hooks, etc.) (Aghios Nikolaos and Siteia Museums). At the 15th km. a turn-off right leads to Palaikastro and Zakros. Left a wide, well-paved road leads (3.5 km.) to the fortified monastery of Toplou (18.5 km. from Siteia). The church, dedicated to the Nativity of the Virgin, is the original one around which the monastery, one of the wealthiest in Crete, de-

The Monastery of the Virgin Akrotiriani, which was called Toplou during the Turkish occupation. The east side of the fortified complex with a Renaissance bell tower.

veloped. Large tracts of the surrounding region still belong to it. It has a square shape and is enclosed by a wall 10 m. high. The entrance is through the restored exterior Loggia Gate. After passing through a vaulted passage one enters a small courtyard opposite the church. Incorporated in its exterior wall are three inscribed plaques and one in relief. The one is from the Hellenistic period and refers to a treaty of the 2nd century B.C. between Itanos and Hierapytna arbitrated by the Magnesians of Asia Minor. The other inscriptions refer to the abbot G. Pandogalos, who restored the monastery (17th century). The interior is adorned with well-preserved portable icons, the most important one being "Great Art Thou, O Lord", a work by the painter I. Kornaros which contains 61 painted scenes and an inscription from 1770.

In 1530 the monastery was plundered by the Knights of Malta. In 1612 it sustained heavy damage from an earthquake and in 1646 it fell into the hands of the Turks.

During the Turkish occupation the

Palaikastro was one of the most important Minoan towns.

"Great Art Thou, O Lord", icon by Ioannis Kornaros, 1770. Details, starting at the top. a) The "abyss" or sea with Noah's ark and Jonah cast forth by the whale in Nineveh. b) The rainbow, the animals emerging from Noah's ark, the sacrifice of Noah's family and the story of Cain and Abel. c) King Ahab left, the idolatrous prophets who are making a sacrifice to the statue of Baal in the middle and right the sacrifice of the Prophet Elijah.

"Great Art Thou, 0 Lord", icon by Ioannis Kornaros, 1770. Details, starting at the top: a) Christ calling the Disciples and the Baptism of Saint John the Forerunner, extension of the Baptism of Christ, central subject of the icon and the Hymn. b) The Nativity of Christ. c) Aged figure, personifying the element of water, a boat navigated by Christ and to the left the Meal of the Pharisees.

monastery was a refuge for the persecuted and a centre for revolutionary movements. The monks continued this tradition during the German occupation when an underground radio transmitter operated there. The abbot Sylignakis paid for this daring act with his life when the German authorities discovered the transmitter in 1944.

From the monastery the road (paved) goes through an uninhabited area, then heads SE to Vaï. At the 24.5th km. it rejoins the main road from Palaikastro. You turn left for Vaï and after 1.5 km., at the crossroads, follow the right turn-off to the coast, going through the famous palm forest, unique in Greece and known throughout Europe. The palm trees (date palms) go right down to the sea where the sand beach along with the off-shore rocks constantly tempt one to swim. Vaï is scheduled as a National Park and it is forbidden to spend the night there.

Back at the crossroads, take the left turn for the coast, where the ruins of the village of Erimoupolis are located at the side of the ancient town of Itanos (see Historical Review).

You return following the road to Palaikastro, where there is a wonderful beach.

Palaikastro was one of the most important Minoan towns, the ruins of which have been uncovered in the course of extensive excavations, still in progress. From here the steep ascent to Zakros begins. Passing through small hamlets, 19.5 km. along you reach the village of Epano Zakros. There is a small hotel there and a few rooms to rent. From the village square a paved road leads to Kato Zakros (8 km.).

At the exit from Epano Zakros are the ruins of a late Minoan villa excavated by N. Platon. Among the finds were a wine press (Siteia Museum) and a pithos with Linear A script (Herakleion Museum).

During the final 3 km. of the excursion the view is stunning as one gazes at the rocky eastern coast of Crete. On the last turn the archaeological site of Zakros bursts into view to the rear of a cove with a gorgeous pebble beach. To the north rise up rocky hills. Building is not allowed in this region, which is a scheduled Archaeological Site, but on the shore there are three or four refreshment bars and restaurants and several houses with rooms to rent.

The archaeological site contains the fourth largest Minoan palace of Crete and a part of the town. It lies opposite the Levant and Egypt, which explains the importance of this Minoan centre.

Archaeological Site of Zakros

The archaeological site at Zakros was first mentioned by Spratt in 1832. In 1901 the English archaeologist Hogarth began excavations on the slopes of the NE hill, above the palace, and discovered houses from the Minoan period. In 1961 Professor N. Platon began systematic excavations which are still in progress today.

No Neolithic remains have been found at the site. The oldest ones are from the New Palace period and have been located at several spots. The new palace must have been built around 1600 B.C. and destroyed in 1450 B.C. N. Platon attributes this destruction to tidal waves caused by the explosion of the volcano on Santorini (pumice has been found).

This palace was the only one of all the Minoan palaces where no signs of subsequent occupation have come to light. It had an area of 8000 sq. m. The arrangement of its spaces is in general the same as the other palaces with a Central (1) and a West Court (2).

The entrance today is on the NE side, where there is a paved road that connects the palace to the harbour. On the left are workshops (3) and the famous bronze foundry (4). There is a hill N. of the palace. Buildings were uncovered on its slopes, perhaps palace annexes used as dwellings by the nobles and officials.

Zakros. Aerial view of the archaeological site.

Four wings of apartments were discovered around the Central Court (I).

The royal living quarters with large, well-lighted rooms (5 and 6) were found in the E. wing. The Cistern Hall (7). lined with lime trass plaster, in the middle of a large room (probably the Throne Room) is impressive.

The basin filled with water from a spring (just as today) while a pipe conveyed the excess water outside. On one side are eight steps which create the impression that this was a pool. What is certain is that it had a ceremonial character. On the S. side of the basin is a second well (8).

On the N. side of the palace were servants' quarters and a large room with columns, perhaps a kitchen (9) because cooking utensils were found there. A lustral basin (10) was also found and to the NW storerooms with many jars and other vases (II).

The W. wing was devoted to religion, as in all the Minoan palaces. The Ceremonial Hall (12) had an opening from the Central Court in its N. corner. Polychrome columns (their bases have been preserved) help up the roof. The interstices of the floor, filled with red plaster, created a variety of patterns and the walls were also decorated. Many religious artefacts were found in this room. In another room, called the Banqueting Hall (13), were found many drinking vessels, probably for wine. A relief fresco adorns its walls, forming a frieze with spirals and rosettes (Herakleion Muse-

um) and its floor was also decorated. The Central Shrine (14) was excavated in the W. wing; it is small in dimensions and was probably only used by the priest. There is a ledge in the shrine near which were discovered libation rhytons and other religious artefacts.

A door in the W. wall of the Central Shrine leads to the Room of the Repositories (15); it has low clay partitions creating storage areas for cult para-

Vaï. The largest palm forest in Greece and known throughout Europe.

phernelia. To the E. of the shrine was another lustral basin (16) where a veined marble amphora was found.

To the W. of the shrine was the Archive Room (17) where tablets in Linear A were discovered and S. the Treasury (18). Here were found clay and stone objects, libation rhytons, ewers, lamps and sacred symbols.

Objects made of precious metals were not found, which suggests that the residents managed to remove them at the moment of the great catastrophe.

In the S. wing is the craft section of the palace with a variety of workshops. Proceeding to the SE corner of the Central Court we find another fountain (19). In the adjacent well (20) was found some fruit in a vessel, obviously an offering to the deity. A small cup contained olives which had been preserved for centuries in the water.

Maronia, a picturesque village.

SITEIA: Excursion 13

Piskokephalo (4 km.) - Praisos (18.5 km.) - Ziros - Lithines - Kapsa Monastery - Makryyalos - Aghia Photia - Hierapetra (70 km.).

You exit south from the front of the Museum and head toward Lithines. At Manares (2.5 km.) there was a Minoan villa contemporary with the new palaces. The stairway in the south part has been well-preserved. A turn-off left at the 5th km. leads to another Minoan villa near the village of Zou, known for its springs from which Siteia draws its water. At the 4th km. you reach Piskokephalo; a narrow road right (a sign points to Chrysopigi) leads to Achladia (5 km.) where a Minoan villa from 1450 B.C. and a well-preserved tholos tomb from 1300 B.C. have been discovered.

From Piskokephalo the road continues on to Moronia and Epano Episkopi, seat of the bishopric of Siteia during the 16th century. At the entrance, a road left (the arrow points to Ziros) cuts through a fertile valley and reaches Nea Praisos (18.5 km.) 4.5 km. later. Following the arrows, you reach the ruins of ancient Praisos, homeland of the Eteocretans.

The Italian Archaeological School began excavations here in 1884 and the British School continued in 1901. The ancient town was spread over three hills, that is there were three acropoleis. During the excavations the foundations of a temple, Hellenistic houses and tholos tombs were found. The town

Kapsa Monastery.

was destroyed by the inhabitants of Hierapetra during their long drawn-out war.

From Praisos the road continues on for Ziros by way of Chandra, traversing plains with vineyards and olive groves. There are old churches in the environs of Ziros, the most important being Saint Paraskevi, with frescoes. On the lintel is an inscription and the date 1523.

Returning to the village of Armenoi on the left, you reach the village of Etia just before the main road; this was the fief of the Venetian family De Mezzo from which remain the ruins of a three-storey villa, partially restored, considered to be one of the most representative examples of Venetian architecture in Crete.

You begin to see the Libyan Sea at Lithines 4 km. later, a sign points left to a dirt road leading to the coastal Monastery of Kapsa. It is not known when it was founded. The church is dedicated to Saint John the Baptist (Aghios Ioannis Prodromes). His name day is celebrated on the 29th of August with a great festival at the monastery.

At the exit from the village of Makryyalos, signs lead to a Minoan villa which was excavated by K. Davaras in 1970. Finds from it are on display in the Aghios Nikolaos Museum. The villa is from the Late Minoan period and was destroyed by fire. A villa from the Roman period was also excavated in the same area, by the archaeologist N. Papadakis. Twenty-four km. later you reach Hierapetra (see Excursion 10).

Makryyalos, a village with a wonderful beach.

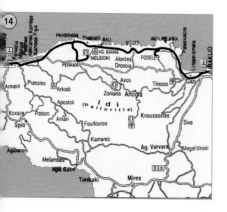

HERAKLEION: Excursion 14

Aghia Pelagia (18.5 km.) - Fodele (26 km.) - Bali (50 km.) - Panormos (58 km.) - Melidoni (71 km.) - Rethymnon (80 km.).

Leave from the Chania Gate for the expressway. In contrast to the old national road, the new one, for its greater part, runs along the sea. Small side roads to the right lead to the beautiful and highly frequented shores of the Cretan Sea.

At the 9th km. you can enjoy one final panoramic view of the bay and the town of Herakleion.

At the 18.5th km. a sign points right to Aghia Pelagia (2 km.), a picturesque cove with large hotels and a fine sand beach.

At the 26th km. an exit left leads through orange groves to the village of Fodele (3 km.) formerly considered to be the birthplace of Domenicus Theotokopoulos or El Greco – known for its oranges of the finest quality. You cross

Fodele and to the right, in a valley, is a Byzantine church of the Virgin (1383); it is cruciform with a dome and was built on the foundations of an old basilica. Paths through the olive grove lead to the church.

Back on the main highway you reach the borders of the Prefectures of Herakleion and Rethymnon at the 31st km.

At the 50th km. is the exit for Bali where coves and small harbours are found and sandy beaches protected from the winds. During antiquity the cove was used as the harbour of Axos.

At the 51st km., on a knoll above the road with a beautiful view of the beach,

The byzantine church of the Virgin at Fodele.

is the Monastery of Saint John the Baptist founded in 1635 by the descendants of the Archondopouli. The feast days are June 24 and August 29.

At the 58th km. is the exit for the village of Panormos (1 km.), a coastal town built between two bays on the site of ancient Panormos where a large Early Christian basilica has been excavated. The town was also probably a port of Axos. From Panormos a road left leads to the country town of Perama (7 km.) from where you continue to the village of Melidoni (4 km.).

Northwest of the village (at a distance of approximately 2 km.), a paved road leads to the Melidoni cave, one of the most important caves in Crete with majestic vaults and impressive stalactites. The cave is firmly bound to the history of the Cretan revolutions.

Here, in January 1824, 324 women and children and 30 revolutionaries were suffocated when the Turks blocked the entrance with straw and wood, doused it with olive oil and sulphur and set it afire.

At the 65th km. you can begin to see the White Mountains from the road as well as the marvellous beach of Rethymnon, 12 km. long, where many large hotels and camping sites have been built. At the 69th km. this road joins the old national road.

At the 75th km. is a turn-off for Arkadi (see Excursion 15). Rethymnon is 6 km. further west.

THE MELIDONI CAVE OR GERONTOSPILIA

The cave lies 2 km. NW of the village of Melidoni (Prefecture of Rethymnon), at a height of 229 m., and is connected to it by road. During the Minoan period it was a place of worship, shown by the potsherds that were found there along with a Late Minoan double axe. The giant Talos, Hermes Talaios and Zeus Talaios were worshipped there. Traces of an inscription from the 3rd century B.C. concerning the worship of Hermes are preserved on the right rock of the entrance. Modern history speaks of the death by suffocation of 370 inhabitants of the village in January 1824; this was caused by the smoke from a fire the marauding Turks set at the mouth of the cave because the villagers refused to surrender. Some of the bones that were left have been enclosed in a monument inside the cave.

Aghia Pelagia. Lovely coves with large hotels and beautiful sand beaches.

Fodele. Built in a valley, this village is known as the place where Domenicus Theotokopoulos (El Greco) was born.

Enormous drapery-like stalactite at the end of the left section.

RETHYMNON

View of Rethymnon with the fortress of Fortetsa on the west side of the town.

Rethymnon, population 20,000, is the capital of the Prefecture of the same name and is 59 km. from Chania and 80 km. from Herakleion. It lies along the north coast, having to the east one of the largest sand beaches in Crete (12 km.) and to the west a steep, rocky coast-line. But 10 km. further west another large, sand beach begins.

There are quite a number of Venetian buildings in Rethymnon as well as old churches which were turned into mosques during the Turkish occupation. Several of the minarets still exist, which give a somewhat Oriental flavour to the town, but after the Moslems left the mosques became churches once more.

On the top of a rock on the west side of the town is the fortress of Fortetsa. Rebuilt, it commands the lovely Venetian harbour which has a splendid lighthouse.

Rethymnon does not have an airport but it does have daily connections with the airport at Chania (midday and evening with buses of Olympic Airways).

Public buses are used to make connections with the harbour of Souda as well as the rest of the market towns and villages of the Prefecture of Rethymnon. During the summer, tourist agencies organize cruises to Santorini but there is no direct boat service to Piraeus.

In the town and its environs are found hotels of all categories, two well appointed camping sites on the large sand beaches to the E., restaurants, tavernas and night clubs. The seat of the new University of Crete is at Rethymnon. Its Faculty of Letters has given new impetus to the already existing intellectual tradition.

Throughout the year various activities are organized which draw a large crowd from the various parts of Crete as well as from abroad. These activities include Carnival, the Kledonas celebration on the name day of Saint John (Midsummer's Day) when groups light bonfires at various points of the town, the wine festival in July, theatrical and musical performances in August-September and finally the Arkadia, 8-9 November which is a local holiday featuring sports contests, a Mass and parades.

History of the Town

Present-day Rethymnon must have been inhabited during the Late Minoan III phase, as is shown by a tomb from this period which was excavated at Mastabas, a southern suburb of the town.

Present-day Rethymnon is built on the ruins of the ancient town of Rethymna, from which it took its name.

Rethymnon.
View of the harbour.

Mosaics from Byzantine and Roman times have been found. Rethymna was an autonomous city with its own currency but during Roman times it declined. Mosaics from the Roman and Byzantine periods have been found. The Venetians understood the importance of the site and the town; they endowed it with walls and a fortress (Fortetsa) on the end of the small headland west of the harbour. On Fortetsa was an ancient temple dedicated to the goddess Artemis.

Fortetsa was built between 1573 and 1583 by the Venetian engineer Pallavicini. It has strong walls reinforced by four bastions. Civic buildings, the governor's quarters, barracks and an ammunition store were built inside the fortress. The walls, the reservoirs and the ruined governor's quarters have been preserved from the Venetian structures. There is also a small church as well as a mosque which suggests that the Ottomans used the fortress after the conquest of Rethymnon in 1645. The area inside the walls is open to visitors only on certain days and for a few hours.

At the foot of Fortetsa is the old town with narrow lanes and Venetian and Turkish buildings which have frequently been restored or repaired.

North of Petychaki Square is the Rimondi fountain (1626), which is interesting from an architectural and sculptural point of view. Right next to the public gardens is the Guora gate, of equal interest.

The finest Venetian monument is the Loggia from the end of the 16th century (Arkadiou St.) where the Archaeological Museum of Rethymnon was formerly housed and which is now the Municipal Library.

Venetian and Turkish buildings have been preserved in Rethymnon, particularly in the old town with its narrow streets.

Fortetsa, the fortress built by the Venetians, has strong walls which are fortified by four ramparts.

Church in the interior of the fortress.

The Venetian Rimondi fountain is of interest from both an architectural and a sculptural point of view.

THE ARCHAEOLOGICAL MUSEUM OF RETHYMNON

In 1989 the exhibit of the Archaeological Museum was transferred from the Venetian Loggia to the former Turkish prison, at the entrance to the fortress of Fortetsa, which has been specially re-arranged for this purpose.

The new exhibit, on which work is still in progress, comprises the basic kernel of the old museum, augmented by finds from more recent excavations in the prefecture and explanatory material (maps, plans etc.).

Exhibits from the old museum include: Neolithic finds from the Yerani cave (on the road from Chania) and the Ellenes Amari cave such as figurines, spear-heads, stone and bone tools, jew-ellery, clay figurines and pottery. Minoan axes (from the villages of Ellenes, Orne and Phouphoura), worshipping goddesses (from Saktouria and Pagalochori), sealstones and clay vases (1400-1200 B.C.) (from the Armenoi cemetery). Bronze artefacts (from the village of Atsipades), discs and mirrors (from the Idaian Cave), gilt jewellery and sealstones, as well as clay larnakes lavishly decorated with fish and octopuses from various parts of the prefecture.

The cases on the right contain Egyptian finds and interesting red-figure vases.

From the Hellenistic and Roman periods come a collection of glass vessels, sealstones, lamps and figurines, as well as marble heads, a headless female statue, a sculptural group of a Satyr and Dionysos, and part of a statue of Pan.

A ship from Roman times that was raised from the bay of Aghia Galini contained a naked bronze warrior, a bronze bust of a woman, a bronze figurine of a horse, etc.

Finally, there is an important numismatic collection which contains coins from various regions and periods.

Gold coin from
Hellenistic Knossos.

Clay lamp with a cockfight depicted in relief. 2nd-3rd century A.D.

From the small Egyptian collection. Bronze statuette of Isis. 18th dynasty (1700-1400 B.C.).

Red-figure pelike with applied white colour. 4th century B.C.

Pictorial motifs on a clay sarcophagus (larnax) of the Late Minoan III B period: facing birds (detail).

Another detail from the same larnax: octopus.

Clay figurine of goddess with raised arms and bell-skirt. Late Minoan III B period. Pagalochori, Rethymnon.

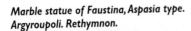

Bronze statuette of a helmeted youth, Graeco-Roman period. From the Aghia Galini shipwreck, Rethymnon.

Marble statue of Faustina, Aspasia type. Argyroupoli. Rethymnon.

Marble statue of Aphrodite, Genetrix type, Graeco-Roman period. Argyroupoli. Rethymnon (ancient Lappa).

RETHYMNON: Excursion 15

Arkadi Monastery (24 km.).

A turn-off right, 5 km. E. of Rethymnon on the old road, leads to the Arkadi Monastery. A short way before the village of Adele (8 km.) a turn-off right ends in the traditional settlement of Maroula which has a lovely view of the north coast. Going on you cross the villages of Pigi and Loutra.

Late Minoan III cemeteries have been found near the villages of Maroula and Pigi. From the villages of Kyrianna and Ammato a narrow winding road through dense olive groves leads to the Arkadi Monastery, which is a holy monument to the national liberation fight of the Cretan people against Ottoman suzerainty.

Because it was difficult to reach, Arkadi was a centre of revolutionary activity. Thus in 1866, when the Great Revolution broke out, the leaders of the rebels gathered there to direct the struggle. The leader of the Turkish forces asked the abbot Gavriel Marinakis to expel the committee of revolutionaries otherwise he would destroy the monastery. When Marinakis refused, the pasha gathered an enormous expeditionary force and on November 7, 1866 set off for Arkadi. There were 964 people in the monastery, of whom only 325 were armed rebels the rest being women and children. After resisting for two days and seeing that the defence was crumbling, the defenders of the monastery set fire to the powder magazine and were blown to bits along with many of the Turkish attackers. The holocaust at Arkadi became a symbol of the

sacrifices made by the Cretan people in the cause of liberty.

According to an inscription the monastery was built during the 14th century. It has a fortress shape with massive outer walls, 1.20 metres thick and covers an area of 5200 sq. m. The church, which is dedicated to Saint Constantine and the Transfiguration of Christ, was completed in 1587.

Today it is without a doubt the most important and best preserved building of the entire complex.

In the 18th century the monastery was at its highest point, both economically and spiritually. Historians of the period speak not only of its enormous storerooms, which were full of produce and barrels of tasty wine, but also of its magnificent library.

Other buildings in the monastery enclosure are the Refectory, the Hostel, the monks' cells, etc. Most of them have been restored. There is also a small museum with a few Byzantine icons, vestments, photographs, etc., as well as an ossuary for the bones of the dead from the holocaust of 1866. There is a tourist pavilion outside the monastery.

The magnificent entrance to the historic Arkadi Monastery.

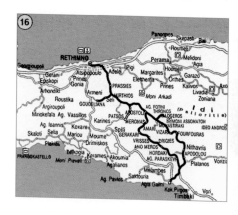

RETHYMNON: Excursion 16

Amari region. Thronos (19 km.) - Apostoli (25 km.) - Kaloyeros - Monastiraki (35 km.) - Apodoulou (53 km.) - Return from Aghia Paraskevi - Aghios Ioannis (56 km.) - Yerakari (41 km.).

This excursion takes one through the villages and the greater part of the beautiful province of Amari, known for its marvellous Byzantine churches.

Leave for the valley of Amari, 3 km. E. of Rethymnon, on an uphill road. At the 6th km. there is a lovely view, right, of the church of Saint Eftychios. At the 8th km. is the pretty village of Prasies with Venetian houses. The church at the cemetery, dedicated to the Virgin, has wall-paintings from the 14th century. A magnificent view of the valley spreads out before it. At the 11th km. a turn-off right for Myrthio, Goulediana joins the main road Rethymnon - Spili - Aghia Galini (Excursion 3). At the 14.5th km.

the valley of Amari begins. At the 17th km. there is another fork to the right. A rough stretch of road for 9 km. leads to Patso. West of the vil-lage is the cave of Aghios Antonios where there was an important sanctuary from the Middle Mi-noan to the Roman period. At the 28.5th km., at a high point where the Amari and the Stavromana rivers divide, is the village of Apostoli. It is believed that the Romans captured the Ten Saints (Aghioi Deka) here, which is why it is called Apostoli. There are frescoes from the 14th and 15th centuries in the church of Saint Nicholas. The visitor has a marvellous view of Psiloreitis from its terrace.

Continuing along the public road, about 1 km. further on is the small vil-lage of Aghia Photeini where there is a good view of the valley, which is formed between Psiloreitis to the east and Ke-dros to the west at an elevation of 400-500 m.

Amari, because of its abundant spring water, is covered with fruit trees. It is also well-known for its plump table olives. Olive cultivation is the main industry in the province. The Amari val-ley, with around 40 small villages, is the natural route connecting the north and south coasts of Crete and was a refuge for the persecuted as well as a revolu-tionary centre during the Turkish occu-pation and World War II.

You continue left from Aghia Photei-ni. At the first turn a sign points to the village of Thronos (1 km.) built on a sec-

The church of Saint Nicholas in the village of Apostoli, with wall-paintings from the 14th and 15th centuries.

tion of the ancient city of Sibrytos or Sibryta. The city was built on successive levels on the slopes of the hill. Its possessions covered the entire province of Amari and Aghios Vasileios while ancient Soulia, the present-day Aghia Galini, was its harbour.

In the middle of the village of Thronos, the frescoed church of the Virgin is built on the ruins of an older basilica. The frescoes that are left are from the 14th and 15th centuries. Other interesting churches are saint John the Theo-logian with wall-paintings from 1347 and Saint Paraskevi from the 15th century, near the village of Kaloyeros.

At the 35th km. is the former monastery of Asomati (340 m. a.s.l.) where there has been an agricultural school since 1931 in a region dense with olive trees, vineyards and fruit trees. A turning right leads to the village of Monastriraki, where a very important Minoan settlement has been discovered, and the church of the Archangel Michael. The road goes on to Amari, the capital of the province of Amari. Outside the village is the church of Saint Ann, with

The church of the Virgin in the village of Thronos, built on the ruins of an older basilica.

The mountain village of Kaloyeros.

the earliest dated wall-paintings in Crete (1225). The main road goes on to Vizari (360 m a.s.l.). At Ellinika (2 km. west of the village) K. Kalokyris excavated a triple-aisled basilica from the 7th century. At the 43rd km., in the centre of the village of Phouphoura (460 m. a.s.l.), is the church of the Virgin with frescoes from the 14th-15th century.

At the 53rd km. to the left, on the last turn before the village of Apodoulou (450 m. a.s.l.), is a Late Minoan tholos tomb excavated by K. Davaras. In ongoing excavations in the area other Late Minoan III tholos tombs have been revealed, as well as a very important settlement, established as early as the Middle Minoan period. Immediately after the village of Apodoulou, a well-paved public road to the left leads to the villages of Kamares - Xaro - Aghia Varvara (see Excursion 3). Another road continues on S. to Aghia Galini.

To complete the tour of the valley, one goes N. and reaches the village of Aghia Paraskevi 4.5 km. later. In the centre of the village, and next to the new church, is a small Byzantine church with frescoes dated 1516.

The road continues on through the mountain villages of Chordaki, Ano Meros, Drigies and Vryses. There is a panoramic view of the south coast facing the Libyan Sea.

From Yerakeri one goes on to the village of Meronas to visit a church dedicated to the Virgin with frescoes from the 14th century.

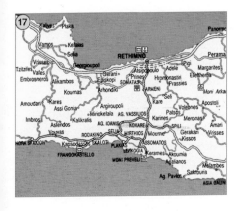

RETHYMNON: Excursion 17

Armenoi (11 km.) - Spili (30 km.) - Melambes (50 km.) - Aghia Galini (62 km.) - Asomati (30 km.) - Crossroads for Preveli Monastery (37 km.) - Plakia (37 km.) - Sellia - Frangokastello - Chora Sphakion.

You leave from the street at the side of the Municipal Gardens heading south for Spili - Aghia Galini. At the 2nd km. is a panoramic view of the town of Rethymnon and Fortetsa. At the 9th km., at the junction with the road to Somata, lies the Late Minoan III cemetery of Armenoi, excavated (work still in progress) by the archaeologist Yannis Tzedakis.

This is the largest organized cemetery of rock-cut tombs (the majority unplundered), which fact implies the existence of a significant town in the region. Numerous vases, clay sarcophagi with interesting representations, weapons and minor objects have been recovered.

The village of Armenoi, the agricultural centre of the region, was settled in 961 by Armenian soldiers of the Byzantine general Nikephoros Phokas.

At the 20th km. a turn-off right leads to the villages of Aghios Vasileios, Aghios Ioannis and Sellia. The public road leads to Spili (30 km.) (430 m. a.s.l.) seat of the metropolitan, with dense vegetation, plentiful water, picturesque houses and four old churches, and continues on to Melambes (50 km.) and Aghia Galini (62 km.) (see Excursion 3).

After the crossroads at the 20th km. there is another crossroads with a sign pointing to Koxare and Plakia. The narrow, winding road passes through the barren landscape of the Kourtaliotikos ravine (2 km.) to reach the village of Asomati, brithplace of the Tsouderos family.

Spili. Village in a lush green setting with plentiful water, picturesque and old churches.

One km. after the village there is a turn-off left for the Preveli Monastery. The winding road goes down to the Libyan Sea where there is a panoramic view with the Paximadia islets opposite.

You suddenly come upon the Preveli Monastery at a turn in the road (500 m. away). Only two monks live there today. Down through the ages its fortified site made it a refuge for the persecuted and

Sellia. Mountain village, about 30 km. outside Rethymnon.

Skaloti. Small village on the road to Frangokastello.

a centre for revolutionary movements. In World War II remnants of units of the British Commonwealth forces, who had taken part in the Battle of Crete, escaped from here. The Monastery church is relatively recent (1836), but there is a fountain at the entrance to the coutyard dated 1701, indicating that the Monastery existed during the Venetian occupation. Treacherous paths lead down to an enchanting but sheer coastline with "secret" coves.

You return to the turn-off south of the village of Asomati and continue left up to Lefkogia. At the exit from the village (at the crossroads), you take the asphalt road to the left straight to Plakia (37 km.). This is a small, charming summer resort spot with modest hotels and rooms to rent which has developed rapidly. On the return along the same road you turn left for Myrthio (400 m. a.s.L). The road to the NE is uphill and the landscape stunning.

At the 3rd km. you reach the entrance to the Kotsyphos ravine from where a turn-off right leads, by another road, back to Aghios Vasileios and then Rethymnon.

Continuing on, 3 km. after the turn-off, you reach the village of Sellia (280 m. a.s.L), where in the Revolution of 1896, the Turks, who were trying to infiltrate southern Crete, were defeated in a bloody battle. At the 12th km. you reach the mountain village of Rodakino, built amphitheatrically on two promontories. Here, on May 24, 1821, the

The impressive Preveli Monastery, a refuge for the persecuted and of many revolutionary movements.

first flag of the Greek War of Independence was raised by the abbot of the Preveli Monastery, Melchisedek Tsouderos. Left is a turn-off for Frangokastello, reached by an asphalt road (3 km.). In front of the fortress stretches a marvellous sand beach with shallow water, protected by headlands.

Frangokastello was built by the Venetians and lies practically on the beach. It has a rectangular shape with square towers at each corner. Its walls are very well preserved. The Turks built various structures in the interior which are half in ruins today. Returning to the main road, we head west, passing through small villages nestled at the southern foot of the Sphakia mountains. The road is asphalt paved. The view of the narrow seaside plain with Frangokastello in the distance is impressive. At a distance of 11 km. from Frangokastello we come upon the main Chania - Chora Sphakion crossroads. The road to the left, after 3 km., brings us to Chora Sphakion. It is a picturesque, enclosed harbour where the

Frangokastello, with quite well-preserved masonry, built by the Venetians practically on the shore. A beautiful sand beach spreads out before the fortress.

small boats from Aghia Roumeli dock,, in summer, bringing the hikers from the Samaria Gorge (see Excursion 22). From here buses collect them for the return trip to Chania or Rethymnon.

Once the buses leave the small harbour returns to normal, and the vacationers staying in rented rooms or the small hotel can enjoy the quiet and calm of this beautiful place. On a nearby hill are the remains of an old fort.

After the Battle of Crete during World War II, the locals helped the New Zealand and Australian rearguards escape from here on the night of May 31. 1941.

Chora Sphakion. Charming little harbour, where small craft land during the summer months.

The exit from the Kourtaliotikos ravine. The dry landscape of sharp rocks has a special kind of beauty all its own.

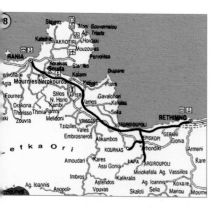

RETHYMNON: Excursion 18

Georgioupoli (21.5 km.) - Vryses (26 km.) - Chania (59 km.). (The new national road follows the coast while the old one goes inland passing through semi-mountainous villages).

Exit Rethymnon on Igoumenou Gavriel St. heading west. The new national road follows the coast till Gerorgioupoli Hill (21.5 km.). The large, sandy beaches are not built up as in eastern and central Crete (there is a camping site in the region of Dramia). On the coast is the an-cient city of Hydramia.

At 13.5 km. there is an exit to the village of Episkopi (3 km.). Before the village a turn-off west leads to the village of Kournas and from there a dirt road goes to Lake Kourna, one the two fresh-water lakes in Crete. From Episkopi, continuing S., you reach Argyroupoli, which is built on the site of ancient Lappa, of which only a few ruins are left today. Lappa, a Dorian town, was destroyed in

67 B.C. but was reoccupied until the Arab occupation. Graeco-Roman statues from Lappa are on display in the Archaeological Museum of Rethymnon.

At 21.5 km. a slip road right leads to the coastal village of Georgioupoli, which has some limited tourist facilities.

At 26 km. a turn-off left goes to Vryses. The highway right goes to Vamo, the capital of the province of Apokorona.

At 44 km., on the right side of the road, stands a large Venetian fortress, known by its Turkish name Itzedin (today the Chania prison).

At 48 km. a turn-off left (3 km.) leads to ancient Aptera (see Excursion 20) while to the right is the bay of Souda. You follow the south shore of the bay which to the north borders on the Akrotiri peninsula (see Excursion 19).

At the entrance to Souda bay two small islets stand out; in antiquity they were called Lefkes. The Venetians built one of the most important fortresses in Crete on the larger one to protect the bay from hostile and pirate ships. The latest fortification techniques were used in its construction so the Turks were not able to conquer it. Thus, for half a century after the conquest of Crete, the fortress of Souda continued to be occupied by the Venetians and perse-cuted Christians took refuge there. A treaty finally turned the fortress over to the Turks in 1715.

To the rear and on the south side of the bay is the harbour of Souda, which during the past few decades has developed rapidly. It is only 6.5 km. from Chania and is the main gateway to the sea, not only for Chania but for the whole of western Crete. This is the place where the large car ferries from Piraeus dock.

From the harbour the road continues west to Chania. A turn-off S., immediately after the harbour in the direction of the airport, leads to the cemetery of the British Commonwealth forces from World War II where the bones of 1497 soldiers, mainly New Zealanders and Australians who fell in the Battle of Crete in May 1941, have been laid to rest.

CHANIA

Chania is the second largest town in Crete (50,000 inhabitants) and is unquestionably the one which has preserved more of its old character than any other. Around Kasteli and the harbour, many buildings and even entire neighbourhoods from the Venetian and Turkish periods have been preserved in good condition. The new part has been built according to a modern plan with wide streets, parks and fine buildings. Eleftherios Venizelos is particularly honoured here; he was born in the village of Mournies near Chania and is buried a little way outside the town, at Akrotiri (see Excursion 19).

Chania is the starting point for a visit to western Crete, which does not have the wealth of archaeological sites of central and eastern Crete but is unequalled in natural beauty.

Chania is connected by air with Athens by four flights daily. Chania airport (14 km. from the centre of the town) is at Sternes, Akrotiri and fulfills the requirements of an international airport; charter flights arrive there in summer direct from abroad. From the airport urban buses and those of Olympic Airways set off for the town (terminus

Georgioupoli. Seaside village with some tourist facilities.

Kourna lake, one of the two in Crete.

at Tzanakaki St. opposite the Public Gardens). At the airport are car rental agencies and taxis for all parts of the island.

Chania has daily boat connections to Piraeus via car ferries which leave from the harbour at Souda. The departure from Piraeus is late in the afternoon, arriving at Souda in the morning where local buses take the travellers to the centre of the town dropping them off in front of the Public Market.

In the town and environs of Chania are many hotels of all categories, a youth hostel (33 Drakonianou St.) as well as many restaurants and tavernas in the centre, particularly at the harbour where there is a good deal of evening activity in the summer.

The closest beach is at Nea Chora (20 minutes on foot but there is also a bus from 1866 Square for Kalamaki or Galatas). Other beautiful beaches relatively close are on the road to Kisamos (Kasteli). (see Excursion 24).

Chania is connected to Rethymnon, Herakleion and the provincial centres of western Crete by frequent bus service.

Visits to the sites of the prefecture and the archaeological sites of Crete are organized by travel agencies (information at the offices of EOT or your hotel).

The celebration of the anniversary of the Battle of Crete is held during the last week in May and is the high point of the year in Chania. The day of the anniversary is a holiday and is honoured with a Mass, parades and folk festivals. A host of people from all over the island gather at Chania (for this week in particular it is necessary to reserve a hotel room). Recently these activities have been periodically held at various other centres of the prefecture.

History of the Town

Chania is built on the site of ancient Kydonia. Excavations that were begun in the neighbourhood of Kasteli in 1965 by the archaeologist I. Tzedakis reveal that this site was inhabited in Late Neolithic times and throughout all phases of the Minoan period. In New Palace times (Middle Minoan III - Late Minoan I) Kydonia emerged as a very important centre of Minoan civilization. Traces of a possible palatial installation have come to light: archive of clay Linear A tablets, a clay sealing with representation of the town and ruler, and, most recently, a lustral basin with wall-paintings. During the Middle Minoan III period also, when building continued on top of the ruins of 1450 B.C., Kydonia experienced a second floruit and the wonderful products of its pottery workshops were in demand over a large market. Life continued unabated in all subsequent periods and the city spread beyond the hill, as far as the present-day commercial centre. Kydonia played an important role in historical times and enjoyed a pre-eminent position in the Roman and Byzantine periods. Chania was rebuilt during the Venetian occupation and developed economically and

intellectually. Excavations are hampered by the town's present needs.

At Kastelli (the hill which commands the harbour), in the fortress, the Venetians built a palace, cathedral, theatre and houses for the nobility. In 1537 the fear of a Turkish invasion forced the Venetians to enclose the entire town with a wall. The architect of the walls was the Italian Sammicheli, who had also fortified Herakleion, but the walls of Chania were not as successful for the town only held out against the Turks for two months (1645). In 1851 the Turks transferred the seat of the Ottoman administration of Crete to Chania. Throughout the Cretan revolutions the Moslem population of the countryside shut itself up in the fortified town of Chania, which the rebels lacked the means to capture. On more than a few occasions the Moslem mob expressed its fury by slaughtering the Christians inside the walls and pillaging their houses.

With the liberation of Crete from the Turks in 1898, Chania became the capital of the Cretan Republic with Prince George as High Commissioner.

Tour of the Town

The Public Market, a magnificent structure of cruciform type, is located in the centre of the town (1897 Square). It was built at the beginning of the present century (1911) and houses, grocery stores, butchers' shops, a fish market and vegetable stalls. Tzanakaki St. begins at the Public market and contains banks, trav-

Chania harbour. The domed building is the Turkish mosque.

Around the harbour of Chania, with its old Venetian and Turkish buildings, are many shops.

Chania. The Venetian lighthouse, restored by the Egyptians.

Chania, the second largest town in Crete, has retained its character more than any other town.

el agencies and the offices of Olympic Airways, and the Public Gardens. Right next to the Gardens, on Sphakianaki St. are the Historical Archives of Chania. NE of the Gardens is the beautiful neighbourhood of Chalepa where the residences of Prince George and Eleftherios Venizelos were.

Chalidon St. is a picturesque street which leads to the old town and the harbour with second-hand shops, leather and tourist shops. Further on Chalidon St. passes before the large cathedral church of the Holy Trinity. In the square is a statue of the Ecumenical Patriarch Athenagoras. The domed building on the NW corner of the square was the Turkish baths. Exactly opposite, in the renovated Venetian church of Saint Francis, is the Archaeological Museum. Chalidon St. ends at the harbour; the one-storey renovated Venetian build-

ings and Turkish houses contain restaurants, tavernas and night clubs.

In the renovated mosque from 1645 are housed the offices of EOT on the eastern side of the pier of the harbour. Kastelli hill lies behind EOT, due east.

The harbour is protected by a Venetian breakwater, built of huge stones. In the centre of the breakwater are the ruins of a fortress, while the pride of the harbour is the Venetian lighthouse,

restored by the Egyptians. The impressive Arsenals (shipyards) built by the Venetians at the end of the 15th century are preserved in good condition on the east and south sides of the harbour. Of the original 23 vaulted structures which covered the shipyards only 9 are left today. There are other fine buildings from the Venetian occupation on the NW side of the harbour, such as the Renieri Gate on Theophanous St., a side-street off Zambeliou St., and the Venetian Megaron with a coat-of-arms and Latin inscription at 43-45 Zambeliou St. The adjacent Theotokopoulou St. is very picturesque with folk art shops. In general, a stroll through the old town presents many opportunities for revealing photographs among the Venetian buildings. Finally, at the NW end of the harbour is the renovated Firkas tower, where the Maritime Museum is housed, as well as a summer theatre where dramatic performances are presented.

Firkas is a monument emotionally tied to the Liberation of Crete. The flag of the Great Powers was raised on this fortress on February 16, 1897, when Crete was proclaimed an autonomous republic. The Greek flag was raised on the same pole on December 1, 1913 by King Constantine in the presence of the leading figure in the Liberation of Crete, Eleftherios Venizelos, celebrating the union of Crete with the rest of Greece.

Picturesque little tavernas and a host of restaurant and nightclubs give a special flavour to the waterfront.

THE ARCHAEOLOGICAL MUSEUM OF CHANIA

The museum is housed in an imposing building, the renovated Venetian church of Saint Francis on Chalidon St.

It contains impressive finds from the region of Chania and all of western Crete from Neolithic to Roman times. The painted larnakes of the Late Minoan period, vases and figurines from the Early Minoan, Middle Minoan and Late Minoan periods, vases and implements from the Geometric period, statues from the Hellenistic and Roman periods, as well as an exquisite Roman mosaic floor, are all outstanding. Most of the displays are uncatalogued and no photographs are allowed. There are explanatory notes on the cases.

Starting from the left:
Cases 1,2,3,4: Neolithic and Minoan vases from the Platyvolas cave. In *Case 4*: of special interest is one of the largest known tripod *pyxis*.
Case 5: Stone tools and vases.
Cases 6-9: Mainly Early Minoan, Middle Minoan and Late Minoan vases.

Cases 10: Tablets with ideograms and seal-stones with Linear B writing from Chania.

Cases 11, 12, 13, 14: Late Minoan pottery from Kasteli, Chania.

Cases 23, 24, 25: Proto-Geometric and Geometric vases from various regions.

Cases 17, 29: (in the centre of the room). Late Minoan tools, daggers, mirrors and a double axe from Chania.

Case 26: Large Geometric vases from the Gavalomouri cemetery.

At the back of the room, three mosaic floors of the 3rd century A.D. from Chania.

Around these floors are an impressive collection of sculptures of youths from the Asklepeion at Lissos, a small Aphrodite from Kydonia, a philosopher

Beautiful "Tanagraia" head, Praxiteles type, of fine off-white clay with a twisted wreath and ivy leaves. Its polychrome and gilded decoration can still be seen. Found in a rock-cut tomb at Chania. Late 4th century B.C.

from Elyros and a delicately sculpted youth from Lissos.

Continuing down the right side from the back of the room toward the entrance, *Case 39* contains Classical and Hellenistic figurines. The small clay model of a 5th-century B.C. shield is striking.

Case 32: Clay vessels from the 6th to the 3rd century B.C.

Case 30, 28: Dedalic figures.

Case 27: Geometric vases and figurines and two children's games.

Cases 33, 36: Archaic and Hellenistic vases and figurines.

Cases 37: Pyxides, vases, figurines from the Classical and Hellenistic periods.

Case 38: Glass vessels from Graeco-Roman times and unprocessed glass paste from Tarra.

Case 18, 19, 20: Clay and metal vessels of the Late Minoan period from Chania.

Case 21: Late Minoan bronze flask with Linear A writing.

Detail of a clay larnax with polychrome decoration: on one side a deer hunt and on the other Cretan ibexes. From the Late Minoan III (1400 - 1200 B.C.) cemetery of Armenoi, Rethymnon.

Spherical flask – unusual
ceramic type. Late
Minoan III period.

Polychrome glass
perfume bottles of
alabastron shape in the
so-called Phoenician
style. Offering in
a female burial in the
family tomb at Chania.
Late 4th century B.C.

Marble statue of Artemis, Graeco-Roman period. From the sanctuary of Diktynna – a pre-Hellenic goddess identified during historical times with Artemis – at Menies, Kisamos.

Small marble statue of Aphrodite of the Knidos type, late Hellenistic period. Chania (historical Kydonia).

Head of an Archaic figurine with
diadem, from the Axos cemetery,
Rethymnon.

Female figure with interesting clothing.
The polychrome colours of her
garments have been preserved.
An example of a group of early
Hellenistic figurines in various styles
from the family tomb in Chania.

Poseidon and Amymone from the mosaic floor of another Roman house of the 3rd century A.D. from Chania.

The Roman "Dionysos House" in Chania yielded two wonderful mosaic floors of the 3rd century A.D. with depictions from the Dionysian cycle. Shown here, the personification of summer (detail).

Main design from the mosaic in the same house. The myth of the discovery of Ariadne in Naxos by Dionysos is depicted.

CHANIA: Excursion 19

Akrotiri (Venizelos tombs 4.5 km.) - Monasteries of Aghia Triada (14 km.) and Gouverneto (18 km.).

Akrotiri is the peninsula to the NE of Chania which protects Souda Bay from the north wind. On Akrotiri are the tomb of Eleftherios Venizelos, the monasteries of Aghia Triada and Gouverneto as well as Chania airport.

Leave Chania on Eleftheriou Venizelou St. in the direction of the airport. At 4.5 km. a turn left lead to the hill of Profitis Ilias where stand the monument and tomb of Eleftherios Venizelos and his son Sophokles. The tomb is impressive in its simplicity; it is at the spot that he himself had designated with a panoramic view of the town of Chania that he loved so much. Continuing on the road to the airport you turn left, following the signs, to Aghia Triada (14 km. from Chania).

The Monastery of Aghia Triada is at the base of Tzobomylos hill on a beautiful site densely planted with olive trees, vineyards and cypress trees. It was built in the 17th century by two Venetian monks of the Tzangaroloi family who had adopted the Orthodox faith. In the middle of the monastery is a cruciform church with a dome, dedicated to the Holy Trinity (Aghia Triada) with two side-chapels to the Life-giving Source (Zoodochos Pigi) and Saint John the Theologian. The facade of the church with its Doric columns reflects strong Venetian influences. The tall campanile, which dominates the surroundings, was built in 1864. In the 19th century there was a theological school at the monastery.

The hill of Profitis Ilias where are situated the memorial and tomb of Eleftherios Venizelos.

Gouverneto Monastery.

Four km. from Aghia Triada is the Gouverneto Monastery. The road is unsurfaced in the begining but becomes paved as it starts to climb.

The fortress-like enclosure of the monastery has the shape of a quadrangle with four square towers at the corners. In the middle of the enclosure is the beautiful domed church dedicated to the Presentation of the Virgin Mary, its facade decorated with Venetian sculpture. It has two side-chapels dedicated to the Ten Saints and Saint John the Stranger or the Hermit (Aghios Ioannis o Xenos or Erimitis). A path (30 minutes) leads to Spilia, where Ioannis lived and died. Coming down the path,

after about ten minutes, you pass a first cave, Arkoudiotissa, with a chapel to the Virgin at the entrance and a stalactite to the rear. Research by the archaeologist K. Davaras proves that Artemis, transformed into a bear (*arkouda*) was worshipped in this cave. The present-day chapel is dedicated to the Virgin Arkoudiotissa.

Continuing along the path you encounter ruins of the Catholico Monastery. The cave which contains the grave of Saint John the Hermit is at the end of the stairway. (Ten minutes further on you reach the rocky shore where you can swim). The return to Chania is by the same road or, completing the tour of Akrotiri, through the villages of Stavros and Kounoupidiana.

The Monastery of Aghia Triada of the Tzangaroloi.

THE CAVE OF GOUVERNETO OR SAINT JOHN THE HERMIT

It is located at Aviakia, Kydonia at a height of 800 m. a.s.l. In this same region the Kyverneio Monastery (Latin, Gouverneto) once flourished but was destroyed by pirates. This explains how the cave got its distinctive name. To ensure their safety the monks were obliged to build a new monastery – with the same name – about half an hour from the previous one; this new monastery is still standing in excellent condition. Right of the entrance to the cave is a small church, hewn out of rock, dedicated to Saint John the Hermit where many pilgrims gather on his name day. Most of them go to the end of the cave where the monk is thought to have lived and died. So pilgrims can approach the cave easily the monks have made a stepped path leading up to the entrance. At the point where the saint is thought to have died, 4 m. inside the entrance to the left, water collects in a cistern and is thought to be Hagiasma (Holy Water).

Enormous drapery-like stalagmites in the centre of the cave.

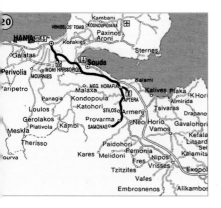

CHANIA: Excursion 20

Chrysopigi Monastery (3 km.) - Aptera (16 km.) - Stylos (38.5km.).

Exit E. on the road to Souda. At the 2nd km. a turn-off right on a picturesque road lined with eucalyptus trees leads to the entrance of the well-preserved Chrysopigi Monastery (open 8 a.m. - 12 noon and 3 p.m. - 6 p.m.). It was founded by the Chartophylakas family in the 16th century. The original Byzantine katholikon is in the middle of the present-day church. The monastery is surrounded by a wall. To the south, near the village of Nerokourou, a Minoan tomb has been excavated.

At the 4th km. you pass the harbour of Souda (see Excursion 18). At the 5th km. you take the national road toward Rethymnon. At 12.5 km. there is an exit right to Aptera. The road is uphill, narrow and winding but paved. At 13.5 km. is the village of Megala Choraphia where a turn-off left leads to the site of ancient

Aptera (2 km.). The reward for this strenuous drive is a panoramic view of the Bay of Souda from the top of the hill (200 m. a.s.L). The road along the small plateau continues on (passing a turn-off right to the archaeological site) to a renovated Turkish fortress which commands the Bay of Souda and the entire coast, having a breathtaking view. To the east lies the coast and the Kyrianis plain. To the south, next to the national road, is the medieval fortress of Itzedin and opposite the Bay of Souda, with its naval station and small islands. On one of them – the islet of Souda – there is still a Venetian fortress. In the background, the horizon is blocked by the Akrotiri peninsula. To the S., there is the incredible massif of the White Mountains, particularly impressive during the winter and early spring months when they truly live up to their name.

On this site, commanding a panoramic view of the Bay of Souda, Aptera, one of the most powerful city states of Crete, was founded in the 8th century B.C. According to tradition, it owes its name to the Sirens who lost their wings (*aptera* = wingless) following their defeat by the Muses in a music contest held here. In reality the city probably took its name from the homonymous epithet of the goddess Artemis, who was worshipped there and is depicted on its coins. Life in the city continued without a break until the time of the Arab conquest, when it was destroyed and abandoned. Of its ruins the city walls (4 km. in length) are particularly impressive, being preserved in several places. They were built in the 3rd century B.C. and their robust masonry indicates the city's greatness in Hellenistic times. In about the middle of the area within the walls is a fenced section with guard, where the ruins of a small temple of Classical times (late 5th-early 4th century B.C.) can be seen, a triple-apsed building of Roman times, associated with the bouleuterion, lies further east. The path behind the Monastery of Saint John the Theologian brings one to the most important monuments on the site, the two vaulted Roman cisterns.

From the Turkish fortress of Itzedin, near the east gate, there is a fine view of the city. On the south side is the theatre (nowadays in poor condition) and elsewhere there are scant traces of ancient temples. Some of the Early Byzantine buildings on the site are quite well preserved.

On returning, outside the walls, to the site of the present-day neighbourhood of Plakalona at Megala Choraphia lies the ancient cemetery.

Many tombs of the Geometric, Hellenistic and Roman periods have been excavated. From Megala Choraphia you can continue on to Stylos (38.5 km.). Before the village of Stylos and after the turn-off to Malaxa, on the left, a section of a Minoan settlement with a pottery kiln and a Late Minoan tholos tomb have been excavated on a hill.

Right at the exit from the village of Stylos, an uphill road (5 km.), winding, paved but not in good repair, leads to the village of Samona (400 m. a.s.l.) where a Late Minoan III settlement is being excavated.

You return by the same road or continue on through Malaxa and Mournies.

The White Mountains.
A mountain range which during
the winter and spring months
is indeed white.

CHANIA: Excursion 21

Vryses (33 km.) - Askyphou (51 km.) - Chora Sphakion (73 km.).

The road crosses the island from N. to S. through the village of Vryses.

Leave east along the road Chania-Rethymnon (see Excursion 18). At the 33rd km. you leave the main artery and follow a paved side road to Vryses, an utterly charming village with plane trees and lush vegetation. The visit to the province of Apokorona begins here. At the 39th km. a branch to the left goes to Alikambos (310 m. a.s.L), where there is a church to the Virgin from the 14th century, painted by Ioannis Pagomenos, with well-preserved frescoes.

Continuing the ascent you reach the Krapi valley. To the south of the valley the ravine Langos tou Katre, the Thermopylae of Sphakia, begins where some of the most brilliant pages of the struggles of the Cretan people during the

Venetian and Turkish occupations were written. The ravine is about 2 km. long, very narrow and rugged with steep slopes covered with ilex and cypress. During the Greek Revolution of 1821, the Sphakiots exterminated nearly 400 Turks here in a battle, thus protecting the region. The view at the exit from the ravine is magnificent. Before you spreads out the deep green plateau of Askyphou, surrounded by high mountain peaks (Kastro. 2218 m. a.s.L, Trypali, 1493 m. a.s.L, and Agathes, 1511 m. a.s.L). The fields are fertile, especially good for potatoes, while , fruit trees, walnut trees and vineyards abound.

At the 51st km., you reach the village of Askyphou (720 m. a.s.l.) where there are rooms to rent. There are also shops, coffee houses and restaurants. It is well worth trying the tasty *myzithropittes* (cheese pies) a speciality of Sphakia.

The road follows the west side of the plateau and begins to ascend once more. At the 54th km. a road left leads to the village Asphendou (770 m. a.s.l.). The main road goes on a little further to the point where the Libyan Sea can be seen.

The descent begins, twisting down the Imvrou ravine which is about 6 km. long with sheer soaring walls. The descent south is winding but safe and offers an enchanting view, while in the background to the east can be seen Frangokastello, the Paximadia islands and the coasts of the bay of Mesara. At the foot of the mountains of Sphakia a turn-

The village of Loutro in southern Crete.

The Imvrou ravine.

off left leads to Frangokastello (see Excursion 17).

Turning right you reach (after 3 km.) Chora Sphakion (see Excursion 17).

Using Chora Sphakion as a base you can visit the villages and sandy beaches of S. Crete, such as Loutro, Aghia Roumeli, Souya, Paliochora and the island of Gavdos.

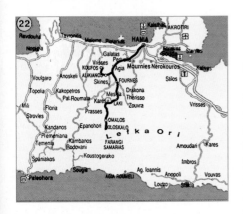

The famous Omalos plateau
(40 km. from Chania).

see also this excursion).

Leave Chania and head west toward Kisamos. One and a half km. later a turn-off leads north toward Alikianos-Omalos. The road crosses the Keriti valley, full of orange groves, for about 15 km. The valley is one of the richest citrus growing areas in Crete with about one million trees. At the 12th km. a branch right leads to the villages of Alikianos (1 km.) and Koupho (3 km.). Before the entrance to Alikianos a. paved road to the left goes to Souya on the Libyan Sea (see Excursion 23).

In Alikianos, on the main road, to the right, is a small, charming Byzantine church of Saint George (13th century) with wall-paintings from 1430 by the painter Pavlos Provatas. Practically opposite, in an enclosure, are the ruins of the historic Venetian Demolino Tower. Continuing on to Koupho, 500 m. before the entrance to the village, on the right, a narrow path (50 m.) leads to the Byzantine church of Saint John (Aï Kyr-Yanni), that has lovely wall-paintings from various periods. The church has been rebuilt and its paintings have been cleaned.

Returning to the main road to Omalos, at the 15th km. you reach the village of Phournes where a turn-off left leads 5 km. later to the village of Meskia, surrounded by orange groves. At the entrance to the village an uphill side road left leads to a small church with well-

CHANIA: Excursion 22

Alikianos (14.5 km.) - Phournes (15 km.) - Lakkoi (24 km.) - Omalos (40 km.) - Entrance Samaria Ravine (44 km.) - Exit at Aghia Roumeli (60 km.).

Many people come to Crete solely to make this excursion and to hike through the famous Samaria ravine.

The excursion combines an ascent by car to the White Mountains up to the Omalos plateau (Xyloskalo, 44 km.) and the descent by foot through the Samaria ravine to Aghia Roumeli on the Libyan Sea (approximately 18 km., around 7 hours on foot).

All those who want to traverse the ravine should go to its entrance (Xyloskalo, 44 km.) with an excursion organized by a tourist agency or on a public bus. It is not possible to go by private car to Xyloskalo with the idea of returning through the ravine on the same day. (For directions on how to return,

preserved wall paintings from the beginning of the 14th century by the painters
Theodorou, Michael Veneris and others.
At the exit from the village is an old
church dedicated to the Virgin, which
was built on the foundations of a basilica of the 5th-6th century, as is testified
by the traces of a mosaic floor.

At the beginning of the 1970s an
enormous modern church in the Russ-
ian style was erected behind the church.

During Hellenistic and Roman times

*The Church of Saint George
(13th century) with wall-paintings by
the painter Pavlos Provatas.*

there was a town here, the name of which is still disputed.

A difficult climb begins after Phournes with many sharp turns, skirting the NW side of the White Mountains and heading toward the Omalos plateau. At the 24th km. you reach the historic village of Lakkoi (500 m. a.s.L), which played an important role in all the Cretan revolu-tions as well as during the German occupation. It is the birthplace of the commander Chatzimichali Yannaris, who was active in the second half of the 19th century.

At the 39th km. you reach the highest point of the excursion (1200 m. a.s.L), go over the pass and start down-hill. Before you spreads out the barren landscape of the Omalos plateau (1080 m. a.s.L). It is enclosed all around by high mountain peaks, which down through the centuries, and especially during the Turkish occupation, have made it an impregnable fortress of Cretan revolutionaries and a refuge of the persecuted. The region was formerly famed for its production of potatoes and cereals but today it is mainly used for grazing land, though stock-raising is slowly declining.

In the centre of the plateau you reach a small settlement of the same name with two or three tavernas which are open during the tourist season. At its entrance, left, on a rise, is the imposing house of Chatzimichali Yannaris and next to it the grave of the rebel leader.

Three km. later you arrive at the south exit of the ravine at the site Xy-loskalo where there is a tourist pavilion and a small hotel. From this points the hikers will begin their descent into the Samaria ravine, which is the longest in Europe. The passage requires 5-8 hours depending on the abilities of each hiker. The walk is tiring because the largest part of it is continually down-hill.

The ravine has been declared a National Park and it is prohibited to stay there overnight.

It commences at Xyloskalo (1227 m. a.s.L). In the beginning the descent is by stairs and then along a well-made and well-marked path. There are two springs and the abandoned village of Samaria along the way. Particularly striking is the point where the ravine narrows to 3-4 metres, the so-called "Portes" (Gates). The absolutely vertical walls, right and left, which at many points are over 500 m. high, are awe-inspiring; this feeling is often enhanced by the whistling of the wind. Throughout the entire length of the ravine the flora is fantastic and bird-watchers will have the chance to spot several of the rarest species. The Cretan ibex, the *kri-kri* as the Cretans call it, still lives here but it is highly unlikely that a human being will encounter one. As the ravine opens up at the exit, 3 km. before the coast, the tired hikers may chance upon muleteers. For a fee they will take you to Aghia Roumeli.

The Samaria ravine,
the largest in Europe.

During the winter the ravine is impassable and the peaks are covered with snow.

At Aghia Roumeli there are only very few rooms to let and some restaurants. The beach is perfect for swimming. The present village is built on the site of the ancient city of Tarra, remains of which date back as far as the 5th century B.C. Ruins of the Roman period are preserved on the west bank of the river. Small boats leave from Aghia Roumeli for Chora Sphakion where buses from the organized tours are waiting for the returning hikers. Public buses also leave from Chora Sphakion for Rethymnon or Chania.

Three times a week there are caiques from Aghia Roumeli to the harbour of Palaiochora (see Excursion 26).

Nevertheless, before the hiker sets off he should get the schedule both for the buses and the boats from the offices of EOT at Chania or Rethymnon. He should have sturdy shoes (boots preferably) for the difficult descent and suitable head covering. The passage through the Samaria ravine is unquestionably a unique experience and the crowning point of a visit to Crete.

Aghia Roumeli, a seaside village with beautiful beaches and rooms to rent.

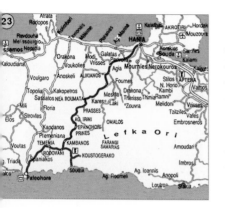

CHANIA: Excursion 23

Aghia Eirene Ravine (44 km.) - Temenia (62.5 km.) - Souya (70 km.).

An interesting excursion to the Libyan Sea. It goes through a varied landscape of the western slopes of the White Mountains. You exit from Chania heading south until Alikianos from where you pass through orange groves to reach the village of Skines. There is an orange festival here in the spring. Countinuing on the uphill road you reach Nea Roumata (26 km., 320 m. a.s.L). After passing through the village of Prases (480 m. a.s.l.) at the 38 th km. a turn-off left, on a dirt road in poor condition (15 km.) leads through the wild and impressive landscape on the Omalos plateau (see Excursion 22). The road to Souya continues on to Aghia Eirene (44 km., 700 m. a.s.l.) on the banks of a mountain torrent of the same name. The ravine of Aghia Eirene begins here (8 km. long). Passing through the villages of Epano-

Temenia.
The church of Christ the Saviour.

Souya. A small village with beautiful sand beaches, built on the ruins of ancient Syïa.

chori and Kabanos you reach the village of Rodovani. East of the village (at the entrance) the ancient city-state of Elyros was built on Kephala hill. The area has not been excavated. During the first Byzantine period, the town was the seat of the bishopric but was destroyed by the Saracens. There is a magnificent statue of a philosopher from Elyros in the Chania Museum.

At the 62.5th km. in the village of Temenia, a turn-off right joins the road Chania - Palaiochora at Kandanos (see Excursion 26). Left from Temenia, the road continues on to Souya.

Two km. before Souya, a dirt road leads to Koustoyerako where during World War II there was a large battle between Cretan resistance fighters and the Germans when the latter shot the

women of the village in the square. Souya, a small village with a gorgeous sand beach, has a modest hotel and rooms to rent. This was the site of the ancient city of SyTa, harbour town of Elyros. Several Roman ruins (baths, sections of the ancient aqueduct, houses and vaulted tombs) still stand, particularly east of the river Souyanos. At the west edge of the settlement a modern church has been erected on the foundations of an Early Christian basilica (6th century) with a wonderful mosaic floor. For the visitor who enjoys walking, nature and antiquities a suprise awaits him west of Souya: ancient Lissos. In an idyllic, verdant landscape, the sole inhabitant is the custodian who guides you to the tiny Doric temple of Asklepios, the ancient theatre and the vaulted tombs.

CHANIA: Excursion 24

Maleme (16.5 km.) - Kolybari) - Crossroads for Spilia (2 km.) and Drakona (4 km.) - Kisamos (Kasteli) (42 km.) - Crossroads for Polyrrhenia (7 km.).

Leave west along Yannari - Skalidi - Kisamou Sts. At 1.5 km. a turn-off left for Alikianos (see Excursion 22). At 2.5 km. left one sees the "Kako Pouli" (literally Evil Bird – a diving eagle), a monument which was erected by the Germans in memory of the German air assault in May 1941. At 3.7 km. a turn-off right for a camping site and after 4 km. a turn-off left for Galatas (2 km.) where there was a major battle, during World War II, pitting Greek soldiers, New Zealanders and unarmed civilians against the German parachutists. The German Witman called it the "Battle of Giants". The road goes along the coast where there are hotels and tavernas next to the gorgeous sandy beaches. Across the way is the island of Aghioi Theodoroi, the ancient Akoitos, which today has become a reserve for the Cretan ibex. At the 9th km. a camping site and at the 10th km. a turn-off to Vryses. The road continues on cutting through orange groves sheltered by tall canebreaks which protect the trees from the north wind.

At 16.5 km. the village of Maleme where the Chania airport was before the war. During the Battle of Crete the Germans dropped a large number of parachutists there and captured it after a fierce battle. There are tourist installations on the site today. Near the village of Maleme a tholos tomb has been excavated from the Post-Palace period.

Immediately after the village of Maleme a road left leads to the German military cemetery where the bones of 4465 German soldiers who lost their lives in Greece during World War II are buried. Adjacent (in the vineyard) stands the Late Minoan III tholos tomb, similar to that at Stylos but of quadrilateral plan.

At the 23rd km., is the village of Kolybari where in February 1897, the head of the voluntary force of Greek troops, Timoleon Vassos, proclaimed the union of Crete with Greece. His bust has been erected in the centre of the village. In the locality Aghia Eirene, south of Kolybari, lies an extensive Late Minoan III settlement.

From Kolybari a crossroad right leads (1 km.) to the Gonias Monastery which was founded in 1618. The original church of 1634 was destroyed by the Turks dur-

The Gonias Monastery,
founded in 1618,
houses a small museum.

The German cemetery in
the village of Maleme
connected with the
historic Battle of Crete.

Aghia Marina - Platanias.

ing the Revolution of 1866. Few treasures were saved. At the monastery there is a small museum where a collection of icons from the 17th and 18th centuries, as well as holy vestments, are on display. Noteworthy icons are the *Crucifixion* and *Saint Nicholas*, painted by Konstantinos Paliokapas in 1637, the *Assumption of the Virgin Mary* from 1728, *Saint Anthony* from 1772, *Genesis* and *Ecce Homo* by D. Sgouros, 1662.

A Turkish shell from the siege of the monastery during the Revolution of 1866 is embedded in the eastern wall of the church. The fountain at the entrance to the monastery bears the date 1708.

Continuing on north, immediately after the monastery left is the modern building of the Orthodox Academy of Crete which carries on a great deal or religious and social activity.

Two km. after the Academy, on a rise which commands the region with a marvellous view of the bay and the coast of Chania, and the island Aghioi Theodoroi, is a simple monument to the Cadets who fell during the German invasion.

Back at Kolybari, a crossroads left leads to the village of Spilia (2 km.). Before the entrance to the village a turn-off right leads to the village of Marathokephala, perched on a hill. At the church of the village you turn left and stop at the first level area on the track

through the fields to follow a narrow path left which leads, after 100 m. to the cave of Aghios Ioannis Xenos. This is the beloved Hermit of the Cretans who in the 11th century founded the Catholico Monastery at Akrotiri of Chania (see Excursion 19). At the entrance to the large cave with man-made stone seats and tall plane trees, is a small chapel de-

dicated to the saint. To the rear of the cave is a stalactite which is considered holy.

In the village of Spilia it is worth visiting the small church of the Virgin (12th century), covered with wall-paintings from the 14th century, on a wooded knoll in the Meriana neighbour-hood.

You continue on to Drakona. Before the entrance to the village a sign points right to a path to the church of Saint Stephen; it is from the 9th century and has wall-paintings.

Two km. from Drakona a sign right (1 km.) takes you to the village of Epi-skopi, Kisamos where you find the impressive church called Rotonda which is dedicated to the Archangel Michael. It has a stepped dome made up of five concentric rings, a design unique in Crete.

The church was the seat of the bishopric during the second Byzantine period and is built on the foundations of an earlier basilica of which a section of the mosaic floor has been preserved.

You return to Kolybari and continue on toward Kisamos, passing a turn-off to Rodopou on the right.

The road, which is difficult to negotiate, in many places follows the course of a paved Roman road and leads to the enchanting cove (Menies) at the edge of cape Spatha. In antiquity this was the most important religious centre in western Crete, with the sanctuary of Diktynna.

At Plakalona (31 km.) you see a valley dense with olive trees, marvellous sandy beaches and in the background the town of Kisamos (or Kasteli as the locals call it).

The town of Kisamos took the name Kasteli from the old Venetian castle there. According to the latest census it has 2800 inhabitants. It is built along a large, sandy beach without a regular plan. Its location makes it the starting point for a visit to the west coast of Crete. It is connected by ship to Kythera and twice a week (Tuesday and Friday) to Gytheion in the Peloponnese. There are small hotels and houses with rooms to rent in the town.

Roman Kisamos stood on the same site as the present town. Excavations in building plots, from 1965 onwards, have brought to light splendid edifices from the ancient city (baths, part of the theatre, villas, tombs) and works of art (statues and primarily mosaics). The mosaic floors of Kisamos are among the loveliest of their kind from the 2nd-3rd century A.D.

The visitor may form his own opinion by visiting the area behind the Health Centre, where excavations are in progress and an archaeological site will be arranged.

During the Early Byzantine period Kisamos was an episcopal see. The Byzantine wall, repaired by the Venetians, is still extant.

A re-exhibition of the Kisamos Archaeological Collection is being mounted in the Veneto-Turkish Commandery and should soon be open to the public.

A visit to ancient Polyrrhenia, 7 km. south of Kisamos, is a worthwhile excursion. Built in a naturally fortified position, the powerful city governed all nearby cities. It claimed to have been founded by the Achaeans, but the earliest remnants found date from the 6th century B.C. Its Hellenistic walls with semicircular bastions are visible in several places, while on the summit of the hill is the citadel with Byzantine and Venetian fortifications. The houses were cut into the rock in step-like arrangement up the hill slopes.

On the flat area at the base of the citadel, where the church of the Ninety-nine Martyrs now stands (built

The town of Kisamos (Kasteli to the locals) built on the site of ancient Kisamos.
Today it is known for its excellent wine.

almost entirely of ancient inscriptions), are the foundations of a temple or telesterion of the 4th century B.C.

In the present village of Kisamos, one of the towers of the ancient fortification and Hadrian's aqueduct, a massive technical feat hewn from the rock, have survived.

Section of one of the fortified towers of the harbour of ancient Phalasarna.

KISAMOS: Excursion 25

Phalasarna (16 km.) - Kephali (31 km.) - Chrysos - Kalitissa to Chania - Return via Topolia (62 km.).

Leave west along the coast road. At the 3rd km. is the protected cove and quay where the ferry boats for Gytheion dock. The road continues into the interior, passing the uninhabited Gramvousa peninsula to the right with craggy steep shores cut by small bays, approachable only by sea. The most beautiful bays are on the NW side opposite the island of Gramvousa.

At the 10th km. is the village of Platanos, where a tomb from the Proto-Geometric period was found when the road was being built. At the entrance to the village a turn-off right to Phalasarna (5.5 km.). There is a magnificent view of the bay with its olive trees and many greenhouses. At the end of the asphalt road on a sand beach several km. long

are two or three small tavernas with rooms to rent. Despite the lack of a tourist infrastructure, the region, because of its natural beauty and its extensive sandy beaches, is especially popular with young people. The last 2.5 km. is a rough dirt road. At the 2nd km. of the dirt road, you come upon, the "rock-cut throne". When it was hewn and what it was used for are still enigmas.

At the end of the road, on the SE side of the small cape, can be seen the ruins of ancient Phalasarna, the westernmost town in Crete, which during the Hellenistic period was a noteworthy commercial naval power. The acropolis is located on the headland, on the north side of the bay. The walls and ruins of the buildings of the city have survived. Due to the relative fall in sea level observed along the south and west part of Crete, the harbour is now on dry land, SE of the acropolis. In recent years one of the defensive towers has been excavated and exposed.

Returning to Platanos, you continue on south to Sphinari. A part of the road,

The Monastery of Chrysoskalitissa, dedicated to the Dormition of the Holy Virgin and the Holy Trinity.

which winds high above the shore, is under construction. At the 16th km. you reach the village of Sphinari where holiday-makers and tourists gather in the summer.

After the mountain village of Kambos, at the 28th km. a turn-off right goes along for 2 km. toward the sea, ending on the coast at Livadia with its lace-like but uninhabited shores. The main road continues on passing through the villages of Keramoti and Kephali. At the south exit of the village is the church of the Transfiguration of Christ (Metamorphosis tou Sotiros) with wall-paintings from 1320. From the village of Kephali a turn-off right (11 km. - dirt road) ends at the Monastery of Chrysoskalitissa, where only a few nuns live today. The church is dedicated to the Assumption of the Virgin Mary and the Holy Trinity. The steep rock, where the cave with the church is, is surrounded by the sea and is 35 m. high. Tradition says that one of the 90 steps which leads to the top is gold, but only those without sin can see it.

Five km. "to the southwest you discover Elaphonisi, a charming islet with a gorgeous sand beach, which is connected to the coast by a shallow ford 0.50-0.80 m. deep.

Return to the village of Kephali and turn right in the direction of Chania. The return route goes through small mountain villages. The village of Elos (500 m. a.s.l.) is at the highest point. From here the road descends gently

Falasarna. Magnificent view of the bay.

without beds, crossing a fertile valley. At the village Koutsomatados the Topolia ravine begins, 1500 m. long. At the entrance to the ravine, left, at a height of 80 m. above the road is the Cave of Aghia Sophia and a church of the same name (Divine Wisdom). Despite being difficult to reach it is worth noting that the cave was used from the Neolithic to the Minoan period.

Eight km. after the picturesque village of Topolia you reach the main road Kisamos - Chania at the village of Kaloudiana, 3 km. east of Kisamos.

Elaphonisi, a charming islet with a gorgeous sand beach, which is connected to the coast by a shallow ford 0.50-0.80 m. deep.

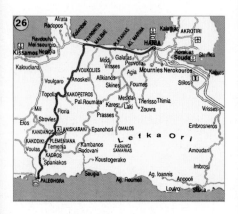

CHANIA: Excursion 26

Voukolies (26.5 km.) - Kakopetro (38.5 km.) - Kandanos (57.5 km.) - Palaiochora (77 km.).

This excursion goes through Selinou province, with its large number of well-preserved and decorated 14th-century Byzantine churches.

You leave on the road to Kisamos (see Excursion 24) to Tavronitis (19.5 km.) where a turn-off left to the south leads to Palaiochora, through a fertile region covered in olive groves and vineyards.

At the 26.5th km. is the village of Voukolies (110 m. a.s.L), the agricultural centre of the region where there is a market every Saturday. There are hotels and restaurants here as well.

After Kakopetro (38.5 km., 420 m. a.s.L), the road continues south through a narrow, fertile valley, with dense olive groves. The region produces cereals,

wine, chestnuts and livestock products. At 57.3 km. you reach the village of Kandanos (420 m. a.s.L), which played an important role in the revolution against the Turks and the resistance against the Germans. On May 23, 1941, when the Germans captured the airport at Maleme and were moving on toward Kandanos, the residents of the area, of all ages and both sexes, fought

the invaders with the primitive means at their disposal. They killed a fair number and the remainder were forced to retreat. The Germans came back the next day and as the resistance fighters had taken refuge in the mountains, killed whomever they found and burned the village. Ancient Kandanos flourished during the Roman period. A large civic building (perhaps a praetorium)

The country town of Palaiochora (Kastelli Selinou of the Venetian period). It has developed into a popular summer resort, because Kastelli attracts thousands of visitors every year.

has been excavated.

The region of Kandanos is well-known for its Byzantine churches which are of great interest.

At the turn-off left for Anisaraki (3 km.), 300 m. from Kouphaloto, is the church of the Archangel Michael with frescoes by Ioannis Pagemenos (1327-28). In Anisaraki four churches from the 14th and 16th centuries stand out: Saint Ann with inscribed wall-paintings from 1457-62 and a noteworthy iconostasis in good condition; Saint John from the 14th century; the Virgin, with quite well-preserved frescoes from the 14th century and architecture showing Venetian influences, and Saint Paraskevi with frescoes from the beginning of the 14th century. From Anisaraki the road continues south and joins the road for Souya (see Excursion 23).

Back at Kandanos and heading south toward Plemeniana, you will see the church of Saint George with inscribed wall-paintings from 1410. At the 64th km., in the village of Kakodiki, next to the modern church of Holy Trinity, is a small church to the Archangel Michael from the 14th century and right next to it Saint Isidores with wall-paintings from 1420.

At the 65th km. a turn-off left to Kadro. At the highest point of the village (one km. from the turn-off) a path right leads to a Byzantine church dedicated to the Nativity of the Virgin with wall-paintings from the end of the 14th century. Above the village there is another church, dedicated to Saint John the Theologian.

Finally, at the 74.5th km. you reach the coast where Palaiochora awaits you, the Kastelli Selinou of the Venetians. The Kastelli was built in 1279 on the tip of the peninsula to control the two bays to the east and west. In 1539 the pirate Barbarossa conquered it and destroyed it. Today it has been renovated and attracts thousands of visitors every year.

The country town of Palaiochora is the second most populous, after Hierapetra, in southern Crete. It has developed rapidly into a summer resort with Class B hotels and many smaller ones as well as rooms to rent. During the summer small ships provide communications with Aghia Roumeli (Samaria ravine) and Chora Sphakion. Similar ships also take visitors to the uninhabited island of Gavdos, in the Libyan Sea, 30 km. off the south coast of Crete.

PREFECTURE OF HERAKLEION

TRANSPORT CONNECTIONS

By air
Olympic Airways, Athens office
tel. 210.9666.666
Athens International Airport
('Eleftherios Venizelos'),
tel. 210.3530.000
Aegean Airlines, tel. 210.9988.300 &
801.11.20000

By sea
Harbourmaster's Office, Piraeus,
tel. 210.4226.000-003
Hellas Flying Dolphins,
tel. 210.4199.000

MUSEUMS & ARCHAEOLOGICAL SITES

Archaeological Museum, 1 Xanthoudi-
dou St, tel. 2810.226092 & 2810.226470
Museum of Ecclesiastical Art, Plateia
Aghias Aikaterinis (St Catherine's
Square), tel. 2810.288825
Historical Museum of Crete,
tel. 2810.283219
Museum of the Battle of Crete and
the National Resistance (1941-1945),
junction of Doukos Beaufort &
Mirambelou Streets
Natural History Museum,
157 Knossou St
Knossos
Archaeological Site, tel. 2810.231940
Phaistos
Archaeological Site, tel.28920.42315
Archanes
Archaeological Museum,
tel. 2810.752712
Malia
Minoan Palace, tel. 28970.31597

Gortyn
Archaeological Site & Archaeological
Museum, tel. 28920.31144
**Limenas Chersonisou
(Port Chersonisos)**
'Lychnostatis' Open-Air Museum,
tel. 28970.23660
Peza & Myrtia district
Museum of the Peza Society,
tel. 2810.741945
Kazantzakis Museum,
tel. 2810.742451
Fodele
El Greco (Dominikos Theotokopoulos)
Museum

USEFUL PHONE NUMBERS

Herakleion
Venizeleio Hospital, tel. 2810.368000
Police Station, tel. 2810.282343
Tourist Police, tel. 2810.283190
Harbourmaster's Office,
tel. 2810.244956
Taxis, tel. 2810.210102
Archanes
Rural Doctor's Surgery, tel. 2810.751882
Police Station, tel. 2810.751811
Malia
Rural Doctor's Surgery,
tel. 28970.31594
Taxis, tel. 28970.31777
Matala
Police Station, tel. 28920.51111
Peza
Rural Doctor's Surgery, tel. 2810.741791

CULTURAL EVENTS

Herakleion
During the summer months the munic-

ipality and local societies put on a large number of cultural events, such as concerts, plays and shows, and exhibitions, in the Kazantzakis Theatre or the Venetian fortress. The feast of the city's patron saint Titus is celebrated on August 25th.

Gortyn
Carnival for the feast of the Ten Saints (Aghioi Deka) on October 10th.

Archanes
The Grape Festival, running from August

10th to August 15th.

Limenas Chersonisou (Port Chersonisos)
Grand Fair for the feast of the Virgin Mary, on August 15th.

Malia
Lenten carnival festivities.

Matala, also Peza
Fair for the feast of St Panteleimon, July 27th.

PREFECTURE OF LASITHI

MUSEUMS & ARCHAEOLOGICAL SITES

Aghios Nikolaos
Archaeological Museum,
74 Palaiologou St, tel. 28410.24943
Museum of Folklore, on the ground floor of the Harbourmaster's Office, tel. 28410.25093

Siteia
Archaeological Museum,
tel. 28430.23917
Museum of Folklore, in the village of Khamezi, and Museum of the Toplou Monastery, tel. 28430.61226

Elounda
Museum of Folklore, tel. 28410.33314

Hierapetra
Archaeological Collection, Plateia Dimarcheiou (Town Hall Square), tel. 28420.28721

Aghios Georgios, in the Plain of Lasithi
Eleftherios Venizelos Museum & Museum of Folklore

USEFUL TELEPHONE NUMBERS

Aghios Nikolaos
Hospital, tel. 28410.55000

Tourist Police, tel. 28410.26900
Harbourmaster's Office,
tel. 28410.22312

Hierapetra
Hospital, tel. 28420.90222
Police Station, tel. 28420.90160

Elounda
Rural Doctor's Surgery,
tel. 28410.41563
Police Station, tel. 28410.41348

Siteia
Hospital, tel. 28430.24311-14
Tourist Police, tel. 28430.24200
Harbourmaster's Office,
tel. 28430.22310

Vaï
Municipality of Itanos, tel. 28430.61204

CULTURAL EVENTS

Aghios Nikolaos
The major celebrations in the course of the year are the Judas Bonfire, the turn of the year, and the Lato Festival.

Hierapetra
The Kyrbeia Festival, taking place in July or August. Fairs for the feasts of the Prophet Elijah, on July 20th, and St Pan-

teleimon, on July 27th.
Plain of Lasithi
Fairs in the neighbouring villages of
Plati (August 30th) and Psychro
(August 31st).
Siteia
The Kornaros Festival, taking place in
July and August. Fair at the Faneromeni
Monastery for the feast of the Virgin
Mary, August 15th. The Grape Festival,
running from August 15th to August

20th. Fair for the feast of the Holy
Cross, on September 14th.
Goudouras, also Ziros
Fair on August 29th.
**Gournia, Koutsounari, Neapoli and
Pachia Ammos**
All these have celebrations for the
feast of the Virgin Mary, August 15th.
Elounda
Fair on August 6th; and cultural events
throughout the summer.

PREFECTURE OF RETHYMNON

MUSEUMS & ARCHAEOLOGICAL SITES
Rethymnon
Archaeological Museum,
tel. 28310.54668
Museum of History & Folklore,
tel. 28310.23398
Museum of Ecclesiastical Art,
tel. 28310.22415
Art Gallery, tel. 28310.55847
Museum of Marine Life,
48 Arabatzoglou St
The Helen Frantzeskaki Folklore
Collection, 17 Regnieri St
Museum of the Aghia Irene
Monastery,
tel. 28310.27791
Preveli Monastery
Museum of Ecclesiastical Art,
tel. 28320.31246
Aghia Galini
Argo Exhibition Centre,
Aghia Galini High School
Adele
Museum of the Arsanio Monastery,
tel. 28310.71228
Anogeia
Gryllos Museum

Arkadi
Museum of the Arkadi Monastery,
tel. 28310.83116
Eleftherna
Archaeological Site
Zoniana
Potamianos Museum, tel. 28340.61087
Plakias
Papageorgoulakis Museum,
tel. 28320.31374

USEFUL TELEPHONE NUMBERS
Rethymnon
Hospital, tel. 28310.27491
Tourist Police, tel. 28310.28156
Harbourmaster's Office,
tel. 28310.22276
Anogeia
Health Centre, tel. 28340.31208
Police Station, tel. 28340.31204
Aghia Galini
Rural Doctor's Surgery, tel. 28320.91111
Harbourmaster's Office,
tel. 28320.91206
Panormos
Rural Doctor's Surgery,
tel. 28340.51203

Police Station, tel. 28340.51203

Plakias & Sellia district

Rural Doctor's Surgery, tel. 28320.31237

Police Station, tel. 28320.31238

CULTURAL EVENTS

Rethymnon

Lenten carnival festivities. Naval Week. The 'Renaissance Festival', taking place in July and August. Wine Festival in mid-July. Fair on June 23rd.

Zoniana

The 'Sphendonia Festival'.

Aghia Galini, also Sellia

Fair for the feast of the Virgin Mary, August 15th.

Eleftherna

Fair on July 20th.

Plakias

Fair at the hamlet of Myrthio, August 6th.

PREFECTURE OF CHANIA

MUSEUMS & ARCHAEOLOGICAL SITES

Chania

Archaeological Museum, 21 Halidon St, tel. 28210.90334

Museum of Folklore, 46B Halidon St, tel. 28210.90816

Byzantine Collection, 82 Theotokopoulou St, tel. 28210.96046

Historical Archives of Crete, 20 Sphakianaki St, tel. 28210.52606

Naval Museum, Koundourioti Quay, 28210.91785

Museum of Chemistry, 34C Venizelou St, tel. 28210.42504

War Museum, 1 Tzanakaki St, tel. 28210.44156

Akrotiri

Museum of the Aghia Triada Monastery, tel. 28210.63310

Museum of the Aghios Ioannis Prodromos Monastery, tel. 28210.64571

Museum of the Kyria ton Angelon Monastery, tel. 28210.63319

Palaiochora

Museum of the Agion Pateron Monastery

Samaria

Natural History Museum, near the entrance to the National Park

Souda Bay

Archaeological Site of Ancient Aptera

Gavalochori

Museum of History & Folklore, tel. 28250.23222

Therissos

Museum of History & Folklore

Kefali

Skalidis Museum

Kolymbari

Museum of the Myrtidiotissa Gonias Monastery

Mournies

Museum of the Chrysopigis Monastery

Plain of Askyfo

War Museum, tel. 28250.95289

USEFUL TELEPHONE NUMBERS

Chania

Hospital, tel. 28210.22000

Bus Station, tel. 28210.91288

Tourist Police, tel. 28210.53333

Taxis, tel. 28210.98700

Sphakia (Chora Sphakion)

Rural Doctor's Surgery, tel. 28250.91214

Police Station, tel. 28250.91205

Harbourmaster's Office,
tel. 28250.91292
Municipal Offices, tel.28250.91131

Samaria Gorge
Warden's post at Xyloskalo,
tel. 28210.67179
Warden's post at Aghia Roumeli,
tel. 28250.91254

Palaiochora
Rural Doctor's Surgery, tel. 28230.41211
Police Station, tel. 28230.41111
Harbourmaster's Office,
tel. 28230.41214

Souda Bay
Naval Hospital, tel. 28210.89307
Police Station, tel. 28210.89316
Harbourmaster's Office,
tel. 28210.89240
Municipal Offices, tel.28210.20501

Aghia Marina
Pharmacy, tel. 28218.60078
Municipal Offices, tel.28210.31363

Akrotiri
Rural Doctor's Surgery,
tel. 28210.63336
Police Station, tel. 28210.63333
Municipal Offices, tel.28210.69800

Almyrida
Municipal Offices, tel.28250.83273

Vamos
Health Centre, tel. 28250.22580
Police Station, tel. 28250.22218
Taxis, tel. 28250.22202

Galatas
Police Station, tel. 28210.32200
Municipal Offices, tel.28210.31363

Georgioupoli
Police Station, tel. 28250.61350
Municipal Offices, tel.28250.61973

Daratsos
Municipal Offices, tel.28210.31363

Elafonisi
Municipal Offices, tel.28220.61544

Kalyves
Rural Doctor's Surgery, tel.
28250.31244
Police Station, tel. 28250.41214
Municipal Offices, tel.28250.32470

Kolymbari
Rural Doctor's Surgery,
tel. 28240.22204
Police Station, tel. 28240.22100

Maleme
Rural Doctor's Surgery,
tel. 28210.62360
Police Station, tel. 28210.62209

Platanias
Pharmacy, tel. 28210.68585
Police Station, tel. 28210.68206
Municipal Offices, tel.28210.61511

Souya
Police Station, tel. 28230.51241
Municipal Offices, tel.28230.51190

Falasarna
Municipal Offices, tel.28220.83043

Frangokastello
Municipal Offices, tel.28250.91131

Gavdos
Rural Doctor's Surgery,
tel. 28230.42195
Police Station, tel. 28230.41019
Commune Offices, tel. 28230.41101
Harbourmaster's Office at Palaiochora,
tel. 28230.41214

CULTURAL EVENTS

Chania
Pan-Cretan Peace Congress and Venizelos Games, in May. Cultural events
and 'green tourism' events, in August.

Kasteli of Kisamos
Lenten carnival festivities. Events

throughout the summer. In August, Wine Festival and the Theocharakis Games.

Palaiochora
Music festival in August.

Souda Bay
Lenten carnival festivities. Events throughout Naval Week in June.

Sphakia (Chora Sphakion)
Fair for the feast of the Virgin of Thymiani, on the last Sunday in May. Events throughout the summer.

Falasarna
Fairs on July 29th and August 12th.

Frangokastello
Fair for the feast of St Nikita, on September 15th.

Aghia Marina
Fairs, on the mainland, on July 17th, and on the islet of Aghioi Theodoroi, on June 8th.

Akrotiri
Fair at the Aghiou Ioanni Monastery, August 29th. Fair at Sternes and Kounoupidiana, September 8th.

Alikianos
Fairs on May 21st and September 14th.

Vamos
Vamos Festival of cultural events, throughout August. In April, 'Periwinkle Night', at which snails and firewater are served.

Voukolies
Numerous events throughout the sum-

mer. Fairs on September 14th and December 12th. Market on Good Friday.

Vryses
Fair on July 7th. Fair at the village of Alikampos, August 15th.

Elos
Chestnut Festival partying in October.

Epanochori
Fair on August 24th.

Kalyves
Fair on August 15th.

Kolymbari
Events throughout the summer. Fairs on August 14th, on August 29th, and on the feast day of the Holy Cross, September 14th.

Kournas
Lakeside events throughout the summer. Fairs on May 5th and August 29th.

Maleme
Fair on January 17th. Events to mark the anniversary of the Battle of Crete.

Fourni
Fair on July 27th.

Megisti Lavra Monastery
Fairs on July 5th and August 15th.

Souria
Fair for the feast of the Prophet Elijah, on July 20th.

Stylos
Fair on August 29th.

Cave church of Aghia Sophia, Kissamos
Great fair on Easter Tuesday